# The ABCs of
# Netscape Composer

# The ABCs of
# Netscape®
# Composer

Michael Meahdra

SYBEX®

San Francisco - Paris - Düsseldorf - Soest

Associate Publisher: Amy Romanoff
Acquisitions Manager: Kristine Plachy
Acquisitions & Developmental Editors: Dan Brodnitz and
Bonnie Bills
Editor: Krista Reid-McLaughlin
Technical Editor: Rael Dornfest
Book Designer: Catalin Dulfu
Graphic Illustrator: Inbar Berman
Electronic Publishing Specialist: Kate Kaminski
Production Coordinator: Robin Kibby
Proofreaders: Duncan Watson and Charles Mathews
Indexer: Matthew Spence
Cover Designer: Design Site
Cover Illustrator/Photographer: Sergie Loobkoff

Screen reproductions produced with Collage Complete.

Collage Complete is a trademark of Inner Media Inc.

Library of Congress Card Number: 97-67206
ISBN: 0-7821-2065-2

Manufactured in the United States of America

10 9 8 7 6 5 4 3 2 1

# Acknowledgements

Its gotten to be a cliché to say that a book such as this is a team effort. But, cliché or not, it's true. I've been fortunate to work with a great team: the people at Sybex. My thanks to Kristine Plachy, acquisitions manager, and Dan Brodnitz and Bonnie Bills, aquisitions editors, for helping develop the concept for this book and working out all the details that made the project possible. Krista Reid-McLaughlin, associate editorial supervisor, has managed to be a delight to work with, even as she fulfilled her separate responsibilities of cleaning up my prose and maintaining the schedule. Thanks to Rael Dornfest for his diligent work as technical editor and for his many excellent suggestions. Thanks also to Robin Kibby, production coordinator, and Kate Kaminski, electronic publishing specialist, for their thoroughness and speed.

A special thanks goes to Brenda Kienan and Dan Tauber for sharing the knowledge and resources developed during the writing of their books, *Surfing the Internet with Netscape Communicator* and *Mastering Netscape Communicator*, also published by Sybex.

I'd also like to thank the organizations and individuals that have generously allowed me to reproduce portions of their Web pages as illustrations in this book.

# Contents at a Glance

# Table of Contents

# Introduction

The Internet and the World Wide Web is all the rage. It seems like you can't read a magazine or watch a news broadcast without seeing evidence of the way this new communication medium is influencing our daily lives. We surf the Web at work, at school, at home, and even at cybercafes.

It's not surprising that a growing number of people are looking for ways to participate in this phenomenon. For many of those people, it isn't enough to view the information and ideas prepared and published by others. They want to contribute something of their own—they want to become publishers as well as readers of Web pages. However, they don't want to get a degree in computer science just to be able to create a Web page.

If you belong to this group of would-be Web publishers, then this book is for you. Its purpose is to show you how to create and publish Web pages using the tools provided in the most popular Internet communication software on the market—Netscape Communicator. You can use these tools to create simple projects such as a personal Home page or a Web page for a club, church, or organization. Or you can use the same tools to create a whole corporate Web site. You can create Web pages for limited distribution on a private intranet, or make your Web pages available to the world on the Internet.

## What Is Composer?

Netscape Communicator is the set of Internet communication programs built around the famous Netscape Navigator Web browser. Composer is the Web-page-creation component of the Netscape Communicator suite.

For some time now, the name Netscape has been synonymous with the leading application for viewing pages on the World Wide Web. It's true that Netscape's flagship product—Navigator—is the market-leading Web browser. However, that program has grown and evolved into something much more than an application for just viewing Web pages. Navigator now leads a collection of companion programs that make up the Netscape Communicator suite. Communicator includes the tools you need to not only view Web pages, but to create them as well; plus, there are components to handle e-mail, news, and live conferencing.

Netscape Communicator is composed of six separate programs that each handle a specific aspect of your Internet communication needs. Although they are separate programs for separate tasks, all the Communicator applications are designed to work together and complement each other. The components of the Netscape Communicator suite are as follows:

**Navigator** is the latest version of the legendary leader of Web browsers. This is the primary program to use for surfing the Web and viewing Web pages on the Internet and on local intranets.

**Composer** lets you create your own Web pages and publish them on a Web server for all the world (or all of your workgroup) to see. Composer's WYSIWYG (What You See Is What You Get) editing environment makes creating and editing Web pages as easy as using a word processor.

**Messenger** handles all your e-mail and does it with full support for richly formatted e-mail messages using HTML. Now your e-mail can look as good as your Web pages.

**Collabra** is the tool for reading and posting articles on Internet discussion groups, called newsgroups, and for collaborating with coworkers in corporate workgroups.

**Conference** provides real-time voice and video conferencing.

**Netcaster** delivers news, sports scores, stock reports, and channels your favorite content to your desktop automatically.

Because this book is about Web publishing, it will focus on Composer and the tools and capabilities provided by that program. However, you shouldn't forget that Composer is part of the larger family of Communicator programs, and that other components of the Communicator suite will come into play from time to time as you expand your Internet experiences.

## How This Book Is Organized

This book is organized into four main parts, plus a collection of appendices at the back. Part One is an overview of Web publishing and the issues you'll need to think about before you start creating Web pages. Part Two covers the basics of creating a Web page with Composer and how to work with text, images, hyperlinks, and tables. Part Three gets into more advanced topics such as multimedia, sophisticated page layouts, and manually editing HTML code. Part Four is where you'll find information on publishing your Web pages and publicizing your site.

## Part 1: Gearing Up for Web Publishing

- Chapter 1, *Getting to Know This New Publishing Media*, gets things started with a brief history lesson and an overview of the technology that makes the World Wide Web possible.
- Chapter 2, *Planning a Web Site*, lays the groundwork for the essential forethought and planning that is a necessary ingredient in a successful Web site development project.
- Chapter 3, *Understanding the Elements of Page Design*, explores the design elements that make up the Web page designer's palette.

## Part 2: Building Your Own Web Page with Composer

- Chapter 4 is titled *Getting Off to a Quick Start*, and that's exactly what it does. This chapter shows you how to use the Netscape Page Wizard and Netscape Templates to create a simple Web page and gets you started with configuring Composer and saving your first page.
- Chapter 5, *Working with Text*, shows you how to use Composer's text-formatting tools and explores how to create headings, bulleted lists, and more.
- Chapter 6, *Adding Images*, explains the techniques for adding pictures and other images to your Web page.
- Chapter 7, *Getting Linked Up*, explores hyperlinks and shows you how to create links from text or images on your page to other Web pages and to specific target locations on a Web page.
- Chapter 8, *Working with Tables*, demonstrates how to create and edit tables using Composer's built-in table tools.

## Part 3: Using Advanced Design Tools

- Chapter 9, *Adding Sound and Motion with Multimedia*, shows you how to spice up your Web pages with sounds, video clips, and animations.
- Chapter 10, *Creating Multicolumn Layouts with Tables*, demonstrates how to use Composer's table-editing tools to create Web pages with magazine-like page layouts with multiple columns of text and graphics.
- Chapter 11, *Getting Your Hands Dirty: Editing HTML*, shows you how to manually enter HTML tags for those times when you want to do something for which Composer doesn't supply a convenient button or dialog box option.

- Chapter 12, *Going Beyond the Limits of Composer*, is a survey of some of the Web page features that Composer doesn't support with its built-in editing tools, and what is involved if you decide you want to use some of these techniques on your Web pages.

## Part 4: Publishing Your Web Site

- Chapter 13, *Posting Your Pages on the Web*, shows you how to publish your Web page by using Composer's built-in tools to copy files to the Web server.
- Chapter 14, *Publicizing Your Site*, shows you some of the things you can do to attract visitors to your Web site.

## Appendices and Glossary

- Appendix A, *Composer's Other Role in the Communicator Suite*, is a brief look at the role Composer plays in creating richly formatted messages for e-mail and newsgroup articles.
- Appendix B, *HTML Dictionary*, is where you can find explanations of the codes Composer places in the HTML source document that defines your Web page.
- Appendix C, *Essential Links*, is where you can find the Web addresses for some important Web sites, including the Netscape corporate site, an assortment of search engines, and, of course, the Sybex site where you can find more of the links mentioned in this book.
- The Glossary is a handy place to look up simple definitions for some of the terms and buzzwords you find in the text.

# Part 1

# Gearing Up
# for Web Publishing

# Chapter 1

# EXAMINING THIS NEW PUBLISHING MEDIA

- **A brief history of the World Wide Web**
- **What is HTML?**
- **Understanding the role of the browser**
- **Who publishes on the Web?**
- **Using HTML documents**

This book is about Netscape Composer, the Web publishing component of the Netscape Communicator suite. But before we get into the specifics of using Composer to create Web pages, we need to examine this new publishing medium—the World Wide Web and its in-house cousins that reside on corporate intranets.

Before you set out on a trip, you need to have a destination in mind, select the route you plan to take to get there, and have a purpose for making the trip in the first place. Similarly, before you set out to create a Web page, you need to consider what the World Wide Web is all about and why you want to publish a Web page on the Internet or an intranet. You need to plan your Web site development project, and you need to think about the elements that make up a Web page and how to use them to distribute your message.

The first part of this book (this chapter and the two that follow) will cover the background information you need to consider before creating our own Web pages. This chapter briefly examines the World Wide Web, and the role of Web browsers and HTML documents. It introduces many of the terms and concepts you'll use as you create Web pages. Chapter 2, *Planning a Web Site*, explores the issues involved in planning a Web site. And chapter 3, *The Elements of Page Design*, presents the design elements you can use to build your Web pages.

# A Brief History of the Web

Not so long ago, the World Wide Web didn't exist. The Internet, which had originated as a system for connecting universities, research centers, and government facilities, was just beginning to emerge into the broader realm of business and personal communications. The idea of interconnecting computers and computer networks to exchange information was starting to catch on, but the information flowing through the wires of the Internet was mostly plain, unadorned text. You could exchange e-mail messages and newsgroup articles, or read text documents located on remote computers—but it was generally all text and no pictures. To send anything other than plain text across the Internet, you needed special utility programs to copy the files and you'd probably need another program to view each file type after you got it.

At a time when computer users around the globe were used to graphical user interfaces (like Windows and Macintosh), fancy word processors, and desktop publishing, the Internet was stuck in a text-only world. Bummer!

Then, an amazing thing happened. Some clever people created a system for viewing text files that contain special formatting codes. This system consisted of a file format for documents, a viewer to display documents, and a protocol that allows a server to provide access to the documents at the viewers request.

With this new system, it was possible to view a page of nicely formatted text, complete with different type sizes, boldface, italics, and even colored type. So, the text looked better and was more readable than the plain text displayed in a monospaced font that was common before. Also, the page could include graphics. The program could detect a reference to a separate graphics file in the text document, automatically download that graphic, and display it onscreen as part of the page. Not only that, the new viewer supported hypertext links—the ability to click highlighted text and allow the viewer to jump to another page of related information.

Hypertext wasn't new; it had been around in help files and the like for several years. However, on the Internet, hypertext took on a new dimension. A hypertext link could jump to another location on the same page or to another page entirely—and that page could be located anywhere on the Internet. Hypertext links could lead from page to page to page and back again like the interconnected threads of a spider's web. The global scope of the Internet let the web extend around the world. Out of a combination of formatted text, graphics, and hypertext, the World Wide Web was born.

It was an idea whose time had come. The World Wide Web caught on and helped fuel the explosive growth of the Internet. Together, the Internet and the World Wide Web have become a dynamic new communication medium, one that is having a noticeable impact on our society.

# What Is HTML?

HTML—HyperText Markup Language—is the language of the World Wide Web. Basically, HTML is a set of codes that can be embedded in a plain text document to control how a Web browser will display that document onscreen. HTML codes control everything from text formatting (bold, italics, text sizes) to graphics and hypertext links.

HTML has its roots in another markup language, SGML (Standard Generalized Markup Language), which is a cross-platform file format for word processing and desktop publishing documents. Like SGML, HTML is a cross-platform file format. Unlike a word processing file, an HTML file includes no proprietary or platform-specific codes, or special characters. Instead, an HTML file contains only plain ASCII text that is common to all popular computer platforms.

Formatting instructions are embedded in the text of an HTML file using regular text characters surrounded by angle brackets. For example, the <b> and </b> tags turn the bold text attribute on and off respectively. In an HTML document, you would place the tags on either side of the text that you want to appear in bold, like so:

```
Some text can be <b>bolder</b> than the rest.
```

The Web browser will interpret anything in angle brackets as formatting instructions rather than text. When it appears in the Web browser window, the line above will look like this:

Some text can be **bolder** than the rest.

Of course, this is a very simple example. While some HTML tags are simple, others can be quite complex with references to external files and elaborate formatting options.

> **NOTE** HTML started out as a relatively simple—and limited—set of tags for basic text formatting and for defining hypertext links and graphics. As the Web has gained popularity, HTML has evolved. Numerous formatting options and other features have been added to HTML, and new extensions to the language are being proposed all the time. Unfortunately, not all Web browsers and HTML editors support all the latest additions to the language.

## Editing HTML

Since an HTML file is really just a plain ASCII text file, you don't need a special program to create the source document or a Web page. Any word processor (such as Word for Windows or WordPerfect) or text editor (such as Windows NotePad) can do the job. Unfortunately, if you used a word processor or text editor to create a Web page, you would need to manually add arcane HTML codes to a text file in order to produce even the simplest page. However, HTML editing is like many other tasks—having the right tools can make the task so much easier.

Composer is the HTML editing component of the Netscape Communicator package. It makes creating and editing HTML documents as easy as using a typical word processor. You don't have to work with plain ASCII text documents, which have strange codes embedded in the text, to give the browser formatting instructions. Instead, Composer provides a WYSIWYG (What You See Is What You Get) view of your document that simulates the way the document will appear in a browser window. You can select text and objects by clicking and dragging (just as you do in a word processor), and add formatting by choosing menu commands or by clicking toolbar buttons (just as you do in a word processor). You can see the results immediately in the Composer window without having to save the text file and open it in a separate program. It really is just like using a word processor, except that the finished file is saved in the HTML format instead of a word processor file format.

Of course, behind the scenes, Composer is creating an ASCII text file that contains not only your document's text, but also all the HTML tags necessary to effect the formatting options, hypertext links, and other elements that you specify. In addition, Composer automatically adds the codes for the page headers required by the HTML standard to each document you create. If you're the adventurous type, you can peek at (and even edit) the raw HTML file with all the codes that instruct the browser how to display the page. But that isn't necessary because Composer makes it possible to create and edit attractive Web pages and richly formatted messages without typing, or even seeing, a single HTML tag.

# Servers and Protocols

Servers and protocols sound like (and are) technical terms used by system engineers and computer geeks. The details of the types of servers and protocols that make the Web work can be complicated, but the basic concepts are simple and easy to understand. Fortunately, the basic concepts are all you need to know in order to create and maintain a Web site.

## The Role of the Server

A server is simply a computer that provides a service to other computers. The server may make files available from its hard disk or queue up print jobs for a printer. In the case of a Web server, the server stores all the files (HTML files, graphics files, and so on) for a Web site on it's hard drive and sends those files out over the Internet in response to requests from Web browsers.

To be effective, a Web server must be available to handle requests from Web browsers anytime of the day, any day of the week. That means the server must be up and running around the clock with a full-time connection to the Internet. For this reason, Web servers typically are separate computers, dedicated to the task, and are maintained by system administrators who specialize in such things. It's usually not practical to use a standard personal computer as a Web server—especially if you access the Internet through a dial-up connection.

Because you'll create your Web pages on a different computer than the Web server, you'll need to copy the finished Web pages to the server to make them available for other people to view with their Web browsers. This process is called publishing or posting your Web pages and Composer includes features to make it fast and easy.

**NOTE** See Chapter 13, *Posting Your Pages on the Web*, for details on how to transfer your finished pages to a Web server.

Web servers usually have addresses such as www.sybex.com. The only thing you need to know about a Web server is its address—the address you use to access Web pages on the server, and the address you use when you publish Web pages by copying them to the server's hard disk.

**WARNING** Often, the address you use to view pages from a Web site and the address you use to publish pages to that Web site will be different. Check with the system administrator to get the correct address for posting the Web pages you create.

A single computer can be configured to function as the Web server for multiple Web sites. Each Web site will be housed in a separate directory on the Web server. Often, the directory path will be part of the address for Web pages on that site (as in www.server.com/~yourname/homepage.html). Sometimes, a Web site address will include its own domain name (such as yourname.com in the address www.yourname.com) even though it is actually housed in a directory on an Internet service provider's server. The domain name makes the Web site appear as though it resides on a dedicated server; but it's all just smoke and mirrors, an illusion created by some minor technological sleight of hand.

# What Is a Protocol?

A protocol is just a set of rules and procedures that two computer programs can use to communicate with each other. You may have heard of Transfer Control Protocol/Internet Protocol, or TCP/IP, the protocols that form the foundation of the Internet. Another protocol, HyperText Transport Protocol, or HTTP, makes the Web run by providing the mechanism for handling requests for Web pages and hypertext links and delivering them over the Internet or an intranet.

The HTTP protocol does its job quietly, behind the scenes. The only evidence of the protocol that most Web surfers see is the http:// at the beginning of many Web addresses.

Although the HTTP protocol is by far the most common protocol used on the Web, a lot of Web browsers are capable of handling more than just hypertext documents. So, you may occasionally use another protocol when surfing the Web or creating a Web page. For example, the File Transport Protocol, or FTP, provides the means to copy files from one computer to another across the Internet. There are separate FTP utilities available for handling file transfers, but Navigator (and most other popular Web browsers) can do the job without outside assistance. An address that starts with `ftp://` entered into Navigator's Location or as the target of a hyperlink tells Navigator to use the FTP protocol to download the specified file.

> **NOTE**    **Composer can use either the HTTP or FTP protocols to copy files to the Web server when you publish your Web pages.**

# URLs Explained

One of the exciting things about the World Wide Web is the ability to open and view any of the millions of Web pages located on servers scattered around the world. All you need to do is enter the correct address (or click a link containing the address) for the Web page you want to view. The system works because each Web page has a unique address—called a Uniform Resource Locator (URL)—and all the Web servers and browsers are programmed to work with addresses in the URL format.

The URL tells the Web browser where to find any resource file available on the net. That resource could be an HTML file for a Web page, a graphic file, a sound or animation file, or just about anything else.

A complete URL consists of four parts: the protocol, server, path, and file name. For example, in the following URL: `http://www.sybex.com/directory/sample.html`

- **http://** is the protocol
- **www.sybex.com** is the address of the Web server
- **/directory/** is the path
- **sample.html** is the file name

Many URLs consist of just a protocol and a server. The directory, the filename, or both are omitted. If part of the URL is missing, the Web server will simply complete the address with default values. If there is no path specified, the server will look in the root directory. If there is no file name supplied, the server will open the default file (usually `index.html`) at the specified location. Sometimes, you can get by with dropping the `http://` protocol from a URL. If you don't specify a protocol, Navigator will use HTTP as the default. As a result, if you want to use the HTTP protocol to open the default Web page in the root directory of a specific server, the URL can be reduced to just the server address (such as `www.sybex.com`).

# Understanding the Role of the Browser

Of all the components of the World Wide Web, the one that most people are familiar with is the Web browser. A Web browser, such as Netscape Navigator, isn't some mysterious software running on a server someplace, it's a program you run on your own personal computer that enables you to view Web pages.

On the surface, a Web browser seems to be a simple viewer for displaying Web pages. A Web browser is that, but it's also much more. There's a lot happening behind the scenes.

## Conducting Locate and Display Missions

When you enter a URL in Navigator's Location box, the program goes to work to locate the Web page you've specified. First, it must search the Internet to find the correct Web server, then it must establish a connection and request the Web page. Next, Navigator begins downloading the HTML file containing the text and formatting codes that describe the Web page. In addition to the HTML file, Navigator must identify and download graphics files, multimedia files, and other resources that make up the Web page.

Downloading the files that make up a Web page is just part of the Web browser's task. Remember, a Web page is not a single, preformatted document. The browser must assemble all of the separate page elements and display them properly onscreen as a single page. That's no small task. First, the text from the HTML file must be sized, formatted, and word-wrapped to fit within browser's viewing window. Then, the browser adds graphics and other elements to build the Web page on your screen. Depending on what's on the page, the browser may need to call on plug-in utilities and other system resources to play back or display some page elements.

After the Web page appears on your screen, the browser isn't finished. The program must monitor every movement of your mouse over the page to detect any interaction with hyperlinks. If you click a hyperlink, the browser must take the appropriate actions to display or play the target of hyperlink.

All these steps are required just to display a simple Web page. In addition, the Web browser provides a multitude of other options and features, such as the ability to print Web pages and maintain bookmarks for convenience, and store copies of recently-used files in a cache on your hard disk to improve performance.

# Who Publishes on the Web?

The short answer is: you do—you, and lots of other people, organizations, and companies.

At first, only a few technically savvy individuals had the knowledge necessary to publish Web pages. But, that situation has rapidly changed. Now, almost anyone can publish on the Web. After all, the technology is not too formidable. At its simplest, a Web page's HTML file is just text with a few embedded codes. As a result, it's possible for anyone with a text editor to create an HTML file that will produce a simple Web page. Also, many tools, such as Composer, are available to make creating a Web page easy and fun.

Creating Web pages is the easy part. What you really need in order to publish on the Web is access to a Web server The immense popularity of the World Wide Web has spawned a brisk market of services that provide access to Web servers. Web server access is available at modest cost from Internet service providers across the country. In fact, many Internet service providers offer Web site hosting as part of the package of services they include with basic Internet access accounts.

Popularity and easy access to the enabling technology has made the Web a very democratic place. Almost anyone can create and publish a Web site—and sometimes it seems that almost everyone does. The World Wide Web is made up of large corporations, small businesses, government agencies, universities, schools, political organizations, charities, clubs, special interest groups, and thousands of individuals.

Basically, anyone with a computer, an Internet connection, and something to say can have a Web site. On the World Wide Web, you'll find everything from corporate image sites, to product information sites, to sites devoted to hobbies and special interests of all kinds. Some people even publish family albums and personal newsletters on the Web for their family and friends.

## Publishing on an Intranet—the Not-So-Wide Web

Web servers on corporate intranets offer another, parallel, Web publishing medium. Web publishing on an intranet uses the same technology as the World Wide Web on the Internet; it's just available to a different audience.

Anyone with Internet access and a Web browser can access a Web page posted on the World Wide Web. In contrast, intranets are more restricted. They are usually available only to coworkers connected to the same local area network.

You can use the same tools—Composer and Navigator—to create and view HTML documents on an intranet that you use to create and view Web pages on the Internet. Whether you're creating or viewing Web pages, the only difference between an intranet and the larger Internet is the address of the Web server and who will be able to access it.

Working on an intranet opens up the possibility of using the technology to share documents with coworkers. And, because your intranet is likely to be an internal network with restricted access, you can do so without worrying about outsiders getting access to documents that were intended for colleagues, not the general public. On an intranet, you can publish documents that would be inappropriate on the larger World Wide Web.

Intranet Webs can serve as company bulletin boards and reference libraries. For example, the human resources department can post company policies, employee manuals, and training materials. The sales department can post price lists and news of new customers and projects. Workgroups can post status reports on projects and share documents. The computer support staff can use the Web to make help files available to users throughout the company. And someone will probably post a page of announcements to stir up interest in a volleyball league or share pictures taken at the company picnic.

# Finding Other Uses for HTML Documents

The HyperText Markup Language and HTML documents were developed for the World Wide Web. So, it's natural to think of HTML documents as Web pages. But HTML has worked its way beyond the Web and is proving to be immensely useful in a growing list of applications, such as:

- Web pages on the World Wide Web
- Limited-access Web pages on intranets
- E-mail. It can emerge from the doldrums of plain text to become as richly formatted as Web pages. Messenger—the e-mail component of the Netscape Communicator suite—can display messages that include HTML codes and all the features those codes make possible.

- Newsgroup articles. Like e-mail, they can be formatted with HTML. Collabra—the newsgroup and collaboration component of the Netscape Communicator suite—lets you create and view messages and articles in the HTML format.

Like HTML itself, Composer can be used for more than just Web pages. Composer isn't just a Web page creation tool, it's an HTML document editor. In fact, Messenger and Collabra automatically invoke a customized version of Composer to create their messages.

# Chapter 2

# PLANNING A WEB SITE

- **Setting your goal**
- **Defining your target audience**
- **Organizing information**
- **Making your site browser-friendly**
- **Intranet publishing: special considerations**
- **Building and maintaining your Web site**

Presumably, you've been surfing the Web for a while, getting to know this new communication medium. You've been observing, watching, learning, and visiting a variety of Web sites, good and bad. You've seen the power of hypertext links, become engrossed in compelling content, and experienced the excitement of animation and multimedia. You've also been disappointed by some of the utterly useless sites that litter the Web.

Now you have some ideas of your own. You have a mission, a message to share with others—you want to publish your own Web site. Perhaps you want to promote your business, espouse a noble cause, or just publish a family newsletter. Maybe you have information you want to share with the world, or you just need to share data with members of your workgroup on a local intranet.

Whatever your reasons are for wanting to create a Web site, you're probably anxious to start learning to use Netscape Composer. However, before you begin the nitty-gritty work of creating Web pages, you need to consider some overall issues. This chapter will get you started and will touch on some of the preliminary planning steps that are essential to successful Web site development. It's sort of like taking a trip. Before you set off, you must have a clear picture of where you are going and a plan for the route you intend to take to get there. Otherwise, you're likely to spend a lot of time wandering aimlessly, and you'll never reach your destination.

# Setting Your Goal

Like any other project, a Web site begins as a concept. The Web site has (or should have) a purpose, a mission, and a reason for existence. This goal should be your guiding principal as you design your site, and everything about the site should support it. It often helps to sit down and write out a sentence or two articulating the purpose of your Web site. Perhaps your goal is to generate sales leads for a new product, or provide technical support for your customers, or furnish employees of your company with information on employee benefits and company policies. If your main goal is very broad, such as creating an online presence to build name recognition and prestige for your company, be sure to work out the approach you plan to take in achieving that goal.

The purpose of having a written goal for your Web site is to help keep your work focused. As you go through the process of developing your Web site, return to your goal from time to time for a reality check. If some aspect of your site doesn't match up to the stated goal, then something needs to change—either revise the aberrant content or restate your goal.

After you decide what you want to accomplish with your Web site, you can begin selecting and developing content. You can write the text, find or draw graphics, and locate other sites you plan to link to. You can also begin developing ideas for what you want your site to look like.

# Defining Your Target Audience

When you define the goal of your Web site, a picture of your target audience should begin to emerge. Defining the target audience is an essential step in any design project, and Web publishing is no exception. You need to determine (or at least guess) who will be viewing your Web site. You need to consider the viewers' background and previous experience, their interests, their tastes, and why they might be visiting your site. One important aspect of the target audience that is unique to Web publishing is the audience's access to your Web site—the speed of their Internet connection, the capabilities of their Web browser software, and the technical expertise of the viewers themselves can all impact how you present the content on your Web page.

If your Web site exists solely as a personal statement or creative exercise, you may think you can ignore the target audience and design your site based on your own tastes and preferences. Actually, in that case, what you are really doing is defining your target audience as yourself and a small circle of friends and other kindred spirits. That's a valid approach—as far as it goes—but it's rather limited.

In practice, most people who publish on the Web do so to get their message out to a larger audience. Your goal should be to reach that audience as effectively as possible. All your Web site design decisions should be based on the needs and wants of the viewers that you envision as your target audience.

For instance, things that make a Web site fun for an audience looking for entertainment might be annoying distractions for a serious-minded researcher looking for information. A lot of graphics and multimedia effects might be just the ticket for creating an exciting Web publication on a corporate intranet where you can reasonably expect everyone to access the site via a speedy local area network. The same content may prove too slow to download practically over a dial-up connection to the Internet.

The keys to successfully communicating with your audience is to first identify the audience, and then to anticipate that audience's reaction to the various elements of your Web site design, so you can select the most effective options. You can tailor almost every aspect of your Web site to the intended audience, from the way you organize information to the kind and number of images to the colors and fonts you use.

# Organizing Information

Once you've laid out a goal for your Web site and defined its target audience, you can begin to think about its content and how you want to present it. The best way to start developing content for your Web site is to organize your assets. Obviously, you'll want to gather up any existing documents and images you want to work with, but your assets can also include corporate-style guidelines and samples of publications in other media, information on Web sites you admire (and may want to emulate), samples of

Web sites you hate (so you can analyze what makes you hate them and avoid the same pitfalls), clip art collections and information on sources of Web art, media, and special effects. Think about the message you want to convey and which types of images, text, and other content might be appropriate. (Is it fun and lighthearted or seriously corporate?) Take inventory of what you've got and determine what is usable, what will need to be modified, and what will need to be created from scratch.

**NOTE** Make sure you have the legal right to use any materials you plan to include in your Web site. For more information, a U.S. copyright law page published by Cornell University is at: `http://www.law` `.cornell.edu/topics/copyright.html`.

**NOTE** Don't expect to publish on the Net via your PC with a dial-up connection to the Internet. To actually publish a document for public viewing on the Web, you'll need access to an HTTP or FTP server. If you're connected to a corporate LAN, your network administrator is probably the one you need to see about getting access to the Web server. If you use a dial-up connection to access the Web, check with your internet service provider. Most internet service providers can provide access to an HTTP or FTP server at little or no additional cost. See Part 4 of this book, Publishing Your Web Site , for procedural details on posting your Web pages to a Web server.

## Creating a Storyboard

With all the materials and information you want to work with in hand, sit down with paper and pencil (or some nifty drawing software) and plot the site out (see Figure 2.1). Storyboard (sketch) your home page and each page it will link to; include all the elements you're considering (text, images, buttons, hyperlinks), and don't be afraid to make adjustments. If your original concept doesn't flow nicely, can it and start again. You can't do too much advance planning.

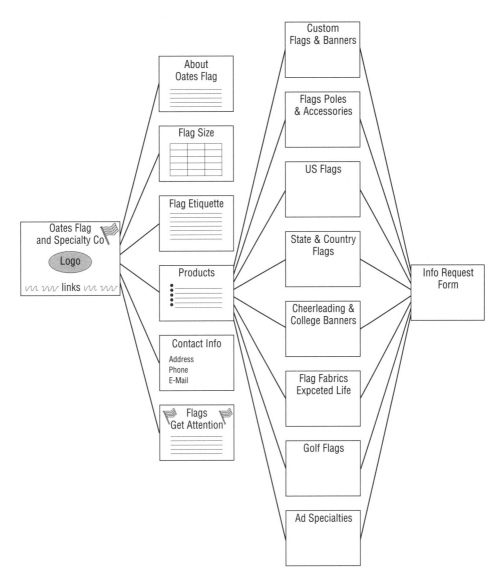

**FIGURE 2.1:**   Sketching out a plan for your Web site helps you visualize how all the parts interrelate.

As you plan your Web site, you need to work on two different levels. First, you need to plan the flow of the information and the appearance of the page itself. Second, if your Web site will be anything more than a single home page, you need to design a map of the site as a whole so you can visualize how all the pages relate to each other and how they work together to create an organic whole.

Remember that the Web thrives on hypertext links and Web users don't expect to read an entire Web site like a novel, moving from page to page in a linear fashion. They want to jump quickly to an item that interests them and then move on to something else. Viewers may enter your Web site at any point via a link from another site. So, you need to design each page of your Web site so that it stands alone and yet is part of a larger whole.

## Working Out a Directory Structure

A very simple Web site may consist of a couple of HTML files and a few images. If that's all you need, you can store all the files in a single directory. Anything more complex will probably need some file management—you'll want to organize your files into subdirectories to make them easier to identify and maintain. For example, you might want to set up separate subdirectories for graphics and multimedia files as shown in Figure 2.2. For really large sites, you may want separate subdirectories for different sections of the site, each of these sections would then have their own subdirectories for things like images, multimedia files, java applets, and such.

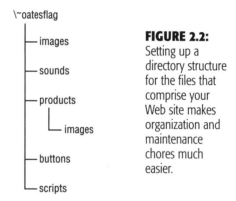

**FIGURE 2.2:** Setting up a directory structure for the files that comprise your Web site makes organization and maintenance chores much easier.

Setting up a directory structure for your Web site is fairly easy, provided you do it in advance. You must know the correct path for each file you specify in a hypertext link or other reference on a Web page. Entering the correct path information when you define a hypertext link is no problem. However, going back and editing a multitude of links to change all the paths is a nasty chore indeed. It's a nuisance on a small Web site; it's nearly impossible on a larger, more complex site.

To avoid this situation, you can determine what your directory structure will be, and then set up the same subdirectory structure on your local hard disk and on the Web server where you post your Web site. When you define links on your Web pages, you can choose file paths as relative to the home directory for the Web site. (See the *Relatively Absolute Address* sidebar in Chapter 7.) If you use relative addresses and have the same subdirectory structure in both locations, you can create and test your Web pages on your local hard drive and be confident that they will work the same when you post your Web site on the server. In order to do this, copy files from your hard disk to their counterpart locations on the Web server.

**NOTE**    You can set up directories and subdirectories on your local hard drive with your usual file maintenance tools such as Windows Explorer or a My Computer window. However, you'll need to check with the administrator of your Web server for information on creating directories and subdirectories. Usually, you'll be able to create subdirectories yourself within your own Web site, but you may need to use a utility program such as WS_FTP or FTP Explorer to do so. You might even need to perform file maintenance chores such as creating subdirectories from a Unix shell account. In some cases, the Web administrator will have to set up the directory structure for you.

## Making Site Navigation Easy for Viewers

Users need to be able to move around a Web site quickly and easily to locate and access information with a minimum of fuss and bother. If you make your Web site hard to navigate, users will just leave and won't come back.

The most important factor in making your Web site easy to navigate is organization. Designing a well-organized site allows you to present information in such a way that it is easy for viewers to see and understand where things are located and how to find what they need. That's one of the reasons why storyboarding your site is so important.

But good organization alone isn't enough. For the sake of speed and ease of use, consider incorporating into your Web pages navigation aids that provide easy one-click access to key locations and sections of your Web site. You can use text links, buttons, graphic icons, or image maps (clickable images) to identify and link to important destinations, such as the home page, next page, or starting points for key topics. It is essential to make the navigational elements obvious, simple to use, consistent throughout and to place them where they are readily available to help viewers find their way around your site. For example, the buttons on the page shown in Figure 2.3 are present on every page in the site. They provide the visitor with easy and obvious links to other key pages in the site.

**FIGURE 2.3:**   Buttons and other navigation aids help viewers find their way around your Web site.

# Making Your Site Browser-Friendly

As discussed earlier, one of the things you must consider in defining your target audience is how that audience will access your Web site. The speed of the viewer's Internet connections is a big part of the access issue. The other major part of the access question is the capability of the viewer's Web browser software. Different brands and versions of Web browsers have significantly different capabilities. Consequently, as you design your Web site, you must consider the impact of your design decisions on those viewers with less than state-of-the-art browsers (dare I call them browser-challenged).

The HTML standard has evolved rapidly over the last few years. It's undergone some very significant changes in a relatively short time with new HTML standards, new browsers, new features, and new extensions to the language popping up every few months. Each new development has meant exciting new possibilities for Web designers. Each new development has also required changes in browser software to recognize and properly display the new features. As a result, older browsers (and even older versions of the currently popular browsers) may not display all the effects that are possible to produce with the latest browser software and the newest HTML codes and extensions. The leading browser developers seem to be in a race to develop and launch more and more new effects and entice Web designers to use them in the hopes of having their own extensions accepted as the de facto standard of the Web.

The rapid pace of change makes it hard for end users to keep up with the latest thing. By the time a new browser version can be adopted and disseminated to a large group of users (such as a large corporation or the subscribers to an online service), it may have been superseded by yet another version that is newer still. Also, some of the less popular platforms may lag a version or so behind the developments of a more popular platform such as Windows 95. As a result, large numbers of Web users are working with browsers that are one or more versions behind the state of the art and are not capable of displaying the latest, cutting-edge effects.

As you now realize, an important part of identifying the target audience is figuring out what browser versions it might be using. Some of the latest effects simply will not display properly (if at all) in an older browser. Therefore, if you want to use the latest, greatest, and most exciting effects, you will be limiting your audience to those viewers using the latest version of the most popular Web browser. If, on the other hand, you want to make your Web site available to the widest possible audience, you must avoid any effects that require the newest browser version or special add-in software and stick with accepted standards that are widely supported by old and new browsers on all platforms. The choice is yours.

## Conserving Bandwidth

Another factor you will need to consider as you design your site is the size of the files that make up your Web pages. HTML files are generally quite small, even when they contain considerable quantities of text. Images and multimedia files, on the other hand, can be very large.

The time and resources required to move those large files around on the Internet can become a significant design consideration. Frequently, you will be required to pay for the amount of storage space your Web site occupies on the Web server. In addition, you might be charged for the volume of data visitors download from your site. However, the biggest problem is the time it takes for your page to appear in the visitor's Web browser window. The bigger the files, the longer it takes to download them.

Some studies suggest that a Web surfer will wait only about 12 seconds for a page to download. My own observations indicate many people are more patient than that and will wait about twice as long. Still, you can expect to have lost many of your potential viewers if your page isn't on their screens in less than thirty seconds. At the very least, slow downloads interrupt the continuity of the reading experience and make viewing your Web site a cumbersome and frustrating experience for the Web surfers who stick around.

With a direct connection to the Internet, you can download a lot of information in thirty seconds, but moving data through a modem connection is another story. The typical Web visitor accesses the Internet via a dial-up modem connection. 28.8K modems are becoming the standard, but many people still use 14.4K modems. The slower the Net connection, the less data that can be transferred in a given amount of time. Thus, the amount of data that a viewer can download in a limited time using a slow modem connection becomes a limiting factor to what you can put on your Web site. Specific suggestions for dealing with file size/bandwidth issues will be discussed in later chapters, especially in Chapter 9, *Adding Sound and Motion with Multimedia*. For now, you just need to keep in mind that images, animations, sounds, and other cool effects often carry a steep price in terms of file size and, therefore, download time.

# Intranet Publishing: Special Considerations

Generally, any of the techniques and principals that work for Web publishing on the Internet also apply to corporate intranets. One of the only differences between the two is that Web sites on the Internet are available to the world and Web sites and documents on an intranet have a much more restricted distribution—they are available only to other users on the same local network.

Limited distribution can be a good thing. It enables you to publish materials that would be inappropriate for just anyone. For example, a company might post its employee manual, personnel policies, project schedules, and even some confidential cost and pricing information on its intranet. The information would be readily available to employees using the intranet but inaccessible to anyone outside the company.

Because of the differences between the Internet's World Wide Web and Web sites on intranets, you need to think about the kind of documents you're likely to create for distribution in each venue. On the Internet, it's important that each Web site be able to stand on its own. Visitors to your site will probably be strangers, and you can't assume that they will have any prior knowledge of you or your topic. Intranets, on the other hand, are often used as a way for coworkers to share documents and information; you're much more likely to create individual documents and distribute them by posting them on the Web server. There is no need to build elaborate multipage sites to create a context for each document because you can reasonably expect your colleagues to share a common background and knowledge base. A simple page title may be enough to provide all the context that's needed for a page posted on an intranet.

## Centralized versus Decentralized Administration

How an intranet is administrated varies greatly. Some intranets are tightly controlled by a single system administrator or a central administrative group that regulates all access to the network and all materials available on it. Other intranets are much more loosely organized with the central administration providing a basic skeleton system and allowing decentralized administration of the details by various departments and perhaps even individual users.

Posting a Web page on an intranet with a centralized administration might involve submitting a request to a person or a group who has the responsibility for maintaining Web services on the intranet. You might not be allowed to create and post Web pages yourself. More likely, you will be able to create your own Web pages, but you must submit them for approval and testing before they will be posted on the Web server.

In contrast, an intranet with decentralized Web administration might have a very informal approval process for Web pages. A designated person in each department might be able to post Web pages on the server. Or the Web server address might be announced, and anyone on the network would be able to post Web pages by simply copying HTML files to the server.

## Security and the Corporate Intranet

The Internet is pretty much open to the entire world. Anything you publish on the World Wide Web is available to anyone with an Internet connection and a Web browser. With intranets, on the other hand, you can be much more selective in who gets access to what. Typically, a corporate intranet is separated from the Internet by a firewall, a proxy server, or both. The firewall and proxy server act as gatekeepers to protect the intranet from unauthorized intrusions. These intranet security features intercept data that passes back and forth between the intranet and the Internet. They pass along information requested by an intranet user but block outsiders from gaining access to the resources of the intranet.

In addition to insulating the intranet from the larger Internet, network administrators can restrict access to Web servers, directories, and documents so that only certain users can access the documents. Restricting access to documents allows corporations to use the power of the Web to provide easy access for authorized users and, at the same time, protect sensitive or proprietary information in those documents from unauthorized users.

Typically, firewalls, proxy servers, and the various levels of access restrictions are transparent to the intranet user. They are set up and maintained by the network administrator. You'll rarely know they are there (unless you get an access denied message when you try to access a restricted resource). But that doesn't mean you can ignore the difference between the intranet and the Internet or the access restrictions. As a responsible intranet user you must be aware of the differences between e-mail addresses and URLs that are part of your corporate intranet and those that are located on the Internet. It's your responsibility to make sure that any confidential information and sensitive messages stay within the confines of the proper directories on the intranet and don't get addressed to an outside party or other unauthorized person. If your intranet is connected to the larger Internet, your systems administrator has probably set up separate Web servers for the internal system and the publicly accessible Internet. You need to be aware of the difference between the two Web servers and pay particular attention to the one where you post the pages you create. Posting a Web page containing sensitive information intended for internal use to the wrong server could have serious repercussions.

## Maintaining Consistent Corporate Style

Posting Web pages on a corporate site usually means following some corporate rules concerning the content and appearance of the documents. The rules may be quite strict or very loose, but there are usually at least some basic rules about what is considered appropriate. Corporate style guidelines can make the documents on the corporate Web site easily distinguishable from outside Web pages. The guidelines may dictate colors, backgrounds, fonts, graphics, and standard navigation buttons.

# Maintaining Your Web Site

A good Web site is rarely just a collection of static documents. Instead, a Web site is a dynamic entity that needs to be updated on a regular basis. As a result, you can't consider your job finished when you complete the process of planning, producing, and posting a Web site—you must plan to devote time to the continued care and feeding of your Web site as well. From time to time, you'll need to add new information to your Web site. But just as important, you must also cull outdated material (particularly broken hyperlinks).

In short, setting up a Web site isn't likely to be a one time project that you can just finish and forget; it's more of an ongoing commitment. However, like adopting a pet, developing and maintaining a Web site can be a rewarding experience if you're willing to invest the time it takes to reap the rewards.

# Chapter 3

# UNDERSTANDING THE ELEMENTS OF PAGE DESIGN

## FEATURING

- **Setting the stage**
- **One column or two? Deciding on a layout**
- **Presenting text**
- **Following hyperlinks**
- **Creating an image with pictures**
- **Adding tables and frames**
- **Getting feedback with forms**
- **Adding sound and action with multimedia**
- **Page design tips**

As you create the pages that make up your Web site, you can draw upon a palette of design elements such as text, hypertext links, images, tables, and multimedia objects. You can control and manipulate each of the elements to determine attributes such as color, alignment, size, and placement on the page. You can also work with basic text paragraphs or multicolumn layouts, with simple images or fancy animation effects.

However, the factors that make your Web site good or bad, exciting or dull, interesting or boring, have less to do with the complexity of your design or the technical sophistication of your effects, and more to do with providing compelling content with a presentation that is appropriate for the viewing audience. All the formatting options, tricks, and techniques are just tools for presenting information. The important thing isn't the tools themselves, but how you use them to present your information.

Still, you need to have a basic familiarity with the tools at your disposal to use them effectively. That's what this book is about—getting familiar with the Web page creation tools in Netscape Composer. This chapter gets things started with a preliminary look at the page design elements you'll be manipulating. Later chapters will delve into the details of how to manipulate those elements with Composer.

> **NOTE** All the Web page design elements described in this chapter can be viewed with Netscape Navigator but not all of them can be created using Netscape Composer. While Composer makes it exceptionally easy to create basic (and some not-so-basic) Web pages and other HTML documents, the program does not support some of the more complex effects that are possible on a Web page.

# Setting the Stage

An artist starts a painting with a blank canvas. A Web designer starts with a blank Web page that will be the background for all the other elements of the page. That page needn't remain completely featureless—at least, not for long. You can give the background character by defining its color, its texture, or adding a picture or design. And while you're at it, you can define some other colors (such as the default colors for text and hyperlinks) as well. Then the Web page designer must consider the page layout—the arrangement of the various elements on the Web page.

## Considering Colors

The default colors for a Web page are black text on a white (or light gray) background. A simple black and white color scheme is functional, providing good legibility for text on most systems, but it's drab. Adding color to your Web page can make a big difference in how that page is perceived by the viewers.

In traditional print publishing, adding color to a project means adding cost for extra production expenses and passes through the printing press. In the world of computers, on the other hand, color is essentially free. Almost all modern computer systems have at least some color capability, and most can reproduce 256 colors or more. So, using color on your Web pages costs only the time its takes you to select and specify your color choices.

The mere presence of color on your Web page can make the page more interesting. But remember, color must be used very carefully. The right combination of colors can make the page appealing and easy-to-read. In contrast, the wrong combination of colors can produce a page that is an unattractive, illegible mess. In addition, colors can have a strong emotional and psychological effect that must be considered.

The psychology of color and how color can be used to affect moods and perceptions can be an interesting study. While it is beyond the scope of this book, here are a few basic generalizations that can be helpful in selecting colors.

- Warm colors (red, orange, yellow) seem to advance toward the viewer; they tend to convey excitement and energy.
- Cool colors (blues and greens) seem to recede away from the viewer; they tend to evoke feelings of tranquillity.

The number and kind of colors you choose for your Web pages can influence a visitor's perception of your site—even before they read a single word. You can set a quiet, conservative tone (by sticking with basic black and white, and adding a few accents of navy blue or hunter green), or create a feeling of festive excitement (with liberal use of bright, high-intensity colors, especially reds and yellows).

**TIP**

One of the best ways to learn how to use color is to observe how other designers have used color. Study magazines, brochures, annual reports, TV, and other Web pages. Look at the colors used and how they affect your perception of the publication, and the product being discussed.

Color does more than affect moods. Your choice of colors also determines the legibility of the text on your Web page. I can't overemphasize the importance of selecting color combinations that produce legible, easy-to-read text. This point is absolutely critical!

## Contrast

The main factor influencing text legibility is contrast—the relative difference between the foreground (text) and the background. Obviously, black and white provide the maximum dark/light contrast. That's why black and white is the standard for most printed material (such as this book) and the default color combination for many Web pages as well. However, you don't have to go to such extremes to maintain adequate contrast for your text to be legible. For example, you can use black or dark-colored text on a light-colored background such as light gray, light blue, beige, or yellow (see Figure 3.1). Similarly, you could use white or light-colored (light gray, cyan, yellow) text on a dark-colored (dark blue, maroon, dark gray) background. Any of these combinations should provide plenty of contrast between the text and background to make the text easy to read. On the other hand, white text on a yellow background or dark blue text on a black background (such as the sample in Figure 3.2) will be difficult to read (if not almost invisible).

**FIGURE 3.1:**　You don't have to stick with black and white as long as your background and text colors have enough contrast for good legibility.

## Color Compatibility

In addition to the dark/light contrast, you should consider color contrast as well. Graphic artists use a tool called a color wheel to help visualize color relationships. As figure 3.3 shows, the color wheel is a pie chart composed of six equally-sized segments. The colors are arranged in sequence starting with red and going through yellow, green, cyan, blue, and magenta to complete the circle back at red.

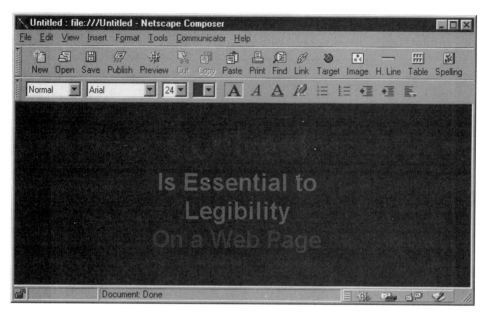

**FIGURE 3.2:**    A lack of contrast between the text and background makes your page hard to read.

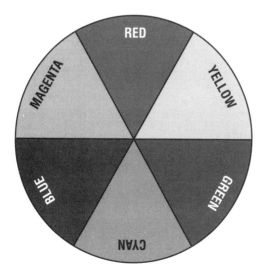

**FIGURE 3.3:**
An artist's color wheel is a valuable reference when choosing colors.

Pairs of colors that are opposite of each other on the color wheel are called complementary colors. Complementary colors exhibit the maximum color contrast and using them together can create visual tension. A color scheme that uses complementary colors can work if one or both colors is subdued. But using full-intensity complementary colors next to each other can create an optical illusion that is very hard to look at—the edge where the colors meet seems to vibrate. Avoid the vibrating color effect for small type at all costs—it's just too hard on the eyes!

Pairs of colors that lie next to each other on the color wheel are called adjacent colors. Adjacent colors have much less color contrast than complementary colors and are, therefore, generally considered compatible or comfortable color combinations—in other words, the colors go well together. The challenge in setting up a color scheme based on adjacent colors is to ensure that there is adequate dark/light contrast between the text and background.

## Should the Background Be Light or Dark?

Contrast is the key to legibility. Black text on a white background delivers excellent legibility due to the contrast between black and white. But what about white text on a black background? The contrast is just as good, but dark backgrounds aren't used as much as white or light-colored backgrounds. Why not?

The prevalence of light-colored backgrounds as a design element can be attributed to habit or tradition—it's what we are used to seeing in other media. Consequently, most people are more comfortable reading black or dark-colored text on a white or light-colored background. So, when you want to emphasize the content of your Web page, it's probably best to stick with the traditional light-colored backgrounds.

On the other hand, using a dark-color background and light text is a good attention-getting technique because it's a bit unusual. If you elect to use a dark-colored background, the color choice becomes very important. Darker colors tend to be more intense than lighter colors and the background color has more impact than the text color because there is so much more of it visible on the page. Therefore, the color of a dark-colored background makes a stronger impression on the viewer than the color of a light-colored background or the color of the text.

### Labeling with Color

In addition to its psychological and aesthetic aspects, color serves a very practical purpose when labeling some elements of the page. This is especially important on a Web page where color helps to identify hyperlinks.

Not only do hyperlinks appear in a different color from the normal text on the page, they are also color coded to show the status of the link. In fact, when you select page colors for a Web page, you specify five different colors:

- Background color
- Normal Text—the default color for all text that isn't a hyperlink
- Link Text—the color of a hyperlink the viewer hasn't visited yet
- Active Link Text—the color of a link that has been selected and is currently loading. (You won't see much of this color. It normally appears for only a second or two.)
- Followed Link Text—the color of links that the visitor has already

> **NOTE** Although these color selections are labeled text colors they apply to the borders around images as well.

You can use color to label other elements of your Web page in addition to hyperlinks. For instance, some designers like to use a different color for headings or for picture captions to help them stand out from the surrounding text. You're free to use any color combinations you like, but beware, using too many colors can be confusing. It's usually best to select a limited palette of colors and to use them very consistently.

> **NOTE** See Chapter 4, *Getting Off to a Quick Start*, for instructions on how to select colors for your Web page.

## Beginning with Backgrounds

In the beginning, there was gray.

Initially, Web page backgrounds were almost always light gray. Actually, viewers could select their own color scheme in most Web browsers, but almost nobody bothered to change the default settings.

When the HTML standard was expanded to include tags that enabled Web authors to specify color schemes for their Web pages, colored backgrounds were created. Any of the standard system colors can now be used as solid colored backgrounds. The advent of colored backgrounds gave Web pages a whole new look; but the changes haven't stopped there.

**NOTE**  See Chapter 6, *Adding Images,* for instructions on how to add background images to your Web page.

## Textures

After a solid-color background, the next step in developing an aesthetically pleasing Web page is the background texture. You can create textures because you can define an image that will serve as the background of a Web page. All the text, foreground images, and other elements of the page appear on top of the background image.

A background image could be a single, large image big enough to fill the entire Web page. But the problem is that the Web designer has no way of knowing the size of the viewer's browser window, so there's no way to be sure how big (or small) to make the background image. Besides, a full-page sized background image would require a large image file that would be slow to download and display.

Therefore, Web page background images are usually small. The Web browser automatically duplicates the background image and displays as many tiled copies as needed to fill the browser window. The effect is similar to the tiled wallpaper·on a Windows 95 desktop.

The repeating background images can be used to produce a variety of patterns. But the technique lends itself to simulating textured backgrounds such as the one shown in Figure 3.4. A very small (and therefore fast to download) image is all that's required to establish a texture such as sand, gravel, paper, or cloth. An image that is little larger is needed to create a more detailed background texture such as wood, leather, or polished stone. A good texture adds visual interest to the page without distracting the viewer from the text.

**FIGURE 3.4:** A textured background can add visual interest to a Web page.

## Watermarks

Of course, background images can do more than just simulate simple textures. The same basic technique can be used to create other effects. One very effective use of a background image is to repeat a logo or other symbol across the page background as shown in Figure 3.5. The result is reminiscent of watermarks on fine stationery, especially if the logo is rendered with a subtle embossed effect. Often, the embossed look isn't required as long as the colors in the logo are sufficiently subdued, so that they stay in their role of as a background, and don't conflict with the text and foreground images.

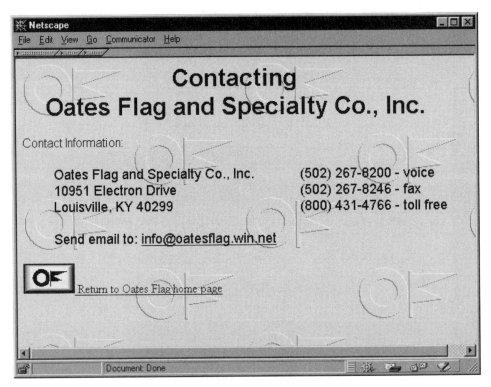

**FIGURE 3.5:**  Repeating a logo as a background image is a good way to give your Web page a strong corporate identity.

## Color Bars

Another very popular background image effect is a color bar running down the left side of the Web page as shown in Figure 3.6. This effect is often combined with a multicolumn page layout. Web designers frequently place buttons or hyperlinks in the left column over the color bar and position the body text in the remainder of the page.

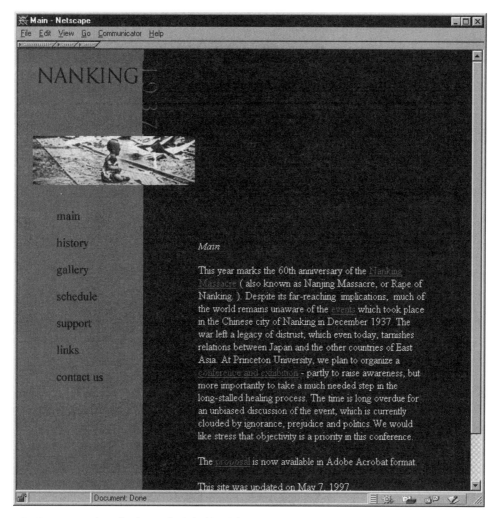

**FIGURE 3.6:** A bar of color on the left side of the page is another popular background image effect.

The color bar effect is achieved by using a background image that is only a few pixels tall but very wide—wider than the widest browser window. Essentially, the background image is a horizontal line that consists of a section of color on the left end (to form the color bar) and the rest of the line is the desired background color. Because the background image is wider than the browser window, the browser's attempt to tile the image results in stacking copies of the background image on top of each other, line over line, to fill the height of the page. (The background image in the graphic below is thicker than necessary and includes a black border to enable you to see how the images are stacked to create the color bar effect.)

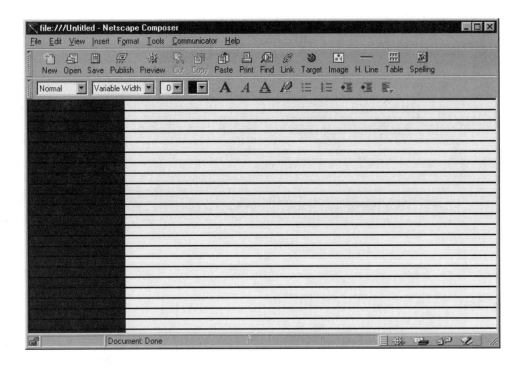

# One Column or Two? Deciding on a Layout

Given the Web's roots in the academic and scientific communities, it's not surprising that HTML and the Web started out as a utilitarian tool. Early Web pages tended to look like a thesis or a submission to a scholarly journal—pages of single-column text with a few illustrations and some formatting to set the headings apart.

As the Web has matured, designers have found ways to apply graphic design principles, developed in other media, to Web page design. Some of the most significant advances have come in the area of page layout—arranging the positions of the elements on the page. Web pages are no longer confined to a single column of text running the full width, from the left to right margins of the page, presenting information in a linear manner.

Now, single-column Web pages, such as the one shown in Figure 3.7, are only one of the options available to a Web author. The single-column page layout is simple, effective, and provides the maximum versatility for adapting to widely varying viewing conditions. It reveals information to the viewer in a linear fashion, as the viewer reads down the page.

**FIGURE 3.7:** The standard Web page layout arranges all text in a single, full-width column.

Web pages can also benefit from the same kind of multicolumn page layouts you commonly see in newspapers, magazines, and brochures. Using multiple columns in the page layout gives the Web page author much more control over how various elements are positioned on the page. As a result, a creative Web page designer can simultaneously add to the page's aesthetic appeal and control the flow of the reader's eye across the page. Multiple columns break the page into smaller sections and they give the Web designer more opportunities to present different information on the same page.

Multicolumn page layouts can range from simple, two-column layouts such as the one shown in Figure 3.8, to three- or four-column page layouts such as the one shown in Figure 3.9. Sometimes, a column doesn't actually contain text; it may exist simply as a spacer to affect where on the page the another column of text will appear.

Multiple columns are produced from an unusual type of HTML tags. The secret to creating multiple-column Web pages lies in the innovative use of the HTML table features. Basically, you just use a large table as a page layout grid and adjust the table settings to make the structure of the table disappear. All that is visible to the viewer then, is text and images arranged in neat columns. The technique works because there is no restriction on what you can place in each cell of a table. A single table cell can contain a whole column of text, complete with images.

**NOTE** See Chapter 10, *Creating Multicolumn Layouts with Tables*, to learn how to create your own multicolumn Web pages.

## Layout with Layers

Tables have been the tool that allows Web authors to have more control over how elements are positioned on a Web page. Now, a new development promises to raise the graphic design bar to a higher level.

A new HTML feature, called layers, will allow Web page designers to specify the exact position of each element on a Web page. Individual page elements can overlap and be turned on or off. Not only that, layers make it possible to control the order in which things appear on the page.

Layers hold the promise of some exciting, new Web page effects. This new development could make tables, as a page layout tool, obsolete. The demo page, shown in Figure 3.10, shows how the viewer can click icons to display or hide different components of the architectural rendering. It brings a new level of user interaction to the Web.

**FIGURE 3.8:** Breaking the text into two columns has a dramatic impact on the Web page layout.

**FIGURE 3.9:** You don't have to stop with only two columns.

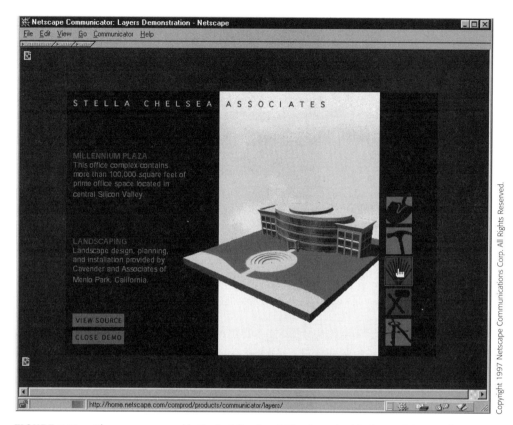

**FIGURE 3.10:**   Viewers can assemble the building by clicking icons in this demo of the new layers feature.

Layers are a new technology—an extension to the HTML standard—that is not yet uniformly supported. Only the latest versions of the most advanced Web browsers can interpret and display Web pages using the layers tags. As a result, it's not yet practical to use layers on a Web page that you intend to publish for the general Web public.

Currently, the latest version of Netscape Navigator can display Web pages using layers. Composer, on the other hand, does not support layers; it has no facilities for defining and manipulating layers on a Web page.

# Presenting Text

Let's face it, most Web pages are mostly composed of text. Consequently, the appearance of the text will have a tremendous impact on the appearance of your Web page.

Before the World Wide Web became popular, most documents viewed on the Internet typically had plain, unformatted text, and they usually appeared in a monospaced font such as courier. It was pretty ugly stuff.

The World Wide Web brought a revolutionary change in the appearance of online documents such as the one shown in Figure 3.11. The combination of HTML and a Web browser makes it practical to display text in proportional fonts and use bold, italics, different text sizes, and other types of formatting similar to what we use when we work with a word processor.

It's interesting to note how text is handled on the Web. Usually, the Web page author specifies text formatting options such as bold, italics, underline, colors, and text sizes in the HTML source code. However, it's the viewer's settings in their Web browser that mostly determines what font will be used to display the text. In fact, HTML originally provided no way for the Web author to select fonts beyond choosing between a variable width or monospaced font. This generic font selection arrangement allows viewers to select from the fonts available on their own systems and choose the ones that display attractively.

**NOTE**  See Chapter 5, *Working with Text*, for an exploration of Composer's text handling features.

Enhancements to HTML give the Web author more control over the fonts that appear on Web pages. Now in Composer, any font can be applied to text in your Web page. If that font is available on the viewer's system, the Web browser will use it to display your page. For example, the page shown in Figure 3.12 uses a casual, handwriting-style font for the list of links in the left column.

The problem with specifying these types of fonts is that the list of universally available fonts is very small. Most systems will have access to some variation of Ariel (or Helvetica), Times Roman, and Courier; but that's about all. There is an assortment of fonts (such as the Comic Sans font used in Figure 3.12) available on the Internet, for use on any Web page. But not everyone has downloaded and installed these fonts. Even if they had, the list of fonts contains less than a dozen basic typefaces plus bold and italic variations.

To address the problem of limited font availability, a new development—dynamic fonts—has emerged. Dynamic fonts stay on a Web server and are downloaded by a Web browser only when needed to display Web pages. This technology holds a lot of promise, but it hasn't yet achieved widespread acceptance. Navigator can properly display Web pages containing dynamic fonts, but Composer contains no features to create pages these fonts.

**FIGURE 3.11:**   The default font in most Web browsers is Times Roman.

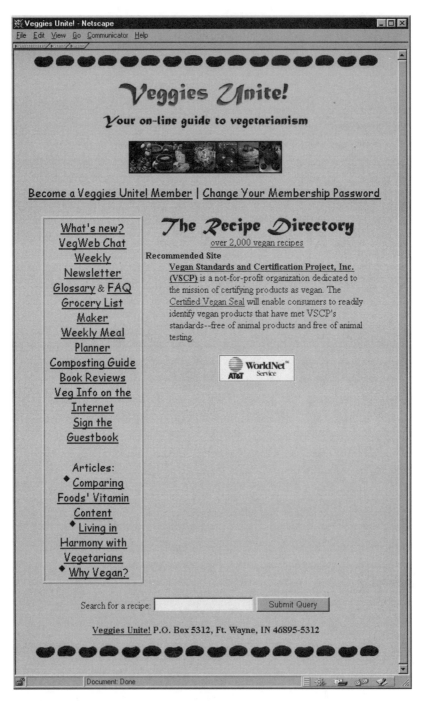

**FIGURE 3.12:** This page uses a non-standard font for the links in the left column.

One sure-fire method of adding a variety of fonts that the viewer will definitely see, is to create a graphic image of text that contains a special font. Then, instead of attempting to format text on the Web page to use the selected font, you simply insert the image in place of the text. Because almost all Web browsers can display images, you can be assured that the viewer will see the text as you intended. This technique, shown in Figure 3.13, works great for logos, headlines, and many other applications. Until dynamic fonts and other font initiatives become mainstream on the World Wide Web, graphic images of text are probably the best way to introduce a variety of fonts to your Web pages.

# Following Hyperlinks

Hyperlinks are the lifeblood of the World Wide Web. More than anything else, it is hypertext links between Web pages that give the World Wide Web it's character and define the Web surfing experience. (It's no coincidence that the language of the Web is called HTML for *HyperText* Markup Language.)

Hyperlinks make the World Wide Web a unique medium. They change the way a viewer can interact with the information on a Web page. Instead of reading a Web page in a sequential, linear fashion, like a traditional printed document, the viewer can interrupt their reading to follow a hyperlink. By jumping from page to page, clicking hyperlink after hyperlink, the process of reading a Web page is transformed into a stream-of-consciousness experience. Because the viewer is an active participant, choosing what they view next, the Web becomes a more engaging medium.

Hyperlinks can lead to almost anything. The target of a hyperlink can be another Web page, another location on the current page, an image, or any other computer file available for download from the Web server.

As you design your Web pages, you need to give careful consideration to the hyperlinks you include. Think about what the viewer might be looking for and what they might find interesting. Use hyperlinks to provide a variety of ways to experience your Web page. Sometimes it helps to think of each Web page as an index, or table of contents, to all the targets of all the hyperlinks on the page. It's easy to see how the page shown in Figure 3.14 serves as an index to the link pages. Most Web pages must perform the same function to a lesser degree.

**TIP**   Make your hyperlinks clear, concise, and descriptive to give the viewer a good idea of what they will find, if they follow the link.

**FIGURE 3.13:** To display an interesting variety of fonts, this page uses images of text that needs to appear in non-standard fonts.

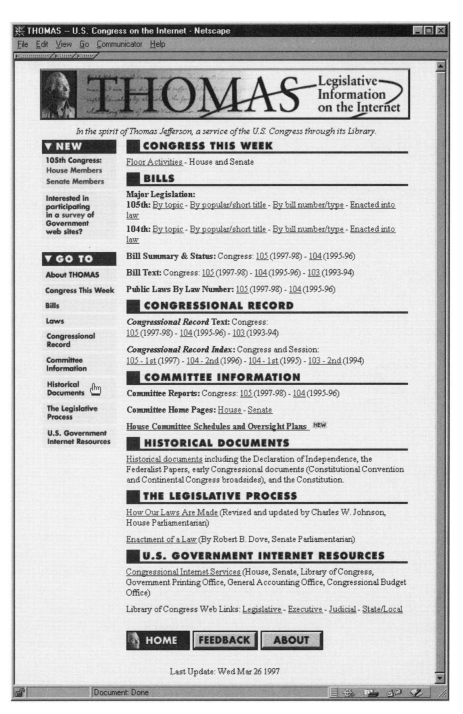

**FIGURE 3.14:**    Many Web pages exist to provide links to other Web pages where the viewer will find the information they seek.

**NOTE** See Chapter 7, *Getting Linked Up,* for information on how to create and edit hyperlinks in Composer.

# Creating an Image with Pictures

Images, as you well know, are another important aspect of the World Wide Web. It's the many Web page images that transform the World Wide Web from a drab world of text documents to the graphically rich experience we all know and love. Perhaps, the original developers of the World Wide Web included the ability to display images so that charts, graphs, and illustrations could be added to the dissertations and research documents they envisioned as typical Web documents. Modern Web authors have put images to use for a wider variety of purposes. Today, images are more likely to be used to add color and visual interest or to create a user interface with buttons and images maps; although, some images can convey essential information as well.

**NOTE** See Chapter 6, *Adding Images,* to learn how to add images to the Web pages you create with Composer.

## Announcing Banner Graphics

A very popular Web page design technique is to start the page with a banner graphic—a colorful image that identifies your site with some distinctive logo or illustration. The idea is, that the strong visual will make a good first impression and be more memorable than a text headline.

For example, as you can see in Figure 3.15, the logo at the top of the page unmistakably identifies the Web site. In addition, each headline on this opening page of the Web site is accompanied by a separate minibanner to give each topic a graphic identity.

While this is a good design approach, its effectiveness is sometimes compromised by slow execution. Images take much longer to download and display than text—especially when a user views your Web site via a dial-up Internet connection over a slow modem. Unfortunately, the viewer may have to wait a significant amount of time for the image to appear.

**FIGURE 3.15:**    Banner graphics identify the Web site and each topic on this page.

The only way to eliminate the problem of slow image downloads is to avoid using images of any kind, and stick to plain text. But, you would then have to sacrifice the considerable power of graphic images. The best approach is to balance the need for speed with the appeal of graphics. Choose images to convey information and not just for their random decorative value. Then, make sure every image is properly sized and compressed to create the smallest possible file, so as to keep download times to a minimum.

These guidelines apply to every image in your Web site, but especially to banner graphics, because the banner is often the first thing a viewer will see. You can't expect viewers to wait too long for that initial graphic to appear.

## Say It with Pictures

Perhaps the most apparent use for images is to add pictures, charts, graphs, and illustrations to a Web page. Scanned photos such as the picture of the young girl on the page shown in Figure 3.16 can, indeed, be worth the proverbial thousand words when it comes to setting a mood. Illustrations can often communicate important information in a way that words alone can't.

In addition to the obvious uses of images as part of the main content of the Web page, they play many supporting roles as well. I've already mentioned a few of them: background images, graphics text, and banner graphics. Images are also used to place logos and symbols on Web pages. There are still more uses for images, just read on.

## Navigating with Buttons

By anchoring a hyperlink to an image, you can create an image that, when the viewer clicks it, will take them to another Web page, download a file, or play a multimedia effect. As a result, the image acts like a button—you click it to make something happen.

This simple concept has a very powerful effect. It allows a Web author to make a Web page function like a graphical user interface. Of course, hyperlinks can be anchored to simple words or phrases of text, but using images can make the interface more intuitive. The buttons in the left column of the page, shown in Figure 3.17, are a good example of images that make effective hyperlinks. Images that look like the buttons we all use to control household appliances and other machines don't need instructions to click here. Their use is immediately apparent. The images of buttons can be labeled with icons, simple text (as in the figure), or a combination of both (as in the banner at the top of the page in the figure).

**FIGURE 3.16:** Pictures can convey data, but they also set a mood, which is sometimes equally as important.

**FIGURE 3.17:** The images of buttons make excellent anchors for hyperlinks. They seem to scream "Click Me!"

Using hyperlinks anchored to clickable images is a great way to provide viewers with simple, easy to understand navigation aids that help them find their way around your Web site. But all the images that anchor hyperlinks don't have to look like buttons. Signs provide another useful passageway. Images of icons and symbols, such as the ones shown in Figure 3.18, can be just as effective as rectangular button images in leading viewers to follow hyperlinks.

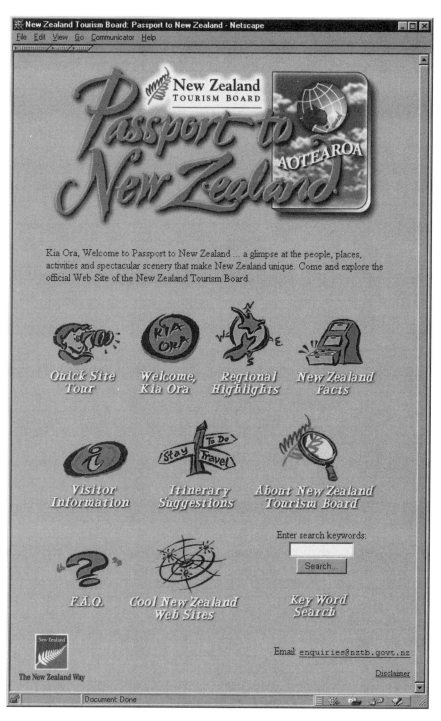

**FIGURE 3.18:**    Images of icons and symbols also make good buttons when anchored to hyperlinks.

## Finding Your Way with Maps

If an image that anchors a hyperlink is called a button, what do you call an image that anchors several different hyperlinks? The answer is an image map.

An image map is just an image that has been divided into smaller sections each of which can serve as the anchor for a separate hyperlink. As a result, clicking different portions of the image can take the viewer to different hyperlink targets.

The opening page of the Sybex Web site (shown in Figure 3.19) is a good example of an image map. The virtual desktop is a single image that contains hyperlinks to the major areas of the Web site. Click different parts of the image to take you where you want to go. For instance, to go to the online catalog page, click the shelf of books on the left side of the image; to go to a page where you can learn more about the company, click the Sybex logo on the computer screen in the middle of the image.

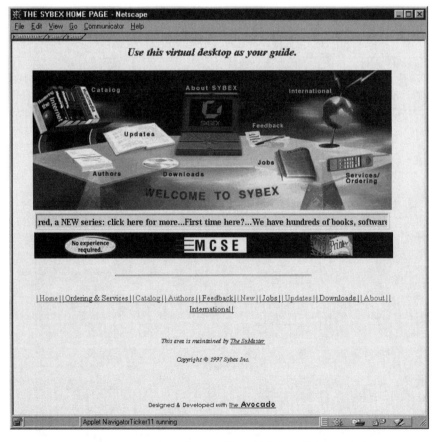

**FIGURE 3.19:** An image map is one image with multiple hyperlinks attached.

Working with image maps is somewhat more complex than working with single images and hyperlinks. Defining the different areas within an image to anchor hyperlinks and setting up those links requires some specialized programming. It used to be that creating image maps required running custom programs on the Web server. Now, it's possible to create image maps that are self-contained within the Web page and function with support from the Web browser—no special server programs are required.

Composer doesn't include any facilities for defining image maps. If you want to create an image map, you'll need to use a separate utility program designed for that purpose. Then, to add the image map to your Web page, you'll need to copy the HTML code generated by the image map program and paste it into the HTML source document for your page. Again, that's not something Composer allows you to do, so you'll need to use an external HTML editor to directly manipulate the HTML source code. After you add the code for the image map to your page, you can edit other portions of the page with Composer without worrying about trashing the image map in the process.

# Adding Up Tables

A table is a way of organizing text or numbers by arranging them in columns and rows. You see tables everywhere. Invoices, bus schedules, calendars, and spreadsheets are examples of tables.

Tables might be common, but they weren't easy to produce using early versions of HTML. The way the Web browser wraps lines of text to fit within the browser window made it impossible to align text into columns by simply inserting extra spaces. To meet the need for reliable, nicely formatted tables on Web pages, newer versions of HTML have instituted special tags for defining tables. The HTML table features have become a powerful tool for Web designers.

Using table tags, you can create a table such as the one shown and Figure 3.20. Composer includes table creation features that enable you to create and edit tables quickly and easily; and your tables needn't be as plain as this example. You can change the background and the grid lines of a table, change the text formatting, and add images and other elements (including another table) to any table cell. Tables can even serve as a page layout tool to produce multicolumn layouts.

**NOTE**    For information on how to use Composer's table creation tools, see Chapter 8, *Working with Tables.*

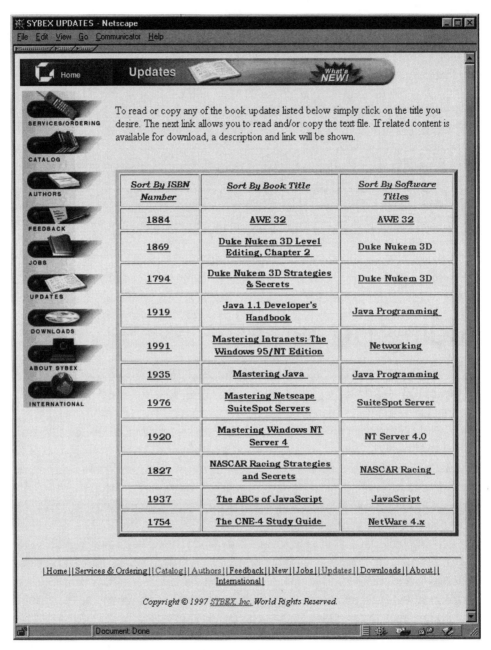

**FIGURE 3.20:** Creating tables is easy with the tools provided by Composer.

# It's a Frame Up

Frames are an HTML feature that enables the Web author to divide the browser window into smaller, separately scrollable windows. Each frame acts almost like a separate browser window. The viewer can scroll and move about in one frame without affecting other portions of the Web page. One good use of frames is to create a toolbar of navigation buttons that remain accessible onscreen no matter where you scroll in the frame. For example, the text labels in the left column of the Netscape developer's site, shown in Figure 3.21, are just such a group of hyperlinks. Those links, and the banner at the top of the page, are in separate frames and remain fixed in place as the viewer scrolls through the text in the other frame.

| NOTE | Visit GroundZero's site at `http://groundzero.com` for a several examples of frames in use. When you're ready to tackle frames yourself, visit Netscape's guide at `http://home.netscape.com/ assist/net_sites/frames.html`. |
|---|---|

Frames are definitely an advanced Web page design technique. Using frames effectively requires careful planning and an understanding of the programming principles involved in making frames work. Composer does not support frames; so, if you want to use frames, you must do it on your own.

# Getting Feedback with Forms

Web pages can include forms that allow viewers to submit information to the Web server for processing. For example, the Web page shown in Figure 3.22 includes Web form components that enable the viewer to specify the search parameters of the site's database of books.

Web forms work pretty much like their paper counterparts. You fill in the information and submit it (but in this case, it is submitted with the click of a button). Anyone who has used dialog boxes will recognize the text boxes, selection lists, checkboxes, and radio buttons that appear in Web forms. Using the form to solicit information, instead of an e-mail message, insures that the data will be submitted in the proper format for efficient processing.

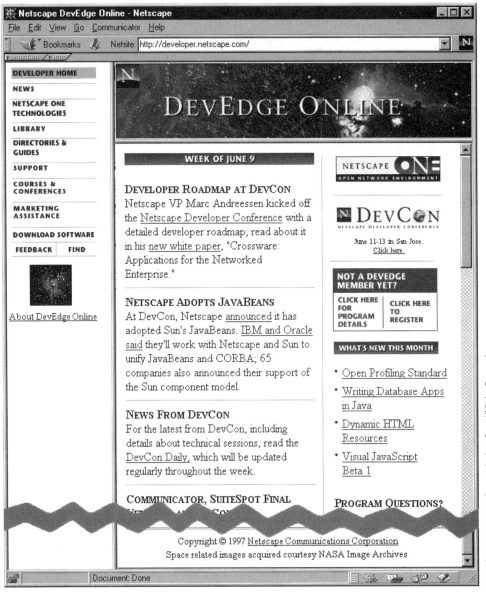

**FIGURE 3.21:** The most common and effective use for frames is to keep navigation links accessible, no matter how the main window is scrolled.

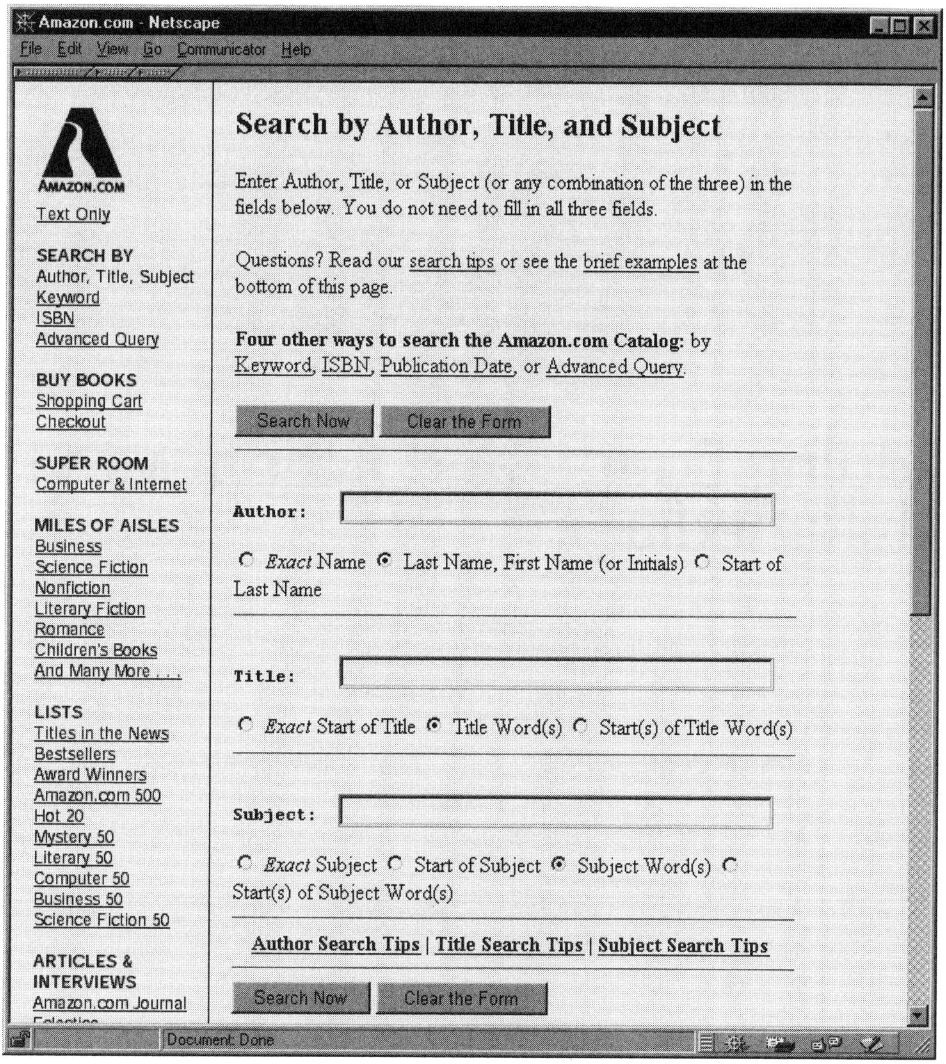

**FIGURE 3.22:**    Fill in the form on this Web page to search for a book listed in the database.

Web forms work with the information processing programs running on the Web server to accept submissions from viewers and send the information to the program or person that needs it. The information gathered from a Web form can be used to generate a response from a program such as a search engine, or it can be stored in a database or forwarded to a human for action.

Web forms are another fairly advanced Web page design technique. You won't find convenient buttons or commands in Composer to facilitate creating Web forms. But, if you're determined to add a form to your Web site, you'll need to do it by manually editing the HTML source code for the Web page.

> **NOTE**
>
> See Chapter 12, *Going Beyond the Limits of Composer,* for information on working with forms and other features that aren't supported by Composer.

# Adding Sound and Action with Multimedia

Web pages can include not only text and graphics, but sounds and moving pictures as well. Incorporating such multimedia elements can add an exciting new dimension to a Web page. It's no longer something you read—it's something you experience.

Multimedia elements can include the following:

- Sounds—audio information such as sound effects, music, and voices that Web surfers can hear when they visit your page
- Movies and Video—pictures don't have to be still; you can see live-action video clips on the Web
- Animation—scrolling text marquees, logos that spin and dance, and illustrations that move are all possibilities on a multimedia enhanced Web page

> **NOTE**
>
> See Chapter 9, *Adding Sound and Motion with Multimedia,* for details of various multimedia options and how to add them to your Web pages.

# Interacting with Multimedia Content

Manipulating multimedia is more involved than dealing with simple text and images. Almost all computer systems can display text and images, but successfully playing multimedia content often requires some special hardware or software. For instance, in order to hear sounds, a viewer's system must be equipped with a sound card and speakers. In addition to the standard Web browser, the viewer may also need a plug-in, helper application, or system software enhancement to play back the Multimedia content.

Unlike images, which have been standardized on a couple of file formats, multimedia content is available in many different (often incompatible) forms and file formats. A few of the most common multimedia formats are supported by either the popular Web browsers or the Windows (or Macintosh) system software. Otherwise, you will need to download and install special playback software for each type of multimedia content you wish to view. Not surprisingly, you'll also need special software to create each type of multimedia content. Some kinds of multimedia content even require that special software be installed on the Web server.

It takes a lot of data to reproduce sounds and motion. So, it's not surprising that multimedia files tend to be very large. Therefore, one of the problems associated with multimedia is the time it takes to download content before it can be played or displayed. Attempts to address this problem range from data compression, to defining animation in scripts that are interpreted by the browser, to a technique known as streaming—a process that enables multimedia content to begin playing as soon as a portion of the file has been downloaded.

Multimedia content is a varied lot. And the techniques for working with the different forms of multimedia are equally varied. In some cases, you can create a multimedia file using an appropriate program; then, you can add a hyperlink from that file to your Web page, just like adding any other hyperlink. When a viewer clicks the hyperlink, their Web browser downloads the file and playback begins automatically, providing they have the required playback software installed. Other forms of multimedia can be added to your Web page like images. Still other multimedia formats require scripts or special codes to be embedded in the HTML source code.

## Just What Is VRML?

Another form of multimedia is VRML, which stands for Virtual Reality Modeling Language. Just as HTML brought hypertext to the Internet, VRML promises to bring 3-D virtual reality to the Web. Using VRML, it's possible to define 3-D spaces in place of the flat 2-D Web pages that make up the regular World Wide Web. Then, a visitor to a VRML site can use a special VRML viewer (or a Web browser equipped with VRML additions) to move through the 3-D space and interact with some of the objects in that space, somewhat like interacting with the hyperlinks on a typical Web page.

So far, VRML use is limited to a small niche occupied by some computer gaming enthusiasts. In the future, the technology may have broader applications, but for now, VRML is essentially an interesting experimental area without many practical applications, outside of games. But you won't be creating virtual reality worlds with Composer; it doesn't support VRML.

# Page Design Tips

One of the best ways to learn about Web page design is to explore the Web, looking at lots of examples of Web pages. You've probably been doing that already, but you may not have really studied the Web pages you encountered. When you see a Web page you like, stop to think about what you like about it. Is it the colors or images that are appealing? Was the layout attractive and effective? Are the buttons easy to understand? How are the various pages of the site organized? Take note of the best ideas and incorporate them into the Web pages you create. Similarly, when you see a Web page you don't like, try to analyze what it is that turns you off. Was the appearance of the Web page unappealing, or was the content disappointing or poorly organized? By figuring out what went wrong with another Web page, you can avoid making the same mistakes.

> **TIP**
>
> When you see a Web page containing a feature you want to emulate, you can get a closer look at how the Web author achieved the effect. When viewing the page in Navigator, choose View ➢ Page Source to open a window displaying the HTML source code for the page. If you want to study the page further, choose File ➢ Save As and save the page as a file on your hard disk for future reference.

**WARNING** Don't just save a Web page on your hard disk and then use it as a template for your own pages. While it's all right to study other Web pages and learn from what other Web authors have done, it's generally considered unethical (and perhaps illegal) to actually copy the code for someone else's Web page without permission.

The following list of tips and general comments about Web page design may help to get you thinking about what makes an effective Web page:

- Web surfers are impatient. Make sure that you present something to grab their attention within the first few seconds after they arrive at your Web site.
- The title for your page is important; make it short, catchy, and descriptive. Also, make sure the title is accurate and that your page lives up to the promise of its title.
- Place important, attention getting items at the top of the page where they will appear on the first screen the viewer sees. Don't expect Web surfers to scroll down the page until after you've captured their attention.
- Keep your Web pages short. If you need to scroll down more than about three screens to reach the bottom of the page, consider breaking it up into more than one page.
- Keep your pages focused. Don't attempt to get everything on one page—use separate pages for separate aspects of a topic and tie the pages together with hyperlinks.
- Don't waste viewers' time by forcing them to wait for images to download that don't add much to the page.
- Make sure buttons and other navigational links behave as the viewer expects them to.
- Use compressed images and other techniques to make your page load as quickly as possible.
- Make your Web site browser-friendly by avoiding HTML tags and features that aren't supported by all the common Web browsers.
- If you include multimedia content that requires special playback software, provide a link to where viewers can obtain the software and instructions for its use.
- Get permission to use text or images created by someone else.
- Sign your work. Give viewers a way to send comments to the Web author by adding a link to your e-mail address to key pages on your Web site.

- Test your page and make sure every link and other feature works before you publish the page on the Web. Test it again by accessing the page from the server using different Web browsers.
- Retest your Web pages on a regular basis to find and fix any broken links.
- Keep your Web pages fresh. Remove any outdated information and add new information from time to time.

There is no formula for guaranteed success at Web page design. What works on one site, under one set of circumstances, may not work equally well under other circumstances. Besides, the Web is a new and exciting medium with lots of experimentation and innovative new developments going on all the time. That's part of the fun of the Web experience!

# Part 2

# Building Your Own Web Page with Composer

# Chapter 4

# GETTING OFF TO A QUICK START

- **Starting and configuring Composer**
- **Using the Page Wizard**
- **Creating pages based on templates**
- **Using Composer to create and edit pages**
- **Peeking behind the scenes: the HTML code**
- **Using Navigator to check your Web page**

The first part of this book covered Web publishing concepts—some background on the World Wide Web, and the elements you'll need to work with to create and publish a Web page. You should already have an idea of where you are going, what kind of Web site you want to create, the audience it should appeal to, and what you want the Web site to accomplish. So, now it's time to begin looking at ways to use the tools at hand to get the job done.

In this chapter, I'll show you how to get started creating simple Web pages with the help of the Netscape Page Wizard and templates. Then, I'll introduce Composer—the powerful publishing component of the Netscape Communicator suite, designed for creating and editing HTML documents. Composer provides a WYSIWYG environment that makes working with HTML documents as easy as using a word processor. Although the obvious use for Composer is to create Web pages, it is equally useful for creating richly formatted e-mail and other messages. (Later chapters will explore the various features of Composer in detail.)

# Starting and Configuring Composer

Before you get started, you should make sure Composer is properly set up and ready to use. Composer is normally installed along with Navigator and the rest of the Netscape Communicator suite, so you shouldn't need to do anything special to add the program to your system.

To launch Netscape Composer, follow these steps:

1. Starting from your Windows 95 desktop, click the Start button in the taskbar.
2. From the Start menu, Point to Programs. When the cascading menu appears, point to Netscape Communicator.
3. The Netscape Communicator menu will then appear, click Netscape Composer.

> **TIP**
> If you have more than one user profile defined for Communicator, the Select Profile dialog box will appear. Select your profile name from the list and then click the Start Communicator button. If you have only one profile defined, this step will not be necessary and Composer will start immediately.

The Netscape Communicator splash screen appears briefly, then Composer starts. You should now see a blank editing window, as shown in Figure 4.1.

> **TIP**
> If you're already running any of the other Communicator programs, you can start Composer by choosing Communicator ➢ Page Composer. The Communicator menu is available in all the Communicator programs.

Formatting Toolbar
Composition Toolbar
Menu bar

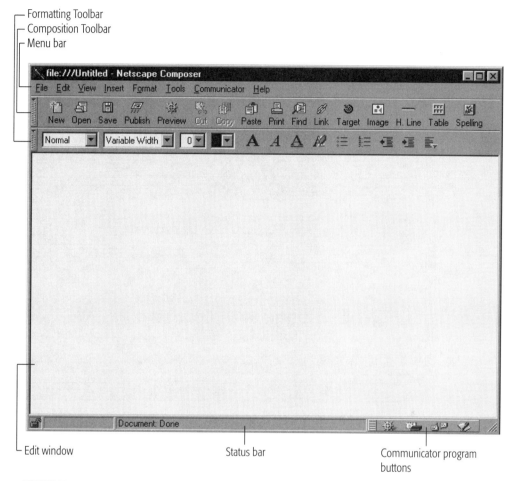

Edit window                    Status bar                    Communicator program
                                                              buttons

**FIGURE 4.1:**    Netscape Composer starts out with a clean, blank page in its edit window.

## Setting Defaults and Preferences

After you've launched Composer for the first time, it's a good idea to check the default settings and preferences to see if they are appropriate for your needs. Most of the default settings are fine for general use, but at the very least, you'll want to enter your name as the author of your Web pages. You can also configure Composer to use predetermined external editors to edit HTML source code and images, and select how you want Composer to display font size choices.

To set the preferences in Composer, follow these steps:

1.    From Composer's menu, choose Edit ➤ Preferences. This will open the Preferences dialog box.

**2.** In the Category list, click Composer.

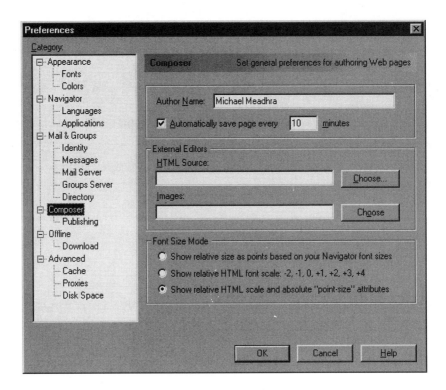

**3.** From this category, in the Preferences dialog box, you can adjust the following settings:

**Author Name:** Enter your name here. Composer will automatically list your name as author in the header of the Web pages you create.

**Automatically Save Page Every *x* Minutes:** You can instruct Composer to automatically save your work at specified intervals. Just check the checkbox and enter the number of minutes between automatic saves in the minutes text box. (The default is 10 minutes, but you can select any interval you prefer.)

**External Editors:** Choose the programs you want for editing HTML source code and Images. Composer relies on these external programs to provide direct, manual editing of the HTML source code and the images you place on your page. Composer doesn't have its own built-in text editor for HTML source code or an image editor for manipulating images beyond placing them on the page and resizing the image. When you choose to edit the HTML source code or an image, Composer will launch the programs listed here to handle the job. (I'll discuss the use of an external HTML editor in more detail in Chapter 11, *Getting Your Hands Dirty: Editing HTML*.)

**Font Size Mode:** Composer can display font size choices in one of three modes, and you can select which mode you prefer here. (Chapter 5, *Working with Text*, will explain the font sizing options in detail.)

> **NOTE**
>
> **For now, you can ignore the settings in the Publishing sub-category that appears under the Composer category of the Preferences dialog box. Those settings come into play only when you publish your page to a Web server. I'll cover them in Chapter 13, *Posting Your Pages on the Web*.**

4.  When you have adjusted the settings in the Preferences dialog box, click OK to close the dialog box and record your settings. Composer will apply the settings (except Author Name) to your current page and will use all these settings (including Author Name) as the defaults for Web pages you create in the future.

With the Composer preferences set, you're ready to begin creating Web pages.

# Using the Page Wizard

Perhaps the easiest way to create your first Web page is to let a wizard do most of the work. The Netscape Page Wizard enables you to create a very basic home page. The page doesn't contain a lot of fancy effects or options. It's just a title, some text, a list of links, and an e-mail contact. You get a choice of backgrounds, rules, and bullets, but that's about all. There is no option for adding fancy graphics, tables, or multimedia. The page you create with the Netscape Page Wizard is suitable for use as a personal home page but it's not going to impress anyone. Still, it's a good way to get started, and you can always edit the page later to add more pizzazz.

No doubt, you've used wizards before—to install and setup software or perform any number of other tasks. Like other wizards, the Netscape Page Creation Wizard gathers information from you, as it leads you through the process of creating a Web page. However, unlike the typical wizard you may have used with another program, the Netscape Page Wizard is not installed on your hard drive; instead, the wizard runs on the Netscape Web site. As a result, you need to use a Web browser to interact with the wizard. Therefore, strange as it may seem, the easiest way to start using Composer to create a Web page is to begin the process in Navigator.

Using the Netscape Page Wizard is simple. You just enter information about what should appear on the Web page into an onscreen form, and the wizard will create a simple home page for you. After the page is displayed in Navigator, you can save the page and use it as is, or edit and refine it in Composer.

## Follow the Wizard

The Netscape Page Wizard makes it easy to create your first home page. First, you'll need to make sure you are connected to the Internet and Navigator (or Composer, or any other program in the Communicator suite) is running. Then, simply follow these steps:

1.  In Navigator, Composer, Messenger, or Collabra, choose File ➤ New ➤ Page From Wizard. This will launch Navigator (if it isn't already running), connect to Netscape's Web site, and load the Netscape Page Wizard page. When the wizard first appears, it looks a little strange (see Figure 4.2). The Navigator window is divided into three frames, but initially only one frame is occupied.

2.  Use the scroll bars on the upper-right frame to scroll down through the introduction. Click the Start button to get things rolling. Now, instructions will appear in the left frame.

    When you click a link in the instruction frame, your choices will appear in the bottom frame. There you can enter text or select an option. A preview of the page you are building will appear in the right frame as shown in Figure 4.3. Some of your choices will take effect immediately when you click them; others won't be reflected in the preview frame until you click an Apply button.

3.  Click the give your page a title link in the instruction frame. Type a title in the text box in the bottom frame and click the Apply button. Watch the title appear in the preview window on the right.

4.  Enter the first block of text by clicking the type an introduction link in the instruction frame and typing the text into the text box in the bottom frame. You can enter anything from a short phrase to a paragraph of text (up to 1000 characters). Click the Apply button to see the effect in the preview frame.

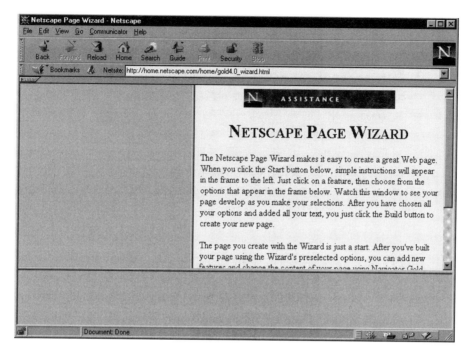

**FIGURE 4.2:**    The initial Navigator Window in Netscape Page Wizard: one frame occupied

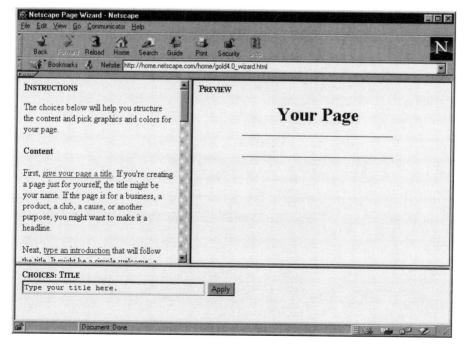

**FIGURE 4.3:**    Instructions, choices and a preview of your page

5. If you want to add links to other Web pages, click the <u>add some hot links to other Web pages</u> link in the instruction frame.

    **a.** In the Name text box in the bottom frame, enter the text that will appear on the page to describe the link.

    **b.** In the URL text box, type the Internet address for the page to which you want to create a link.

    **c.** After entering the Name and URL, click Apply to add the link to the page in the Preview frame.

    **d.** Repeat steps a through c to add other links.

6. Now you have an opportunity to enter another block of text. Click the <u>type a paragraph to serve as a conclusion</u> link and enter the text as in step 4. This block of text doesn't have to be a conclusion. It is simply a text block that sits below the list of hot links.

7. Click the <u>add an e-mail link</u> in the instruction frame, if you want to add your e-mail address to the page. Enter your e-mail address in the text box in the bottom frame and click the Apply button. The wizard adds a mailto link and some accompanying text to the page in the Preview frame. Visitors to your page will be able to create an e-mail message to you by simply clicking this link.

At this point, you have entered all the content for your page. The remaining steps enable you to dress up its appearance.

8. If you're not satisfied with the default color scheme for the page, pick something different by clicking the <u>preset color combination</u> link in the instruction frame. Then, click one of the color scheme samples that appear in the bottom frame. If you want to select colors individually, instead of choosing one of the preset color schemes, click one of the following links:

- <u>background color</u> to select a color for the page background
- <u>background pattern</u> to select a textured image that will be repeated as the page background, overriding the solid background color
- <u>text color</u> to set the color of all text, except hypertext links
- <u>link color</u> to select a color for the text of hypertext links
- <u>visited link color</u> to select a color for the text of hypertext links that have been seen by the visitor

After you click one of these links and then click a color sample in the bottom frame, the wizard updates the preview frame immediately. You don't need to click the Apply button to make your choice effective. If you change your mind, simply click another color sample.

9. You can choose a different bullet to appear in front of the hot link items by clicking the <u>choose a bullet style</u> link and then clicking one of the bullet samples in the bottom frame.

10. Click the <u>choose a horizontal rule style</u> link to display a selection of rules in the bottom frame. There are several choices, so you'll need to scroll the frame to see all the options. Click a rule sample to select it. The wizard will use the selected rule as a separator between text blocks on your page in the preview frame.

    If necessary, you can scroll back up through the instruction frame and click a link to change any of the settings you've entered so far.

11. If you like the page the wizard has built for you, scroll the instruction frame to the bottom and click the Build button. The frames of the Netscape Page Wizard will disappear and your new page will appear in the Navigator window. The results might look something like those in Figure 4.4.

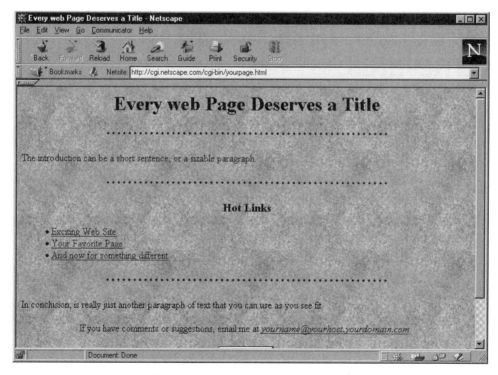

**FIGURE 4.4:** Your newly built page

12. The Netscape Page Wizard has done its job but your newly created page exists only in the Navigator window. You need to save it for future use or open the page in Composer for further editing.

- To save the page on your hard drive, choose File ➤ Save As. In the Save As dialog box, give the page a file name, select the location where you want to save it, and click Save.
- To edit the page in Composer, choose File ➤ Edit Page. This will open a new Composer window and load the newly created page into it.

After the basic, wizard-created page is complete, you can use Composer to edit it. You can either launch Composer and open the file you saved on your hard drive or, while you're viewing the page in Navigator, you can use Navigator's File ➤ Edit Page command to copy the page from Navigator into Composer. Once the page is loaded in the Composer window, you can edit it just as if you had originally created the page in Composer. I'll briefly cover the general editing options later in this chapter and explore specific topics in more detail in subsequent chapters.

# Creating Pages Based on Templates

In addition to the Netscape Page Wizard, Netscape provides another way to get a quick start creating Web pages—templates. Templates are pre-built Web pages complete with a color scheme, layout, and sample text that demonstrate a suggested use. There is no wizard to merge your content into the template. Instead, you simply copy the template to your computer, then open the file in Composer. Begin editing by replacing the sample text, pictures, and links with your own information.

The templates tend to be more sophisticated than the simple home page generated by the Netscape Page Wizard. The templates demonstrate sample Web pages designed to fulfill a variety of different needs. You can peruse them for ideas or use a template as the basis for your own Web page. As this book goes to press, the list of templates includes the following:

- My Home Page
- Resume
- McNab Family
- Flower and Garden Supplies
- Home Sale Announcement
- Human Resources
- Job Listings

- Department Overview
- Product Data Support
- Catering Service
- Travel Club
- Windsurfing Club
- My First JavaScript
- My Calendar

To use one of the Netscape-supplied templates as the basis for your own Web page, follow these steps:

**1.** Make sure you're connected to the Internet and then choose File ➣ New ➣ Page From Template in Navigator or any of the other Communicator programs. This will open the New Page From Template dialog box.

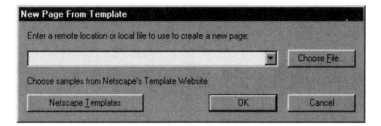

**2.** Click the Netscape Templates button. This will launch Navigator (if it isn't already running), connect to the Netscape Web site, and load the Netscape Web Page Templates page.

**3.** Scroll down past the instructions and click the link of the template you want to use. This will open the template page in Navigator (see Figure 4.5). If necessary, use the Back button to return to the Netscape Web Page Templates page and select a different template.

**4.** When the template you've chosen is displayed in Navigator, pull down the File menu and choose Edit Page. This will open a new Composer window and load the newly created page into it.

**TIP**

You can use any existing Web page as a template—not just the Netscape Templates. To select another page as a template, choose File ➣ New ➣ Page From Template and enter the file name or URL of the page to be used as a template into the text box of the New Page From Template dialog box. A copy of the page will appear in a new Composer window, ready for you to begin editing.

**FIGURE 4.5:** Netscape page templates, like the Product Data Sheet shown here, can serve as the basis for Web pages of your own.

After the page is loaded in the Composer window, you can edit it by substituting your own information for the sample text, pictures, and links in the template. I'll cover how to use Composer's editing options later in this chapter and in the next chapters.

**WARNING** The templates contain text that provides how-to instructions and suggestions. These instructions are just plain paragraphs of text added to the page, so be sure to delete them before saving and publishing a page you've created from the template.

# Using Composer to Create and Edit Pages

Using Composer to create (or edit) Web pages and other HTML documents is like using your word processor. You work in a WYSIWYG environment that provides a reasonable approximation of what your page will look like when viewed in a browser. In Composer, you type your text on a screen that looks and acts like most word processor programs (see Figure 4.6). You can select text and format it using menu commands and familiar toolbar buttons.

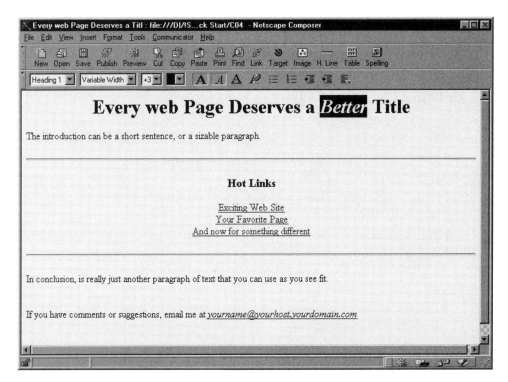

**FIGURE 4.6:**   Editing a simple page in Composer

As you create a page in Composer, you are actually building a text file that contains, in addition to any text on your page, HTML markup codes for text formatting, layout, graphics, and hypertext links. But Composer shelters you from the details of those arcane markup codes. No HTML codes appear in Composer's normal view of your page, and you enter your formatting choices by choosing menu commands, clicking toolbar buttons, and setting options in dialog boxes, instead of by typing markup codes.

## Starting a New Page

If you want to create a new Web page in Composer, you can start off with a fresh, clean slate. Choosing any of the following commands will open a new, empty edit window in Composer:

- In Composer, choose File ➤ New Page ➤ Blank Page.
- In Composer, go to the toolbar and click the New Page button.
- In Navigator, Messenger, or Collabra, choose File ➤ New ➤ Blank Page.

## Editing an Existing Page

If you make changes to an existing page in Composer, there are two ways to go about opening it: You can open a file (whether its on your local hard disk or a URL you access over the Net); or you can load the page you are viewing in Navigator into Composer. (This is the option you will use to edit a template or a Web page created by the Netscape Page Wizard.) Regardless of where the page originated, once you load a page into Composer, it's no different from any other page—you can work with it and edit it using all the same tools and techniques you use to create a page from scratch.

To open a file or URL directly into the Composer editing window, follow these steps:

**1.** In Composer or Navigator, choose File ➤ Open Page. This will open the Open Page dialog box.

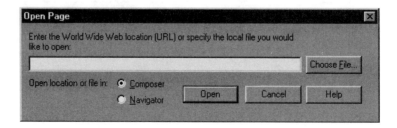

2. In the text box, type the path and file name for a local file, or the URL for a Web page on the Net. As an alternative, you can click the Choose File button to open a dialog box an then select the file.

3. Click the Composer radio button to open the file or location in Composer rather than Navigator.

If you are browsing a Web page in Navigator and want to load that page into Composer to edit, just issue the following command:

- File ➤ Edit Page

Regardless of which technique you use, the effect is the same—the specified file or location will appear in the edit window of Composer.

# Editing the Text (and More)

After you open a page in Composer's edit window, you can begin entering and editing the content. The rest of this book devotes entire chapters to working with the various kinds of content to add to your Web pages, such as text, images, hyperlinks, tables, and other elements. You can use all of these features to edit your page.

However, for simple text changes, you probably don't need to read a lot of instructions. You just click in the edit window to position the insertion point and start typing. You can also drag the pointer across some text to select it; then, press the Delete key or use commands on the Edit menu to Cut, Copy, and Paste text.

# Giving the Page a Title

One detail of Web page design you'll want to think about is what title to choose for your Web page. This will be the name of the Web page and will appear in the browser's title bar when you view the page. The title also shows up as the name of your page when a reader creates a bookmark or shortcut to the page. If you plan to promote your page through the major directories and search engines (such as Yahoo, InfoSeek, and Excite), the page title becomes even more important because that is what the reader normally sees listed in response to their queries.

To change the title of your Web page, follow these steps:

1. Choose Format ➤ Page Colors and Properties. This will open the Page Properties dialog box.

2. Click the General tab, and the options that describe your Web page will be displayed.

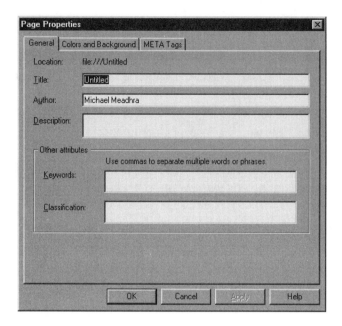

3. In the Title text box, type a title for your Web page. Although the text box will scroll to accommodate a longer title, it's best to keep your title short.

4. Enter your name in the Author text box if it's not already entered as the default when you created a new page.

5. Click OK to close the dialog box and record the new title. The title will appear in Composer's title bar.

## Choosing Your Colors and Background

Another simple change you can make to a new Web page (or a page you are editing) is to select a new color scheme. You can pick a background color for your Web page and colors for regular text and hyperlinks.

> **NOTE**
>
> **You can use Composer's text formatting capabilities to change the color of selected passages anywhere on your page. However, those color changes won't affect the color of hyperlinks.**

### Changing the Background

Most Web browsers usually display pages with a light gray or white background. You can change the background of your page by specifying a color or using an image as the backdrop for the document text. Changing the background color of your page is an easy way to give your page a distinctive appearance and make it more interesting and appealing.

**TIP**

The color and/or image you choose for your background should be in harmony with the color of your text. I've seen quite a few examples of enthusiastic Web authors who pick flamboyant colors for their pages, which become unreadable (or at least unattractive) as a result.

**WARNING**

Not all Web browsers can display custom colors or images as backgrounds. For this reason, you must be sure the design of your page doesn't depend on the background color or image to look good.

### Setting the Background Color

To select a background color for your Web page, follow these steps:

1. Choose Format ➤ Page Colors and Properties. This opens the Page Properties dialog box with the Colors and Background tab displayed. (Click Colors and Background if another tab is selected when the dialog box appears.)

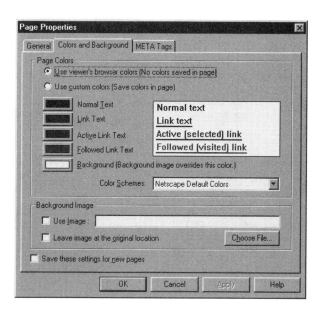

2. Click the Use Custom Colors checkbox. Checking this option will instruct Composer to record your color settings in the HTML source code for your Web page. Otherwise, the viewer's Web browser will display your page using the browser's default color settings.

3. In the Page Colors area, click the Background button. This mini-dialog box is really a list box of color samples.

4. Select a color by clicking the color sample of your choice. Composer immediately closes the list box and updates the sample display in the Page Properties dialog box, so you can preview the effect of your color choice.

5. After selecting a suitable color, click OK to apply the color to your Web page. (Alternatively, you can click Apply to apply the background color setting without closing the dialog box. Then you can continue adjusting other settings such as the text colors.)

Composer will display the specified background color for your Web in the edit window. Most browsers will be able to display your page with the background color as well.

**NOTE**

Most Web browsers recognize the HTML tag to set a background color, but some older or less capable browsers can't interpret that tag. When a viewer accesses your page with such a browser, the browser will just ignore the background color setting and use its own default background color—probably gray or white. Since the older browser will most likely ignore any text color settings as well, your page will remain readable, if not pretty.

## Setting Default Text Colors

Along with the background color, you can also specify default colors for text, thus developing a color scheme for your page. You can specify colors for regular text, hyperlink text, active hyperlinks (ones that have already been clicked), and visited hyperlinks (hyperlinks that have already been activated).

> **WARNING**
>
> **Some Web browsers ignore color settings for page backgrounds and text. Sometimes it's because the browser software doesn't support the feature, or because the viewer has chosen to override color specifications on Web pages and use their own default settings instead. Either way, you must remember that everyone won't see your page in the colors you specify.**

To set the default font colors for your Web page, follow these steps:

1.  Choose Format ➤ Page Colors and Properties. This opens the Page Properties dialog box with the Colors and Background tab displayed. (Click Colors and Background if another tab is selected when the dialog box appears.)

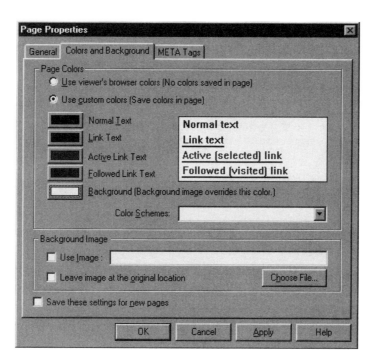

2. Click the button corresponding to the category of text you want to change. You can choose Normal Text, Link Text, Active Link Text, or Followed Link Text. No matter which button you choose, a color list will open where you can select a text color.

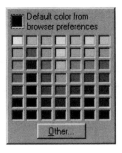

3. Select a color by clicking the color of your choice. Composer will close the color list and update the sample display in the Page Properties dialog box, so that you can preview the effect of your color choice.
4. Repeat steps **2** and **3** as needed to change the other default text colors.
5. After selecting a suitable color scheme, click OK to close the dialog box and apply the colors to your Web page.

**TIP**

After you develop an acceptable color scheme, you can make it the default for all new pages you create with Composer. Simply adjust the settings on the Page Properties dialog box's Colors and Background tab and then check the Save These Settings For New Pages checkbox. Click OK to close the dialog box and apply the settings. Thereafter, Composer will automatically use the same color scheme for any new page you create.

# Saving a Page

After you finish editing your Web page in Composer, you'll want to save the results. The process of saving a file is simple and familiar to anyone who has used other typical Windows programs. Just follow these steps:

1. Choose File ➤ Save As to open the Save As dialog box.

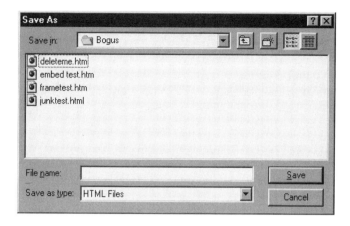

2. Select the location where you want to save the file.

3. In the File Name text box, enter the name of the file. In the Save as Type box, HTML is the only choice.

4. Click the Save button to save the file and close the dialog box.

After you save the file and give it a name, you can just choose File ➤ Save or go to the toolbar and click the Save button to save any recent changes without opening the Save As dialog box.

# Peeking behind the Scenes: The HTML Code

Although Composer's clean interface makes it unnecessary to deal with HTML codes for most page creation, it's interesting and sometimes useful to know what's happening behind the scenes.

Every page you create with Composer is, in reality, an HTML file—an ASCII text file with special codes added to the file to instruct a browser program (such as Navigator) to display the text with certain formatting attributes, or insert a graphic or hypertext link into the page. Unlike the proprietary formatting codes employed by most word processors, HTML codes are standardized, visible, and relatively easy to edit in the HTML document by using a simple text editor such as Notepad, which comes with Windows 95.

Of course, usually you'll want to use Composer when working with your pages becuase it's much easier than editing even the simplest HTML codes in a text editor. However, a basic understanding of the HTML codes in your pages can come in handy in helping you understand how Composer behaves and what happens to your pages as they are viewed with different browsers. Also, editing HTML codes directly is the only way to implement some effects and features that are supported by the HTML standard but not by Composer, such as forms, style sheets, and Java applets embedded in a Web page.

Although Composer hides the HTML codes and shows only the resulting formatted text and other page elements, you can easily peek behind the scenes and see the raw HTML document with all its markup codes exposed. Just pull down the View menu and choose Page to open a View Document Source window, such as the one shown in Figure 4.7.

```
<HTML>
<HEAD>
    <META HTTP-EQUIV="Content-Type" CONTENT="text/html; charset=iso-8859-1">
    <META NAME="GENERATOR" CONTENT="Mozilla/4.0b5 [en] (Win95; I) [Netscape]">
    <TITLE>Every web Page Deserves a Title</TITLE>
</HEAD>
<BODY TEXT="#000000" BGCOLOR="#FFFFFF" LINK="#0000FF" VLINK="#FF0000" ALINK="#FF0000">

<CENTER>
<H1>
Every web Page Deserves a <B><I>Better</I></B> Title</H1></CENTER>
The introduction can be a short sentence, or a sizable paragraph.
<BR> 
<CENTER>
<HR WIDTH="100%"></CENTER>

<CENTER>
<H3>
Hot Links</H3></CENTER>

<DL>
<CENTER><A HREF="http://your.url/goes/here.html">Exciting Web Site</A></CENTER>

<CENTER><A HREF="http://your.url/goes/here.html">Your Favorite Page</A></CENTER>

<CENTER><A HREF="http://your.url/goes/here.html">And now for something
different</A></CENTER>
</DL>

<CENTER>
<HR WIDTH="100%"></CENTER>
```

**FIGURE 4.7:** View the hidden HTML markup codes in this window.

When you examine the HTML source document, you'll see that it consists of the text that appears on your page, plus a bunch of codes enclosed in angle brackets like this:

`<title>`

These codes are called HTML tags and they tell the browser to do things like make some text bold, display an image, or define a hyperlink. The browser doesn't display the tags themselves, only the results of the instructions they contain.

## Every Document Must Have the Required Tags

Every HTML document must include certain tags, which essentially identify the document as an HTML document and, as such, show its beginning and end. Note that even these fundamental HTML tags come in pairs—the <html> at the beginning of the document matches the </html> at the end of the document.

Figure 4.8 shows the HTML source (Figure 4.8a) for a simple Web page and the way that page appears in Composer (Figure 4.8b). In Figure 4.8a, you can see some elements of a basic HTML document. Take note of:

- The entire document enclosed between <html> and </html>
- The header of the document enclosed between <head> and </head>
- The body of the document enclosed between <body> and </body>

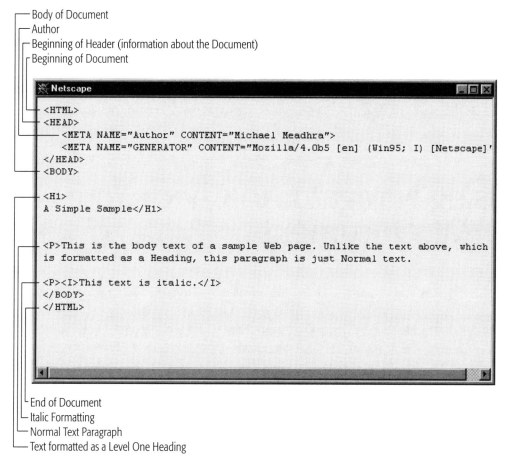

Body of Document
Author
Beginning of Header (information about the Document)
Beginning of Document

End of Document
Italic Formatting
Normal Text Paragraph
Text formatted as a Level One Heading

**FIGURE 4.8a:**    In an HTML-coded document (above) you see tags (within angle brackets) surrounding the element to which they refer.

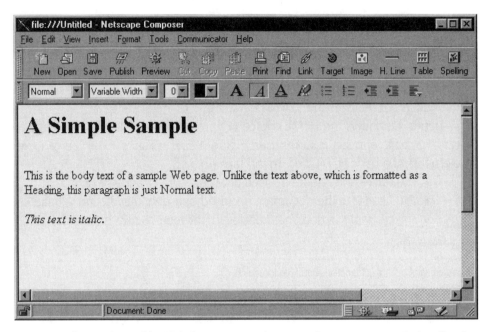

**FIGURE 4.8b:**   In the resulting Web document, you do not see the tags–you see only the effect they have on the document displayed.

# Using Navigator to Check Your HTML Document

So, you've created a Web page and saved it as an HTML file (really, a simple text file containing HTML tags) on your hard disk. You've seen a preview of what your page looks like as you worked on it. However, before you make your Web page available to the public, you'll want to test it in a browser, such as Navigator. To view a page that you are editing in Composer, simply choose File ➤ Browse Page or go to the toolbar and click the Preview button. If you have not already saved the page, Composer will prompt you to do so. Once the file is saved, a Navigator window will open and the page will appear in the browser.

# Checking Previously Saved Pages

You can also use Navigator to view other Web pages stored on your hard disk. To load a file from your hard disk into Netscape, follow these steps:

1.  Start Navigator and choose File ➤ Open File. The Open dialog box will appear.
2.  In the Open dialog box, highlight the file name for your page. (The Open dialog box works here just as it does in any Windows application.)
3.  Click the OK button. The dialog box will close, and in a few seconds your home page will appear on screen in the form of a beautiful Web document!

**TIP** If an old version of your page appears by some chance, select View ➤ Reload from the menu bar to load the latest version of your HTML document into memory.

# Chapter 5

# WORKING WITH TEXT

- **Entering and editing text**
- **Heads up for heads**
- **Assigning text attributes**
- **Using special characters**
- **Getting lined up**
- **Using paragraph styles**
- **Inserting ruled lines**
- **Checking your spelling**

Most Web pages are composed primarily of text—by far the most common element of page design. In fact, the Web started out as a system for formatting and viewing academic documents which usually consisted of pages and pages of text with only an occasional chart, graph, or other illustration. It's come a long way since then, but despite all the glamour and attention lavished on multimedia, animation, and interactive scripts, text is still the backbone of most Web pages.

Read on to learn how Composer allows you to work with text in your Web pages.

# Entering and Editing Text

Working with text is so easy most of the time, you tend to take it for granted. It isn't until you encounter unexpected problems that you realize working with text isn't always trouble free. Fortunately, at its basic level, working with text in Composer is so easy you *can* take it for granted. Just start typing. You'll get very few surprises. As you will see, even some of the more involved text formatting features aren't much more difficult than simple text entry and editing.

## Entering Text

Entering text in Composer is straightforward and intuitive. Anyone who has used a typical word processor will probably feel right at home. Simply start typing to enter text at the insertion point in the Composer window. Composer will automatically word-wrap long lines of text to fit within the window, so there is no need to press the Enter key to end each line. In fact, you should press Enter only at the end of a complete paragraph. This is even more important for Web pages than it is for word processor documents because each paragraph must be a single block of text in order for the viewer's browser to re-wrap that text to fit in the window on each individual's system.

### The Price of Convenience

If you're familiar with other HTML editors and viewers, you'll probably notice that Composer's text handling is significantly different from the way text is typically handled in HTML documents. When viewing an HTML document, a standard Web browser treats any text on the page, that is not otherwise formatted, as body text and wraps the text to fit the width of the browser window. Normal paragraphs are separated by a line of blank space. Furthermore, unless that text is marked with a special `<pre>` tag, the browser ignores all extra spaces, tabs, and normal line breaks in an HTML source document.

The normal way to mark the end of a paragraph in an HTML document is to insert a `<p>` tag at the point in the text where you want a new paragraph to begin. Of course, you don't have to worry about <p> or any other HTML tags if you use Composer. The program will enter all the necessary codes for you. In fact, it enters some extra codes in an effort to make your life easier.

Viewing the HTML source code for a page after you've entered some text in Composer, reveals that each paragraph of text generated by Composer starts with a <br> tag instead of the more common <p>. (The <br> tag indicates a forced line break to end the paragraph but doesn't create a blank line before the paragraph.) Using this paragraph tag instead of the plain <p> paragraph tag allows Composer to function more like a word processor—no blank lines separating paragraphs unless you press Enter twice at the end of the paragraph.

Composer also inserts a special non-breaking space code into the HTML source for your page when you press the space bar. This enables you to increase the space between words by simply pressing the space bar several times. If Composer used the normal space character, the multiple spaces would be ignored by the Web browser. By using the non-breaking space, Composer acts more like a word processor. However, it means that pages prepared in other programs and brought into Composer for editing will behave differently from those created in Composer.

# Heads Up for Headings

After you enter some text, the next thing you'll probably want to do is designate some of that text as headings. Headings are usually (but not always) larger and bolder than the body text of your page.

When you assign a heading style, it is for an entire paragraph. (Technically, any block of text that you end by pressing the Enter key is a paragraph—even if that paragraph consists of only a word or two.) Normally, a heading paragraph will be a short phrase that serves as a title or a headline introducing the topic of one or more longer paragraphs that follow. However, nothing (except perhaps good taste) prevents you from using one of the heading styles on a paragraph containing a longer text passage.

HTML, and therefore Composer, supports six levels of headings. Each level of heading will look different when it's displayed in a Web browser such as Netscape. The standard headings correspond to the headings of a typical hierarchical outline. As a result, the headings work especially well in a document organized in a classic outline style, but they can also work equally well in a variety of other contexts. The highest level (Heading 1) will be the largest, while the lowest level (Heading 6) will be smallest.

**NOTE** The actual appearance of each heading is different from one browser to the next. In other words, HTML allows you to say what text is a heading, but not what the heading will look like when User A accesses it with Netscape, User B with Internet Explorer on a Windows system, and User C with another browser running on a Macintosh system.

To format a paragraph as a heading, simply click anywhere in the paragraph (it isn't necessary to highlight the entire paragraph) and then select the appropriate heading style using either the format toolbar or the menus.

- From the format toolbar, select a heading style from the Paragraph Style drop-down list (the one on the left end of the format toolbar).

- From the menus, pull down the Format menu and select Headings, then choose a heading level.

**TIP** If the Format toolbar isn't visible in the Composer window, pull down the View menu and choose Show Format Toolbar.

Composer will format the paragraph as a heading of the level you selected. Figure 5.1 shows headings as they appear in Composer. Typically, most browsers default to similar formatting for heading paragraphs, however the actual appearance of headings can vary depending on the user's browser settings. Despite differences in browser settings, you can be confident that all Heading 1 paragraphs will be formatted the same in a given browser.

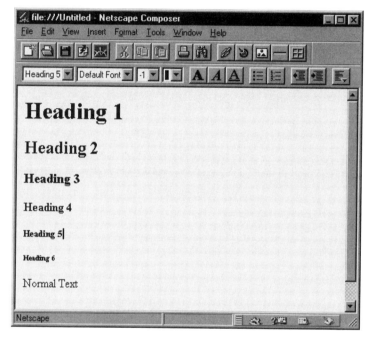

**FIGURE 5.1:**   Heading formats vary from browser to browser, but these samples are typical of the default settings.

**TIP**   See Appendix B, *An HTML Dictionary*, for information on the HTML tags that mark headings in the HTML source code for your page.

# Assigning Text Attributes

You're probably familiar with text attributes in word processors. Formatting details such as bold, italic, and underline, which change the appearance of text and differentiate certain text from the rest, are all known as attributes in a word processor. In Composer you can easily specify attributes such as these.

The types of attributes you can specify using HTML are broken down into two classes:

- Physical attributes
- Logical attributes

The physical attributes specify how text characters will look: italic or bold, for example. They will be italic or bold no matter which Web browser is used for viewing (as long as the browser understands that particular type of formatting). The logical attributes specify the amount of emphasis you want to give to important text and leave it up to the Web browser software to determine what physical attributes to use to make the text stand out from the normal body text. You can choose to make text big, small, emphasize, or strongly emphasized. Different Web browsers will have different ways of displaying logical attributes (some may show strongly emphasized text as bold, others may show it as red or in a slightly larger size, for example).

Composer enables you to format text with physical attributes. In the unlikely event that you want to use logical attributes, you'll need to manually edit the HTML code for your page to insert the appropriate codes.

## Physical Attributes

Applying physical formatting attributes to text in Composer is a very simple process. Just select the text you want to format and then choose the format you want to apply to the selected text. The most complete selection of formatting attributes are available from Composer's menus. From the Format menu, choose Style, and then choose one of the following formatting attributes:

- **Bold**
- *Italic*
- <u>Underline</u>
- Fixed Width
- Super$^{script}$
- Sub$_{script}$
- ~~Strikethrough~~
- Blink

Composer adds the appropriate HTML tags to the source file for your page and displays the result onscreen.

## Removing Styles

If you make a mistake, you can easily return text to its original unformatted state by selecting it, and from the formatting toolbar, clicking the Remove All Styles button.

Almost all the same formatting options you find in the Format menu are also available in the Properties dialog box. You can use the menu commands or dialog box options to achieve the same formatting effects. Use whichever one you find more convenient.

1.  From the Format menu, choose Font to open the Properties dialog box, then click the Character tab.

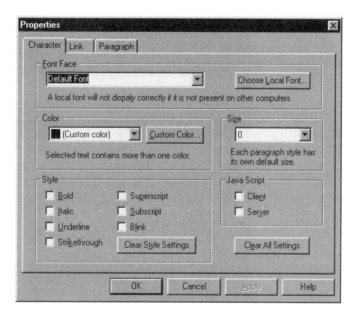

2.  To format the selected text, check one or more options in the Style area then click Apply or OK to apply the formatting. Composer displays the selected text with the formatting you specified.

**TIP**

**Avoid underlining text that includes font size changes within a word or phrase. The size changes will affect the thickness and position of the underline as well as the text characters. As a result, the underline appears jagged and broken instead of a continuous line. There's nothing really wrong with it—it just doesn't look very good.**

Behind the scenes, Composer also adds HTML tags for the formatting attributes on either side of the corresponding text in the HTML source code for your Web page.

The attributes used most—bold, italic, and underline—are also available as buttons on Composer's formatting toolbar. The three buttons are near the middle of the formatting toolbar and each one has a large letter A on it—**A** for bold, *A* for italic, and A for underline. To format text with the toolbar buttons, simply select the text and click the button corresponding to the attribute you want to apply. Composer displays the results immediately.

> **TIP**
>
> **You can apply formatting attributes such as bold, italics, underline, and the rest, to as much, or as little, text as you like. You can apply attributes to a single letter, a word, a sentence, or whole paragraphs.**

> **NOTE**
>
> **See Appendix B, *An HTML Dictionary*, for information on the HTML tags that Composer adds to the HTML source code for your page to indicate formatting attributes.**

## Logical Attributes

HTML has provisions for marking text with logical attributes to give emphasis to the text you feel is important. The way the text actually appears when viewed in a browser depends on the browser's individual way of handling these attributes. Composer doesn't support these logical attributes, but you can manually enter the tags into the HTML source for your page. (See Chapter 11, *Getting Your Hands Dirty: Editing HTML*, for instructions on how to manually embed HTML tags into your page. Also for details on tags, see Appendix B, *The HTML Dictionary*.) The logical attributes that you can use are:

| Logical Attribute | Usual Result |
| --- | --- |
| Emphasis | *Italic* |
| Strong Emphasis | **Bold** |
| Big Typeface | Big |
| Small Typeface | Small |

# Changing Typefaces

As the Web has evolved, graphic designers, as well as Web authors, have sought more control over the fonts used to display the pages they create. Composer supports the ability to specify a font used to display any text on your page. You can specify a font for selected text in much the same way you specify other text attributes such as bold and italics. You can select from one of the short list of standard fonts commonly used on Web pages; or you can select any other font available on your system. Composer will display the text using the font you specify.

Having the ability to choose any of the fonts on your system when designing the text on your Web page sounds like a graphic designer's dream come true. Unfortunately, practical considerations usually restrict your font choices to the same old standard fonts. When a visitor to your Web site views your page, their Web browser displays the page using the fonts installed on the viewer's system. That means the visitor will see the text of your page in the font you specified only if they have the same font installed on their system. If you use a font on your Web page that the visitor doesn't have, the text you formatted will appear in a default font. As a result, if you want to be confident that the font you choose for some text and the font the viewer sees will be the same, you must choose one of the standard fonts that are found in some form on nearly every computer. Unfortunately, that's a short list:

- Times Roman
- Courier
- Ariel or Helvetica

To change the font used to display text in Composer, follow these steps:

1. Select the text you want to format with a different font. Typically, you will drag the pointer across the text to select it. You can select an individual word by double-clicking the word.

2. Choose a font for the selected text using any one of the following techniques:
   - Select the font from the Font drop-down-list in Composer's formatting toolbar.

**WARNING** The Font list in the Formatting toolbar is handy, but it can be awkward to use if you have a large number of fonts installed on your system. It's difficult to scroll through a long list of fonts without inadvertently selecting the wrong font.

   - Click the Format menu, select Font, then choose one of the standard fonts or Other. If you choose one of the standard fonts, Composer will apply the selection to your text immediately. It you choose Other, the Font dialog box will open. Choose a font from the Font list, then click OK to apply your selection and close the dialog box.

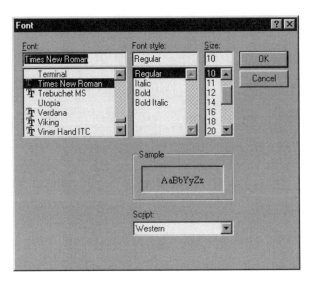

- From the Format menu choose Character Properties or right-click the selected text and a pop-up menu will appear. Choose Character Properties. From the Character Properties dialog box select the Character tab and choose a font from the Font Face drop-down list. Click OK to close the dialog box and apply your font selection.

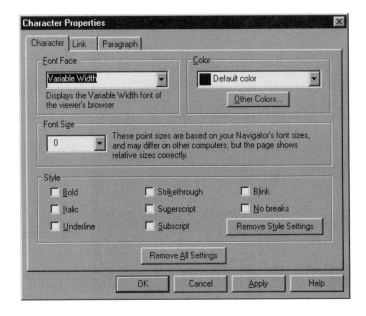

After you make your font selection, Composer will display the selected text in that font. Navigator will also be able to display the text in the font you selected. Just remember that visitors to your Web site may not be able to view your page with the same fonts displayed unless they have the same fonts available. So, the chances are good that visitors will see the text on your page displayed in the default font.

## Web Fonts–for Free

Specifying fonts is futile unless the users who view your page have the specified fonts installed on their systems. Lack of availability of common fonts and inconsistent font names have been a formidable obstacle to the development and acceptance of font specifications for displaying Web pages.

In an effort to address this problem, a group of companies headed by Microsoft have proposed establishing a list of core fonts and encouraging all Web users to install these fonts on their systems for use in displaying Web pages. Microsoft even makes a selection of TrueType fonts available on its Web site for free download in the hope that these Web Fonts will be widely adopted by Web users. The free Web Fonts include the following:

Arial **(Bold)** *(Italic)* ***(Bold Italic)***
**Impact**
Comic Sans MS **(Bold)**
Courier New **(Bold)** *(Italic)* ***(Bold Italic)***
Georgia **(Bold)** *(Italic)* ***(Bold Italic)***
Times New Roman **(Bold)** *(Italic)* ***(Bold Italic)***
Trebuchet MS **(Bold)** *(Italic)* ***(Bold Italic)***
Veranda **(Bold)** *(Italic)* ***(Bold Italic)***

To get the free Web Fonts, go to Microsoft's Web site at `http://www` `.microsoft.com/truetype/` and follow the links to download the fonts.

In addition to the TrueType Web Fonts from Microsoft, there are other proposals to distribute fonts for Web page use. For example, Navigator supports the new dynamic fonts standard that allows fonts to be downloaded as needed—much like images are downloaded. Only time will tell whether any of them can gain wide enough acceptance so that Web authors can specify a font and reasonably expect that the user will see the specified font.

**TIP** See Appendix B, *An HTML Dictionary*, for information on the HTML tags that mark font changes in the HTML source code for your page.

# Changing Font Size

Composer allows you to change the size of the font in your document. You can use this feature to vary text size of an entire paragraph or you can change the size of a single character to create effects such as large initial capital letters.

## Relative versus Absolute Sizes

Traditionally, HTML documents have supported seven different font sizes. A user defines a default text size for their Web browser, then the browser displays text in the default size and in six other sizes (two smaller and four larger) based on variations of the default size. These are called relative sizes meaning that the type sizes are calculated relative to the default size. This system means that you can't specify font sizes in points like you can in most word processors and know that the text will be displayed in that size on the user's screen. Instead, you select one of the seven arbitrary sizes and the user's browser will translate that to a specific display size for the text according to the browser's settings.

The ability to specify absolute text sizes is a relatively new development. Composer now offers you the option of specifying type sizes in points—just like you do in most word processors. Using absolute font sizes gives you access to a wider range of text sizes (from 8 to 72 point) and enables you to exercise more control over the way the text appears on the viewer's screen. However, only the latest versions of the popular Web browsers (such as Navigator 4.0) support absolute font sizes. Viewers with older browsers will see the text displayed in one of the seven standard sizes.

**WARNING** When you use absolute font sizes, remember that the sizes you specify may not be rendered the same way on every viewer's screen. Differences in screen size, video resolution, and browser settings can make all type appear larger or smaller on another system. Font sizes that are small on your screen can be really tiny on another screen and large fonts that fit comfortably on your screen may be huge on a different system.

Composer can record font size attributes on your Web page using relative sizes or absolute sizes, or a combination of both. In addition, Composer gives you the option of changing how the list of font sizes appears on the Composer toolbar and in the Character Properties dialog box. You can configure Composer to display font size options in one of three different ways:

- Relative sizes such as -1, 0, and +2. These are the seven standard font sizes recognized by all Web browsers. Size 0 is the default text size, there are two smaller sizes (-1 and -2) and four larger sizes (+1, +2, +3, and +4).

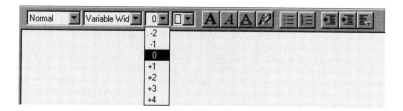

- Relative sizes shown as point sizes. This option presents the seven relative font sizes as a list of point sizes based on the current default font size you have established for Composer and Navigator. For example, if your default size is 12 point, then the relative sizes based on that size are 8, 10, 12, 14, 18, 24, and 36—these are the sizes that will appear in the font size lists. Using this option makes it easy to visualize the effect of choosing different text sizes in your current Web page. Just remember that you're really selecting relative sizes and that visitors viewing your Web page may see the fonts displayed in different sizes, relative to the default size setting in their browsers.

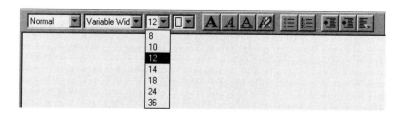

- A combination list of font sizes listing both relative sizes (such as -1, 0, +2) and absolute font sizes (such as 10, 16, and 72-point). This option gives you the most versatility. You can pick relative sizes and absolute sizes from the same list of font sizes. The relative sizes are shown in the same way as if you chose the HTML relative size option. In addition, you have a list of specific point sizes to choose from as well. These are the absolute sizes. Unlike the previous option, when you select a font size expressed in points from this list, Composer inserts HTML codes in your Web page instructing the viewer's browser to display the text in exactly that size, not in a size relative to the browser's default text size. Just remember that only the latest browsers can properly implement this option.

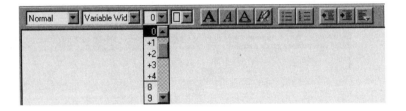

To set how you want Composer to list font size options, follow these steps:

1.	Click Composer's Edit menu and choose Preferences. The Preferences dialog box will open with Composer highlighted in the Category list.

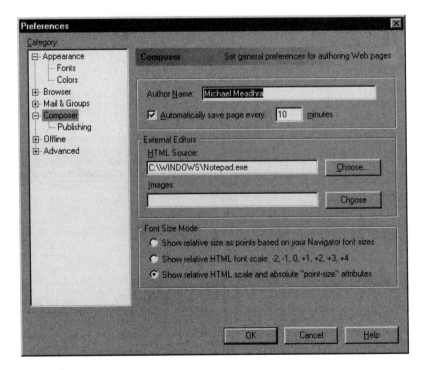

2. Select one of the three options from the Font Size Mode area.
   - The first option–Show Relative Size as Points Based on Your Navigator Font Sizes–does exactly what it says. Composer will list the seven standard, relative font sizes in the font size lists; but they will appear as point sizes based on the default size you set for Navigator and Composer in the Appearance/Fonts category of the Preferences dialog box.
   - The second option–Show Relative HTML Font Scale–prompts Composer to list font sizes in the generic (-2, 0, + 2) form.
   - The third option–Show Relative HTML Scale and Absolute Point-Size Attributes–prompts Composer to list both relative and absolute font sizes in its Font Size lists. (This is the option we chose for the examples in the font size section that follows.)
3. Click the OK button to close the Preferences dialog box and apply your selection.

Composer will use the selected format to show your font size options in the Font Size lists found in the formatting toolbar and in the Character Properties dialog box. Typically, after you set the font size mode the way you like it, you won't need to change the setting.

## Sizing Your Text

Much of the text sizing you do in Composer will be a by-product of using paragraph styles and heading styles. Naturally, a paragraph of regular body text will start out using the default font size. On the other hand, if you assign the heading 1 style to a line of text, Composer automatically increases the size of the text to +3 since that font size is part of the definition of the heading 1 style. You'll need to manually change the font size of text only when you need to override or supplement the font size that is part of a paragraph or heading style.

Changing the font size of text is easy. The process is very similar to applying other text attributes. To change the font size of text, follow these steps:

1. Drag the pointer across the text you want to resize. This will highlight and select it. You can select anything from a single character to a block of several paragraphs of text.
2. Choose the new font size for the highlighted text using any one of the following techniques:
   - In Composer's formatting toolbar click the Font Size drop-down-list, and choose a font size. Depending on your font size mode preference, this list might include relative sizes or both relative and absolute font sizes.
   - Click to pull down the Format menu, select Font Size, and then select a size.
   - Click to pull down the Format menu, select Font, then select Other to open the Font dialog box. Select a size from the Size list box and then click the OK button to close the dialog box. (The Font dialog box always lists absolute font sizes–not relative font sizes.)

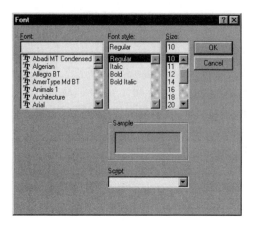

- Click to pull down the Format menu and choose Character Properties (or right-click the selected text and choose Character Properties from the pop-up menu). The Character Properties dialog box will appear with the Character tab displayed. Select a size from the Font Size drop-down list and then click the OK button to close the dialog box.

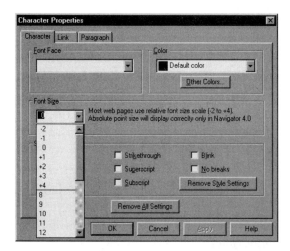

Composer displays the selected text in the new size. The program also adds to the page source for your Web page the appropriate HTML codes to instruct Web browsers to display the text in a different size.

**NOTE** See Appendix B, *An HTML Dictionary*, for more information on the HTML tags Composer inserts into the source code for your page to specify font sizes.

The initial cap effect is one good example of a way to use font size adjustments in your Web page. You can select the first letter of a word, then select a larger size (such as +3) from the Font Size drop-down list in the format toolbar. You might even repeat the process on each word of a title. The result will look something like this:

INITIAL CAPS

# Changing Font Color

Another way you can change the appearance of the text on your page is to change its color from the default. Like the text attributes (bold, italic, and so on) and font size settings, you can apply a color to a single character, a word, a line of text, or an entire paragraph.

Composer offers several ways to specify the font color. Just select the text where you want to apply a color change and then select the color using any one of the following techniques:

- From the Format menu, choose Color to open the Color dialog box. Click a color sample, and then click OK to close the dialog box and apply the color to the selected text.

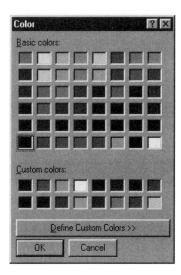

- From the Format menu, choose Font to open the Properties dialog box. Click the Character tab, then choose a color from the Color drop-down-list box, and click OK to close the dialog box and apply the color to the selected text.
- Perhaps the simplest technique is to choose a color from the color drop-down-list box in the format toolbar. Composer applies the color immediately when you make your selection from the list.

You should now see the specified color displayed in Composer. Navigator, and most other browsers can also display the text in color. However, most browsers give users the option to ignore the color settings you added to your page and substitute their browser settings instead. Many users elect this option—perhaps in defense against some of the awful color combinations used on poorly designed Web pages.

# Using Special Characters

Because HTML documents are plain text files, only the basic alphanumeric and punctuation characters are available. Furthermore, some of the standard punctuation characters (such as < and >) are reserved for use as HTML tags. To use any of the reserved characters or special characters such as the copyright symbol (©) and register mark (®) you must insert a special code sequence into your HTML document.

The good news is that Composer will take care of these details for you. You just type the characters you need in your text; Composer will detect any characters that require special treatment and automatically insert the appropriate codes into the HTML source code for your page.

**TIP**

You can use Windows' Character Map utility to insert special characters such as the copyright symbol (©) and register mark (®) into your page. The Character Map utility is one of those optional accessories included (but not always installed) with Windows. In Windows 95, you can usually find it by opening the Start menu and choosing Programs ➢ Accessories ➢ Character Map. To use the utility to insert a special character, simply open the Character Map accessory, click a character, and click Select to copy the character to the Windows clipboard. Then you can return to Composer, position the insertion point where you want to place the character, and paste the character into your page by pulling down the Edit menu and choosing Paste.

# Getting Lined Up

When you enter paragraphs of text, they will show up as left-justified like you're used to seeing most often in print. However, you can change the alignment of a paragraph to make it either centered or right-justified instead of left-justified. Composer lets you change paragraph alignment with a menu command, a toolbar button, or a shortcut key. To change paragraph alignment, click anywhere in the paragraph (or drag across several paragraphs to highlight them) and then do one of the following:

- Click to pull down the Format menu, click Align, and then choose Left, Center, or Right.
- From the Format toolbar, click the Change Horizontal Alignment button at the right end of the toolbar. Then click one of the three buttons (Align Left, Center, and Align Right) that appears.
- Press one of the following shortcut key combinations:
  - Ctrl+L for left alignment
  - Ctrl+E for center alignment
  - Ctrl+R for right alignment

Composer applies the alignment option you specified to the selected paragraph. As shown in Figure 5.2, left-aligned paragraphs align to the left margin; all lines of a right-aligned paragraph align with the right margin of the window; and each line of a center-aligned paragraph is centered in the browser window.

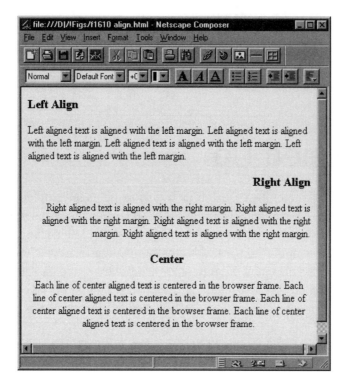

**FIGURE 5.2:**
You can align paragraphs with the left or right margins, or centered in the browser window.

**NOTE** See Appendix B, *An HTML Dictionary*, for information on how Composer indicates alignment options in the HTML source code for your page.

# Using Paragraph Styles

Paragraph styles are really just a set of predetermined attributes such as boldface, text size, alignment, and indents. These styles can be applied to a paragraph of text with one command instead of assigning all the attributes individually. You've already seen paragraph styles in action when you used headings. But paragraph styles can do more than define headings, you can also use paragraph styles to create different kinds of lists and format text as an address.

# Creating Lists

In addition to paragraphs of body text and headings, Composer supports several kinds of lists. You can create and display bulleted (unnumbered) lists, numbered lists, and description (glossary) lists.

> **NOTE**
>
> **In addition to the standard list formats, Composer will let you create two other kinds of lists—menu lists and directory lists. Composer and Navigator do not support displaying these rarely used list formats, but some browsers do. If you decide to use menu lists or directory lists, you can instruct Composer to insert the appropriate HTML tags into your page, but you'll have to rely on another browser to view the results.**

## Bulleted Lists

Of all the kinds of lists, a bulleted list is probably the one you'll use the most. In a bulleted list (sometimes called an unnumbered or unordered list) each paragraph is indented and preceded by a bullet or another symbol. For example, a bulleted list of summer holidays might look like this:

- Memorial Day
- Independence Day
- Labor Day

To create a bulleted list in Composer, follow these steps:

1. Start by entering the text of the list. Type each list item as a separate paragraph and end it by pressing the Enter key.
2. Drag the pointer across all the paragraphs of the list to select them.
3. Apply the Bulleted List paragraph style to the selected paragraphs using one of the following techniques:
   - From the Paragraph Style drop-down list in the formatting toolbar select List Item. The Bulleted List style is the default list type, so Composer will automatically apply the Bulleted style when you choose the generic List Item style.
   - From the Format menu, select List, and then select Bulleted.
   - Right-click the selected text and a pop-up menu will appear. Choose Paragraph/List. The Character Properties dialog box will open with the Paragraph tab displayed. From the

Paragraph Style drop-down list select List Item. Then from the Style drop-down list select Bullet (Unnumbered) List. Click the OK button to close the dialog box.

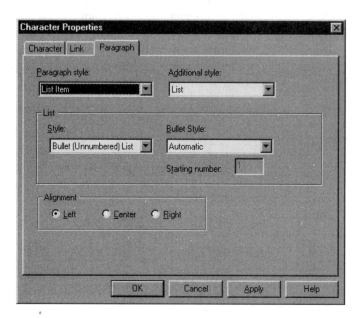

Composer displays the selected paragraphs as a bulleted list. As shown in Figure 5.3, each paragraph is indented and preceded by a symbol—normally a solid circle or dot. Of course, Composer also adds the appropriate HTML tags to the page source for your Web page so that Web browsers will be able to display the list in a similar fashion. You don't have to do anything extra to indent the paragraphs or add the bullet symbol; these are built-in features of the Bulleted List paragraph style.

### Changing the Bullet Shapes

The standard symbol for a bullet preceding each item in a bulleted list is a solid circle. If you want a little variety in your bulleted lists, you can choose another symbol by following these steps:

1.  Select the text of the paragraphs you want to change.
2.  Right-click the selected text and a pop-up menu will appear. Choose Paragraph/List Properties. The Character Properties dialog box will open with the Paragraph tab displayed.

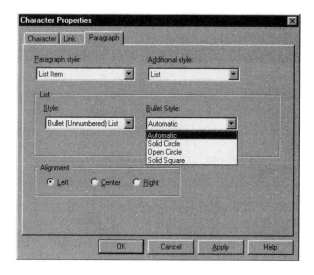

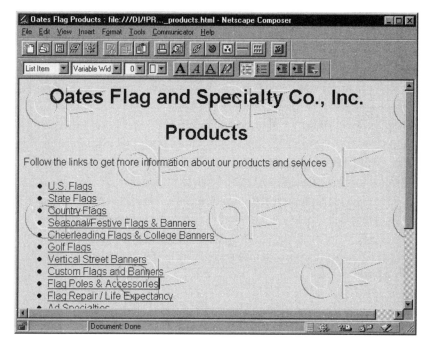

**FIGURE 5.3:** You'll find many uses for bulleted lists on a typical Web site.

3. Select a symbol from the Bullet Style drop-down list. You'll have the following choices:
   - Automatic—allows the Web browser to use its default symbol for bullets
   - Solid Circle
   - Open Circle
   - Solid Square
4. Click the OK button to close the dialog box and to apply your selection.

## Numbered Lists

A numbered list (sometimes called an ordered list) is, as its name implies, a list of items that are each preceded by a sequential number. It's basically the same as a bulleted list, but with numbers in place of the bullets. Actually, the number can be a numeral, a letter, or a Roman numeral. The neat thing about numbered lists in HTML documents is that you just enter the list items as separate paragraphs and define the lot as a list—the browser will take care of adding the numbers when it displays the page. Because the browser adds the appropriate numbers to each item in a numbered list when a visitor views your page, you can edit the list—adding, deleting, and rearranging items—without worrying about renumbering the items.

To create a numbered list in Composer, follow these steps:

1. Start by entering the text of the list. Type each list item as a separate paragraph and end it by pressing the Enter key.
2. Drag the pointer across all the paragraphs of the list to select them.
3. Apply the Numbered List paragraph style to the selected paragraphs using one of the following techniques:
   - From the Format menu, select List, and then select Numbered.
   - Right-click the selected text and a pop-up menu will appear. Choose Paragraph/List Properties. The Character Properties dialog box will open with the Paragraph tab displayed. From the Paragraph Style drop-down list select List Item. Then from the Style drop-down list select Numbered List. Click the OK button to close the dialog box.

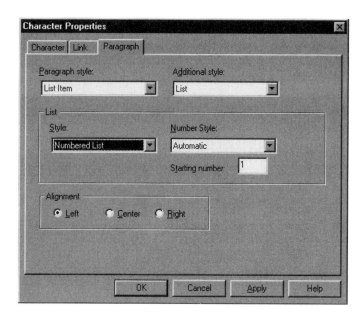

Composer displays the selected paragraphs as a numbered list. Each paragraph is indented and preceded by a placeholder symbol (usually #). When your page is viewed in a Web browser, the browser will replace the placeholder with a number.

### Indenting Text

List styles automatically indent text, but you can also indent text yourself. Just go to the formatting toolbar and click the Decrease Indent or Increase Indent buttons as needed to change how far a paragraph is indented.

### Changing the Numbering Style

The standard numbering style for numbered lists is, of course, numbers such as 1, 2, and 3. If you prefer, you can specify another numbering style such as letters or Roman numerals. You can also define a starting point for the numbering scheme. This is useful when a numbered list is interrupted by other text. You can create one list, add some normal text, and then create another list that picks up where the first list left off so that the numbering continues instead of starting over. To change the number style or starting number for a list, follow these steps:

1.    Select the text of the paragraphs you want to change.

2. Right-click the selected text and a pop-up menu will appear. Choose Paragraph/List Properties. The Character Properties dialog box will open with the Paragraph tab displayed.

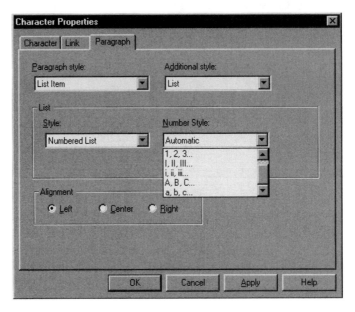

3. Select a style from the Number Style drop-down list. You'll have the following choices:
   - Automatic—allows the Web browser to use its default symbol for numbers
   - 1, 2, 3...
   - I, II, III...
   - i, ii, iii...
   - A, B, C...
   - a, b, c...

4. If you want to change the starting number of the list, type a number in the Starting Number box. You must enter a number here, even if you chose one of the number styles that will label the list items with letters. For example, if you want the list to start with the letter *E*, you would enter **5** in the Starting Number box because E is the fifth number of the alphabet.

5. Click the OK button to close the dialog box and apply your selection.

Composer will apply your changes to the list. However, you may not see much difference. Changing the starting number for a list has no obvious effect in Composer because Composer displays placeholders for the numbers. The numbers don't appear until you view the page in a Web browser. If you changed number styles, the number placeholder in front of each list item will change to reflect the number style. The placeholders for each number style are as follows:

- **#** represents 1, 2, 3…
- **X** represents I, II, III…
- **x** represents i, ii, iii…
- **A** represents A, B, C…
- **a** represents a, b, c…

**NOTE** See Appendix B, *An HTML Dictionary*, for details of the HTML tags Composer inserts into the source code for your page in order to produce the various kinds of lists.

## Creating Description Lists

A description list in a Web document is a special element designed to make it easy to format related items like terms and definitions. In fact, description lists are sometimes called glossary lists because glossaries are the most common application of description lists.

A description list consists of two components: a description title paragraph style (commonly used for a glossary term) and a description text paragraph style (commonly used for glossary definitions). Basically, the description list paragraph styles are just slight variations on the normal text style. The difference between the two paragraph styles is that the Description Title style is not indented and the first line of the Description Text style is indented one step. You can use the description list styles to create a glossary or other, similar list, or you can simply use the styles to create paragraphs of text with and without indents.

Using the description list styles are no different than applying any other paragraph styles to paragraphs in Composer. To apply one of the description list styles, simply follow these steps:

1.  Start by entering the text of the description list. Type each list item as a separate paragraph and end it by pressing the Enter key. Be sure to make the description title (glossary term) and description text (glossary definition) separate paragraphs.
2.  Select the paragraph you want to format by clicking it.

**3.** Apply the appropriate description list paragraph style to the selected paragraphs using one of the following techniques:
- From the Paragraph Style drop-down list in the formatting toolbar select either Desc. Title or Desc. Text.
- From the Format menu, select Paragraph, and then select either Description Title or Description Text.
- Right-click the selected text and a pop-up menu will appear. Choose Paragraph/List Properties. The Character Properties dialog box will open with the Paragraph tab displayed. From the Paragraph Style drop-down list select either Desc. Title or Desc. Text. Click the OK button to close the dialog box.

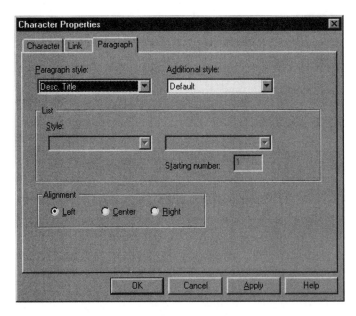

Composer displays the selected paragraph with the style you chose, indenting it the appropriate distance for a description title or description text.

# Inserting Addresses

An address is a special HTML paragraph style that was originally designed for formatting the address of the author of the page (the snail-mail address, the e-mail address, or both). Most Web browsers display an address paragraph in an italic font, smaller than body text. It's handy to have the paragraph style available, so you don't need to add separate font size and italic attributes to achieve the traditional appearance.

To enter an address in Composer, just type the address and then select it. With the text of the address selected, you can apply the Address paragraph style with one of the following techniques:

- From the Format toolbar, click to pull down the Paragraph Style drop-down list, and choose Address.
- From the Format menu, choose Paragraph, and then choose Address.

**NOTE**  See Appendix B, *An HTML Dictionary*, for details of the HTML tags used to indicate address paragraphs in the page source.

# Working with (Un)Formatted Paragraphs

Typically, the text on a Web page appears in a proportional or variable-width font such as Times New Roman. Also, Web browsers follow certain rules such as ignoring multiple spaces and automatically wrapping long lines of text to fit in the browser window. The combination of these features enables Web browsers to display text in a way that is attractive and easy to read, despite significant differences in the size of the browser window and the characteristics of different users' computer systems.

Generally, this is a good thing. However, the developers of the HTML standard envisioned some circumstances in which users might miss the formatting capabilities of a plain text document using a fixed-width font. For example, you might want to simulate the appearance of a text-mode computer screen or create a crude table by using multiple spaces to separate lines of text into columns. The Formatted (sometimes called Preformatted) paragraph style addresses this need.

Selecting the Formatted paragraph style instructs the Web browser to display the text in a fixed-width font. The style also suspends the rules ignoring multiple spaces in text. As a result, text formatted with the Formatted paragraph style behaves much like an old-fashioned typewriter or text in an ASCII text file (the kind you create and edit in Notepad).

In the first versions of HTML, using the Formatted paragraph style was the only way to create a table. Now that table tags are supported by all the popular Web browsers, the Formatted paragraph style doesn't get used much anymore. But it's still available if you need it.

To use the Formatted paragraph style, follow these steps:

**1.** Drag the pointer across one or more paragraphs of text to select them.

2. Select the Formatted paragraph style using one of the following techniques:
   - From the paragraph style drop-down-list in Composer's formatting toolbar select Formatted.
   - Click to pull down the Format menu, choose Paragraph, then choose Formatted.

That's all there is to it. Composer applies the Formatted paragraph style to the selected text. The text appears in the fixed-width font and you can enter multiple spaces to separate words. Of course, in Composer, you can achieve essentially the same thing by simply changing the font in a normal paragraph to the fixed-width font.

# Inserting Horizontal Lines

Horizontal lines (sometimes called horizontal rules or ruled lines) are lines that you can use to separate parts of your document. Adding a horizontal line to your page in Composer takes just a couple of mouse clicks. To place a horizontal line in your document, first move the insertion point to the location where you want to add the rule. Then do one of the following:

- From the Composer toolbar, click the Insert Horizontal Line button (the next-to-last button).
- From the Insert menu, choose Horizontal Line.

**WARNING** Be sure to position the insertion point at the beginning or end of a paragraph before you insert a horizontal line. Inserting a line with the insertion point in the middle of a paragraph will split the paragraph into two—one above, and one below the horizontal line.

Composer inserts a horizontal line at the insertion point and adds space above and below the line as shown in Figure 5.4.

The default horizontal line is four pixels thick, runs the full width of the browser window, and is shaded to create an embossed effect. You can change the appearance of the line by changing the settings in the Horizontal Line Properties dialog box. Simply right-click the line to display a pop-up menu and choose Horizontal Line Properties to

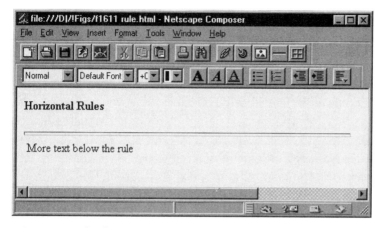

**FIGURE 5.4:** The default horizontal line uses shading to simulate the 3-D effect of an embossed line.

open the dialog box as shown in Figure 5.5. In the Horizontal Line Properties dialog box you can specify the height, width, and alignment for the rule. If the 3-D Shading option is checked, you get a rule with the embossed effect; if you clear the checkbox a solid-colored rule with no shading is generated. After adjusting the settings, click OK to close the dialog box and apply the settings to the rule.

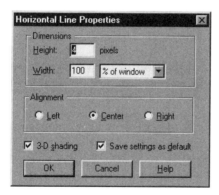

**FIGURE 5.5:**
You can change the appearance of a line with the settings in this dialog box.

**TIP** See Appendix B, *An HTML Dictionary*, for information on the HTML tag Composer adds to your page source to define horizontal lines.

# Checking Your Spelling

Composer includes a feature to help you find and correct those embarrassing spelling errors before you post your page on the Web for the world to see. The Spelling tool is another of those Composer features that will be familiar to anyone who has used word processors. It's easy to use. The hardest part of checking the spelling of a page in Composer is remembering to check every page before you publish it to the Web.

Before you use the Spelling tool for the first time, you must tell Composer what language you are using so the program can use the appropriate spelling dictionary. To do so, follow these steps:

1.  Click to pull down the Tools menu and select Language. The Language dialog box will appear.

2.  Select the appropriate language from the list in the dialog box.

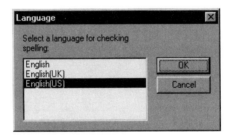

3.  Click the OK button to close the dialog box and record your selection.

Composer will use the dictionary, with the language you specified, to check the spelling in your Web pages. Unless you create Web pages in more than one language, you'll need to make this selection only once.

When you're ready to check the spelling on your Web page, follow these steps:

1.  Select the portion of the page where you want to check the spelling.

    • Drag the pointer across some text to select it. You can select any amount of text from a single word to multiple paragraphs. If any text is highlighted when you start the Spelling tool, the program will check only the highlighted text.

    • By default, Composer will check all the text on the current page. So, to check the entire Web page, you can either make sure all the text is selected (the hard way) or make sure no text is selected by simply clicking some text on the page (the easy way).

**2.** Click to pull down the Tools menu and choose Spelling. The Spelling dialog box will open.

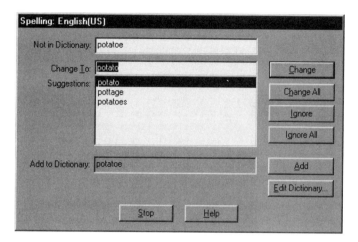

Composer compares the text on your Web page to the words in its spelling dictionary. If it finds a word on your page it doesn't recognize, the program displays the unrecognized word in the Spelling dialog box along with a list of suggested alternatives. Then you can decide how to handle each unrecognized word.

**3.** Composer displays the first (or next) unrecognized word in the Not in Dictionary box. The proposed change to that word appears in the Change To text box. If necessary, you can change the word in the Change To box by selecting a word from the Suggestions list or by typing a new word in the Change To box.

**4.** When the Change To box contains the correctly spelled word, you can tell Composer how to handle the unrecognized word on your page by doing one of the following:

- To replace the unrecognized word with the corrected word shown in the Change To box, click the Change button.
- To replace all occurrences of the unrecognized word with the corrected word shown in the Change To box, click the Change All button.
- To accept the unrecognized word without making any change, click the Ignore button. (Use this option to accept words that Composer didn't recognize but that you know are spelled correctly. This would include names, technical terms, and other words that aren't in Composer's dictionary.)

- To accept all occurrences of the unrecognized word in the selected text without making any change, click the Ignore All button.
- To accept an unrecognized word as correctly spelled and add it to Composer's dictionary, click the Add button. (Use this option to add names and other frequently used words to the dictionary so that Composer will not mark them as unrecognized words in the future. Just be very sure the word is spelled correctly before adding it to the dictionary.)

**TIP**
You can edit the list of words you add to Composer's spelling dictionary. In the Spelling dialog box just click the Edit Dictionary button to open the Personal Dictionary dialog box, where you can perform dictionary maintenance chores. You can type a word into the New Word box and click the Add button to add it to the dictionary. You can select a word from the Words list and then click the Remove button to delete it from the dictionary. When you're through editing the dictionary, click the OK button to record your changes and close the dialog box.

When you click one of the buttons in the Spelling dialog box, Composer takes the appropriate action to replace or accept the unrecognized word and then displays the next unrecognized word from the selected text.

5. Repeat steps 3 and 4 as needed until you've checked all the unrecognized words in the selected text.
6. When Composer finishes checking the selected text, the program will display a message to that effect in place of the Spelling dialog box. Click the OK button to close the message box and conclude the spell check.

Now quickly save your page while you are reasonably confident that it is free of spelling errors. Don't forget to recheck the spelling if you make any changes in the text.

**NOTE**
Composer's Spelling tool just checks spelling. You're on your own when it comes to checking for errors in grammar, style and usage. You can find a good online resource for grammar and style issues at the Crusty Old Slot Man's Copyediting Peeve Page at http://www.theslot.com/. Look into the archive for some real gems of wisdom.

**WARNING**    You won't be able to fix typos or other errors, or add text, graphics, or anything else to your HTML document while you are viewing it with Navigator. If you want to make changes, close Navigator, open up Composer, and make the changes there. Then, you can save the modified file, and reopen it in Navigator to check the changes you just made.

# Chapter 6

# ADDING IMAGES

- Adding images to your page
- Moving and resizing images
- Aligning images
- Dealing with image formats
- Creating textures with background images
- Exploring special image effects

The World Wide Web is more than text pages alone. The HTML standard encompasses images as well as text. As a result, Web browsers such as Navigator can display a rich variety of pictures and graphics along with the formatted text on Web pages. Some images can supply a significant amount of content; and all images, when used properly, add color and visual interest to a Web page.

The images on your Web page can be anything. You can use charts, graphs, and diagrams to illustrate a point. You can use logos and graphic symbols to establish a visual identity for your page. You can use scanned photos and drawings to set a mood or show details. Background images can provide a backdrop as subtle as fine silk or as rich as polished marble.

Composer makes adding images to your Web page easy. With the click of a button or a simple menu choice, you can open a dialog box where you can specify the file name of the image to add to your Web page, and select other options and settings to control how the image will appear on your page. When you click OK, Composer adds the image to your page.

Basically, that's all there is to it. Of course, working with images gets a little more involved when you start exploring some of the effects you can achieve by using the options and settings Composer provides, along with the effects you can incorporate into the images themselves.

What you do with images on your Web page is limited only by your imagination. How you do it is the subject of this chapter.

# Adding Images to Your Page

Most images that are part of a Web page are called inline images. These images typically appear over, under, or beside the text on a Web page (as shown in Figure 6.1). Each image is stored in a separate file. Normally, the images used on Web pages will be in one of two file formats—GIF or JPEG—designed to store graphic information in an efficient, compressed form. (I'll cover image file formats in more detail a little later in this chapter.)

Remember that beneath all of Composer's fancy WYSIWYG trappings, you are building an HTML source file that defines your Web page—and that HTML file is basically text. The inline images themselves are not included in the HTML source file—only an image tag that references the file name of the image file is stored in the HTML document. When the viewer's browser encounters the image tag in the text of the HTML file, the browser loads and displays the inline image as part of the Web page.

You can't position an image at just any random location on the page—it must be positioned in reference to some surrounding text. The image tag can be embedded in the middle of a paragraph of text, placed at the beginning or end of a paragraph, or, more often, placed in a paragraph of its own. The image tag anchors the image in the text. As the text flows from the top of the page to the bottom, the image will appear in its place within the text—moving with the text as it wraps to fit the browser window.

**WARNING**   Although it is possible to place many, many inline images in your document, remember that including them will greatly increase the time required to load and view the document.

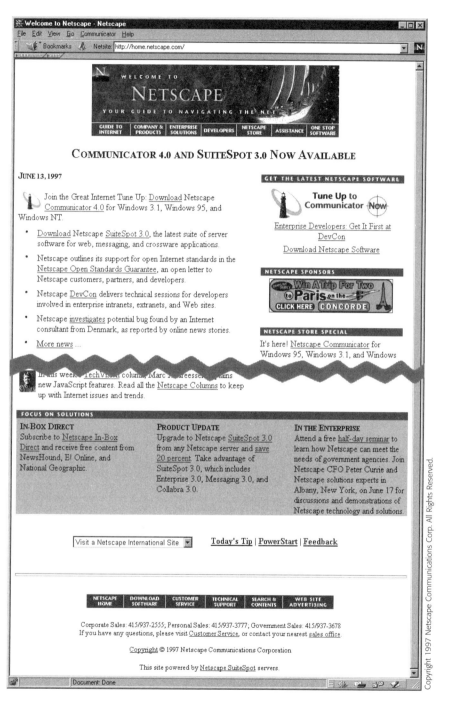

**FIGURE 6.1:** Pictures, logo graphics, and navigation buttons are all examples of images on a Web page.

To add an inline image to your Web page in Composer, follow these steps:

1. Position the insertion point (the same insertion point you use for editing text) at the location on the page where you want to insert the image.

2. From the Insert menu choose Image or go to the Compose toolbar and click the Insert Image button. Either action will open the Image Properties dialog box with the Image tab displayed.

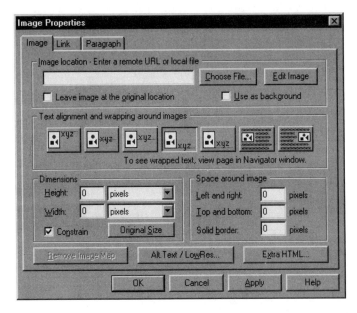

3. In the Image Location text box, type the path and file name of the image file you want to use. Alternatively, you can click the Choose File button to open the Select Image File dialog box. From here select the image file and click Open to insert the file name into the Image Location text box back in the Properties dialog box.

4. Next, click a button in the Text Alignment or Wrapping Around Images area to specify how the image will be aligned on the Web page and the way the text should flow around it. (I'll explore these options in detail in the *Aligning Images* section of this chapter.)

> **TIP**
>
> You can drag and drop GIF and JPEG image files from your Windows 95 desktop or an Explorer window to the Composer editing window. Composer will automatically insert the image into your Web page at the current insertion point location. Later, you can move the image or edit the alignment and other settings.

5. If you want to define a specific size for the image, you can enter values in the height and width text boxes. However, it's usually easier to size an image visually after you place it on the page. You can just click the edge of an image and drag it to make the image larger or smaller. If you do decide to edit size information for the image, Composer provides a couple of tools to make your job a little easier.

- The Constrain option ensures that the image maintains its correct proportions. If the Constrain option is checked, you can enter a new size in either the Height or Width boxes, and Composer will automatically adjust the other setting for you. If you want to distort the image, clear the Constrain checkbox first. Then you can adjust the Height and Width settings independently without affecting the other.
- If your image sizing experiments get out of hand, click the Original Size button. Composer will return the image to the original size recorded in the image file, regardless of the changes you've made since inserting the image.

6. In the Space Around Image area you can specify how much white space there will be between the edge of the image and the closest text. Enter values in the Left and Right text box and in the Top and Bottom text box as needed. In this same area, you can specify the width of a border that will appear around the image. The default value of 0 suppresses display of the border.

Not everyone can view images on a Web page—at least not very quickly. A few people still use text-only systems. Many more users have systems that are capable of displaying images, but slow Internet connections mean that it takes a very long time for images to download and display. These users may elect not to display images as they surf the Web or they may simply follow a hyperlink to another page before the image has time to download. For these users, it's important to supply an alternative preview to the full image while they wait for the main image to appear. HTML allows you to specify an alternative to the image in the form of a text description, a low-resolution image, or both.

**7.** To specify an alternative text or image, click the Alt Text/LowRes button to open the Alternate Image Properties dialog box. In the Alternate Text text box, type the text you want to appear in place of the image.

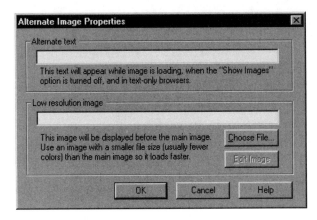

**8.** In the Low Resolution Image text box, enter the file name of another image. Presumably, this will be a lower-resolution version of the same image in a smaller file and will load much faster. When a user views your page, the browser will load the low-resolution image first and then replace it with the regular, higher-resolution image as the larger file is downloaded. After entering the information, click OK to close the Alternate Image Properties dialog box and return to the Image tab of the Properties dialog box.

**9.** Finally, click Apply or OK to add the image to your Web page. Composer will display the image as it will appear in most browsers. However, the text flowing around the image may not be properly rendered. Behind the scenes, Composer adds an `<img>` tag to the HTML source file for your Web page.

> **NOTE**   See the `<img>` tag in Appendix B, *An HTML Dictionary*.

# Moving and Resizing Images

After you add an image to the page, moving and resizing that image in Composer is easy. Moving an image is a simple, intuitive process of dragging the image to a new location on the page. To resize an image, you just drag its border.

> **TIP**
>
> You can edit an existing inline image by right-clicking the image text and choosing Image Properties. This will open the Properties dialog box with the Image tab displayed. You can change any of the settings in the dialog box.

Moving an image changes the location of the `<img>` tag with respect to the rest of the text in the HTML file for your Web page and thus changes what text comes before and after the image. Moving an image does *not* change the alignment (left, right, or center) of the image or how the text flows around it. For that, you'll need to edit the image's alignment settings (I'll show you how in the next section of this chapter).

To move an image, follow these steps:

1. Position the pointer over the image you want to move. Notice that the pointer changes to an arrow with a hand beside it. This is your cue that you can grab the image under the pointer and move it.

2. Click and drag the mouse to move the image. A border appears around the image to show that it's selected and the pointer changes to an arrow with an image icon (the same one that is on the Insert Image button) beside it. As you move the pointer, the flashing insertion point cursor also moves to indicate where the image will be inserted into the text.

> **WARNING**
>
> Since the image must be positioned in relation to the surrounding text, the position of the flashing text insertion point (which jumps through the text on the page) is more important than the pointer (which you can move anywhere on the page).

3. When the insertion point is in the correct position, release the mouse button to drop the image at its new location. Composer moves the `<img>` tag in the HTML source file and redraws the Web page in the edit window.

In some ways, resizing an image is even simpler than moving an image—there is no confusion about the difference between the location of the image tag and the alignment of that image.

You can set the height and width of an image in the Properties dialog box when you add the image to your Web page. You can also edit those same settings at a later time by right-clicking the image and choosing Image Properties from the pop-up menu that appears. The height and width settings on the Image tab of the Properties dialog box enable you to specify the size of an image in pixels or as a percent of the size of the browser window.

Such precise numeric control is nice, but it's usually much easier to size images visually, in relation to the text and the other images on the page. Composer makes it easy to visually resize images by manipulating the image in the edit window—you don't have to open a dialog box. In fact, the process of resizing images will probably seem quite familiar because it's essentially the same procedure you use to resize application windows on your Windows 95 desktop.

To visually resize an image, follow these steps:

1. Select an image in the Composer edit window by clicking it.
2. Position the pointer over the edge (border) of the image. The pointer will change to a double-headed arrow.
   - To change the height of the image, position the pointer over the top or bottom border.
   - To change the width of the image, position the pointer over one of the sides.
   - To change both height and width proportionally, position the pointer over a corner of the image.
3. Click the border of the image and drag it to make it larger or smaller as needed. As you drag, the border changes to indicate the new size, but the image remains the same.
   - Drag the border toward the center of the image to make the image smaller.
   - Drag the border out, away from the center of the image to make the image larger.
4. When the border is the desired size, release the mouse button. Composer redraws the image at the new size (and records the height and width settings in the `<img>` tag for the image in the HTML file).

> **TIP**
>
> If you make a mistake and resize the image to the wrong size (or just don't like how it looks), you can reverse the effect and return the image to its previous size by choosing Edit ➢ Undo or typing Ctrl+Z.

# Aligning Images

The location of an inline image on your Web page is determined by the position of the insertion point when you insert or move the image. That is, the insertion point indicates the location where the `<img>` tag referencing the image is inserted into the text of the Web page. And the location of the `<img>` tag determines where the image falls in the flow of text from the top of the Web page to the bottom—what text comes before the image and what text follows it.

While the location of the `<img>` tag anchors the image in the text, it's the alignment settings that control the finer points of the relationship between the image and the surrounding text.

Basically, there are two kinds of alignment that affect the position of an image on your Web page. They are:

- Paragraph alignment (left, center, right)
- Text alignment (alignment with respect to the text within a paragraph)

The first kind of alignment—paragraph alignment—is easy to understand. The second is a little more tricky, but it's not bad once you get the hang of it.

# Left, Center, Right

Because an image tag is embedded in a paragraph of text, the image will follow the same alignment on the page (left, center, or right) as the rest of the paragraph. If the image is small and located in the middle of a sentence, it will simply take its place like a special character in the text. In that case, the paragraph alignment won't make much difference in the position of the image. However, larger images are a different matter.

Quite often, you'll find that the simplest way to work with an inline image is to place the image in a separate paragraph of its own. Then, you can use the regular paragraph alignment commands to align the image with the left or right margins, or the center of the page. What you are really doing is setting the alignment of the paragraph containing the image, not aligning the image itself on the page. (But that's splitting hairs; the effect is the same.) Naturally, since you're adjusting the alignment of a paragraph, you can do so using any of the same commands you use on plain text paragraphs:

- Choose Format ➤ Align ➤ Left (or Center, or Right)
- Click the Horizontal Alignment button in the toolbar and then click the Align Left, Align Center, or Align Right button.
- Right-click the paragraph (image) and choose Paragraph Properties from the pop-up menu displayed. The Character Properties dialog box will open with the Paragraph tab. Click the Left, Center, or Right radio button in the Alignment box and then click OK.

**NOTE**    For more information, see the text alignment tags in Appendix B, *An HTML Dictionary.*

## Text Flow around Images

In addition to controlling image alignment by setting the horizontal alignment of the paragraph containing the image, you can set alignment options for the image itself. The image-specific alignment options give you a measure of control over the relationship between the image and the surrounding text.

The text/image alignment options can be divided into two groups. The first group controls the vertical alignment of the image compared to the line of text in which it appears. These options really come into their own when working with small images that are embedded in text. Examples would be initial caps at the beginning of a paragraphs and icons or other symbols appearing in the body of a paragraph.

The second group of text/image alignment options enables you to instruct the browser to wrap text around the image. By using these alignment options, you can achieve effects similar to the common magazine and newspaper layouts in which the text flows around the images on the page instead of stopping above the image and starting up again below it.

**WARNING** Composer can't accurately display text wrapping around an image. To see some of the text wrapping effects, you must preview your page in Navigator.

To set the image alignment option for an image, click a button in the Image Properties dialog box. You'll find the buttons in the Text Alignment or Wrapping Around Images area in the middle of the Image tab.

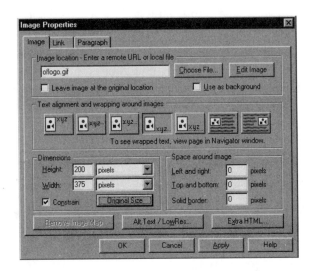

There are seven buttons—five for text/image alignment and two options for wrapping text around an image. To select an alignment option, just click the corresponding button. You can select the image alignment option when you insert the image or any time you open the Image Properties dialog box to edit the image. From left to right, the image alignment buttons are as follows:

| Button | HTML Parameter | Effect |
| --- | --- | --- |
| | TEXTTOP | Aligns the top of the image with the top of the text |
| | ABSCENTER | Aligns the vertical center of the image with the vertical center of the text |
| | CENTER | Aligns the center of the image with the baseline of the text |
| | BOTTOM | Aligns the bottom of the image with the baseline of the text (this is the default alignment) |
| | ABSBOTTOM | Aligns the bottom of the image with the bottom of the descenders (the tails of letters such as *g* and *y* that extend below the baseline) |
| | LEFT | Aligns the image with the left margin and wraps text around its right side |
| | RIGHT | Aligns the image with the right margin and wraps text around its left side |

**WARNING**

**Not all browsers support all of the same image alignment and text wrapping options that Composer offers. The buttons for TEXTTOP, CENTER, and BOTTOM alignment are safe bets. Most newer browsers also support the align left and align right options (the last two buttons). For compatibility with other browsers, you may want to avoid using the CENTER and ABSBOTTOM alignment options.**

> **NOTE**
>
> For information about how the image alignment options appear in the HTML code for your page, see the <img> tag in Appendix B, *An HTML Dictionary.*

When you first begin experimenting with the image alignment settings, you may be surprised (and even a bit confused) by the results you see in the Composer editing window and the slightly different appearance of the page when viewed in Navigator. Remember, the first five buttons affect the vertical alignment of the image compared to the text surrounding the <img> tag for that image. As Figure 6.2 shows, these alignment settings don't affect the location of the image with respect to the text preceding and following the image. The align left and align right settings, on the other hand, can change what text comes before and after the image by pushing the image over to the left or right margin and allowing the text to flow around the image as shown in Figure 6.3.

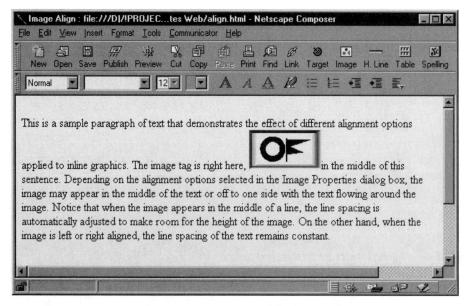

**FIGURE 6.2:** The vertical alignment options don't change where an image falls in a line of text.

You won't be able to preview the effect of the left and right align options in Composer. To see the text wrap around an image, you must view your page in Navigator or another browser.

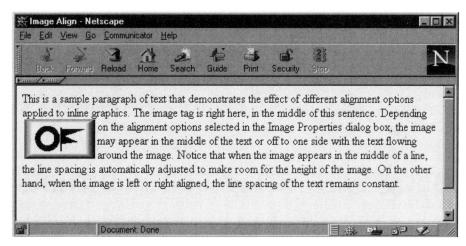

**FIGURE 6.3:** The left and right align options move the image to the page margin and allow the text to wrap around the image.

For your first experiments with the image alignment options, try working with a small image (no more than two or three times the height of the surrounding text) placed in the middle of a paragraph of text. The small image makes it easier to see the effect of the various alignment options on the image's placement and the line spacing of the surrounding text. A larger image can disrupt the page layout by causing text to reflow around the image making it harder to see the effect of the alignment options.

## The Famous Single-Pixel Image Trick

Sometimes, it's the images you don't see that are the most useful.

An old trick among experienced Web authors is to use an image as a spacer to facilitate positioning and aligning text and other images. The trick is to create a tiny image—really just a single pixel—and make it transparent so it won't be visible. Then, you can insert it anywhere on your Web page when you need a spacer to force another element a little farther over, up, or down. You can resize the single-pixel image to occupy any amount of space you need.

# Dealing with Image File Formats

There are many different file formats in use for recording graphics data. It seems like every major graphics program has its own file format. Then there's an assortment of different standard formats used by scanner software, clip art collections, and the like. Dealing with the alphabet soup of file name extensions and abbreviations for file format names is a constant source of confusion and frustration for graphics professionals who must work with multiple file formats.

Fortunately, the World Wide Web community has settled on a short list of file formats that are the supported de facto standards for images. Consequently, any image you create in Composer and want to include as an inline image in a Web document must be in one of two graphics file formats: GIF or JPEG. The GIF file format (sometimes called CompuServe GIF) is the ever-popular standard for Web images. All Web browsers (except text-only browsers) can display GIF images.

Many Web browsers, including Navigator, can also display inline images in JPEG format. JPEG files (which usually have a JPG extension in their file names) are generally smaller in size than other image files, so they appear on screen much more quickly—a real advantage. The drawback for the publisher, however, is that not all Web browsers can display them. If you use a JPEG image, and a user tries viewing your document with a browser that can't handle JPEG files, all the user will see is a little error message where the image should be.

By default, Composer presumes that the images you are adding are GIF or JPEG files. However, you can specify other file types when you insert images. As a result, you can include sounds, movies, video clips, and animations in your Web pages. Composer displays a placeholder icon in the edit window that you can manipulate (cut, paste, move, and edit) in much the same way you do ordinary images.

A third file format, PNG (which stands for Portable Network Graphics), has been proposed as a replacement for GIF files. The leading browsers can display PNG, but the new format hasn't been widely adopted yet. Composer doesn't display PNG files in its editing window but you can insert PNG images as generic objects if you like.

> **TIP** The GIF and JPEG formats both have their strengths and weaknesses. Generally, GIF files perform better for images that contain graphics and sharp-edged areas of solid color. The JPEG format, on the other hand, excels at handling photographs and other images containing lots of colors and shading.

Working with images in only two file formats may seem like a limitation at first, but in practice, it's hardly a handicap. The immense popularity of the Internet and the Web means that every graphics program and utility is likely to have the capability to save or export image files to one of the two supported formats used on the Web. As a result, there is no shortage of options for creating and editing images in the correct format. If you do run across an image that is in the wrong file format (TIF or PCX, for example), it's usually a simple matter to open the image in an appropriate image editing program (such as Photoshop or Paint Shop Pro) and export the image to a GIF or JPEG file that you can then insert in a Web page in Composer.

**Automatic Image Conversion**    In addition to GIF and JPEG images files, Composer allows you to select and import images in one other file format—Windows Bitmap (BMP) files. Composer won't actually use the BMP file, but the program will convert it to a JPEG file. Follow these steps:

1. Use one of the standard techniques to insert an image into your Web page.
    - You can use the Insert ➤ Image command or Image button on the toolbar to open the Image Properties dialog box. Then select a BMP file as the Image Location, adjust other settings as needed and click the OK button to insert the image into your page.
    - You can import a BMP file by dragging its icon from your Windows 95 desktop or Explorer window and dropping it onto your Web page in the Composer editing window.

2. When you attempt to insert a BMP image onto your Web page, Composer will automatically open the Image Conversion dialog box offering to convert the image to the JPEG file format. Click the OK button to accept Composer's offer to convert the file.

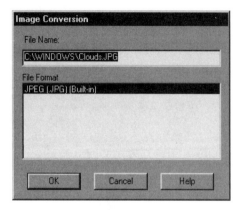

3. Another dialog box—the JPEG Image Quality dialog box—then appears. Select High, Medium, or Low and then click the OK button. (Selecting High creates a higher-resolution image and a larger file. Selecting Low creates a lower-resolution image and a smaller file. Selecting Medium is usually a good compromise between the two extremes.)

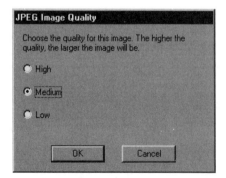

Composer automatically reads the BMP image and creates a copy of the image in a new JPEG file. Then, Composer adds the resulting JPEG image to your Web page.

# Creating Textures with Background Images

So far, we've been considering inline images—foreground images that appear alongside the text on your Web page. However, images aren't confined to the foreground. The HTML standard makes special provisions for using an image to create a background for your Web page. The background image does just what its name implies: It appears in the background with the text and inline images appearing in the foreground. The effect can be interesting and attractive—which probably explains why it is so popular.

The days of the drab gray background are gone. Even solid color backgrounds are plain compared to the effects you can achieve with background images.

You can use any GIF or JPEG graphic file as your background image (any browser that recognizes custom backgrounds can also display JPEG images). For example, many companies like to use dimmed versions of their logos as background graphics—kind of like a watermark in expensive stationery (see Figure 6.4). Another popular technique is to use a background image to simulate a texture such as paper, wood, stone, leather, or fabric (as shown in Figure 6.5).

You might expect that an image large enough to fill the entire background of a Web page would require a very large image file (and you would be right). When creating your background, consider your audience's attention span because an image large enough to fill even a moderately sized browser window would probably require more time to download than most viewers are willing to invest to view your page. Another problem to be aware of is how big to make the background image because there's no way to predict the exact size of the viewer's browser window.

What makes background images practical is that the browser tiles the image you specify as a background to fill up the entire window. That is, it will repeat the image in its original size until it covers the page's viewing area. As a result, you can specify a small, compact image file that will download quickly, even over a dial-up connection. The background image gets downloaded only once. The browser automatically displays as many multiple copies of the background image as needed to fill the background of the page without using the download time or memory resources required by a larger image.

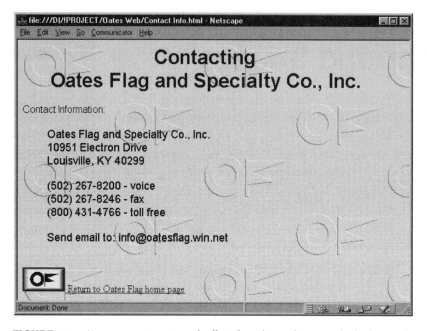

**FIGURE 6.4:** You can create watermark effects by using an image as the background for a Web page.

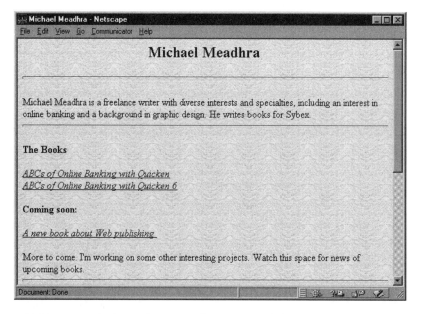

**FIGURE 6.5:** A background texture such as paper or cloth can create a subtle, interesting effect.

**WARNING**  Avoid background images with strong light and dark contrasts. A busy, high-contrast background can make it nearly impossible to find a text color that will remain legible on all parts of the page.

Since the background image is tiled, only a small sample (less than an inch square) is required to create a texture such as paper, cloth, or stone. Textures such as wood grains and veined marble need slightly larger images to create attractive backgrounds. An image of a logo is likely to be even larger, but it's still much smaller than a single page-sized image.

**NOTE**  Because of the way the browser tiles the background image, careful planning is required to create a background image with edges that will blend together to create the illusion of a seamless background texture. This is a job best left to graphics specialists. Fortunately, there are plenty of background texture images you can download from the Web or purchase in clip art collections.

To specify a background image for your Web page, follow these steps:
1.  From the Format menu choose Page Colors and Properties. This opens the Page Properties dialog box. If necessary, click the Colors and Backgrounds tab to display the background image options.

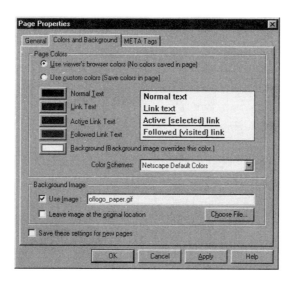

2. Click the Use Image checkbox in the Background Image area near the bottom of the dialog box to select it.

3. In the Use Image text box, enter the URL or file name for the image file you want to use as a background. Optionally, you can click the Choose File button to open the Select Image File dialog box, where you can select the file instead of typing its file name.

4. After specifying an image file, click OK or Apply to apply the background image to your Web page.

Composer displays your Web page in the editing window with the specified background image. It's a pretty good approximation of what most users will see when they view your page in their browser.

**NOTE**
Looking for images to use as background textures? Try these two sites: http://www.solarflare.com/freeart/ or http://the-tech .mit.edu/KPT/bgs.html. You can find plenty more by visiting one of the search engine or Web directory sites and searching on *Web background texture.*

# Special Image Effects

Images can be an incredibly powerful and versatile Web page design tool. You can achieve a tremendous range of effects with images—largely because an image in a Web page can be virtually anything. An image can contain a photograph, drawing, diagram, chart, graph, illustration, logo, symbol, or even text in a special typeface color or arrangement that would be difficult to reproduce with HTML commands. Regardless of the contents of an image, you work with it the same way when assembling your Web page in Composer. When you insert an image, it makes no difference whether the image is a photograph, a logo, or a bar chart. (At least, it makes no difference in the way you insert, move, and align the image in Composer. Of course, the contents of the image can make a big difference in the appearance of your page—and the message it conveys.)

In addition to all the things you can do with regular images, there are a few special effects that can add even more pizzazz to your Web page. Some effects are subtle and others can be quite dramatic. What all the special effects have in common is that they are built into the image file when it is created. The Web browser may need the capability to recognize and display the special effect properly, but you don't have to do anything different to work with the file in Composer—you simply insert the image into your Web page just like any other normal image file.

## Transparent Graphics

An image on a Web page is, by definition, a rectangular shape. That's fine for most images; they tend to be rectangular anyway. However, some irregular shapes, such as the outline of the United States or a corporate logo, don't fit as comfortably within the allotted rectangle.

When you want to create the illusion of an irregularly shaped object without being confined to a rectangle, you can use a special kind of image called a transparent GIF. It's really just a standard GIF format image file with one of the colors (usually the image background) defined as transparent. The transparent areas of the image allow anything that is behind the image to show through. So, if you insert a transparent GIF image in your Web page, the page background will show through the transparent areas of the image. You can also define a zero-width border for the image, and the rectangular shape of the image will completely disappear, as shown in Figure 6.6.

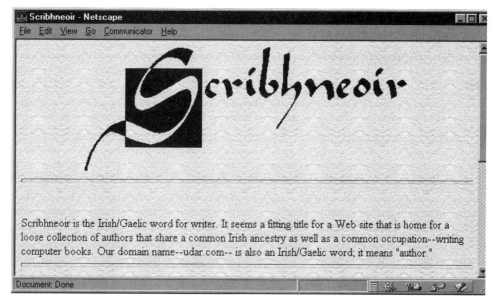

**FIGURE 6.6:** The page background shows through the transparent portions of a GIF image.

# Interlaced Images

An image of any size will take a noticeable amount of time to download and display in the browser window. Normally, the browser will progressively reveal the image a piece at a time as it downloads the information. The progress of an image materializing from the top down can seem frustratingly slow.

An interlaced image provides an alternative way to build the image onscreen in the browser window. An interlaced image first appears as an extremely low-resolution version of the image. It's rough and pixilated, but it fills the rectangular shape of the image quickly. As more data is downloaded, the image resolution improves until the entire image is displayed at its final resolution.

The process of downloading and displaying an interlaced image takes about the same amount of time as it would to display a conventional image. However, interlaced images are generally perceived as downloading faster, because the space is filled immediately and the image gradually gains detail. It's similar to loading a low-resolution image and then replacing it with a high-resolution one, except that the transition takes place in several steps. The viewer may perceive the image as satisfactorily completed before all of the data is downloaded and displayed.

As I write this, only the GIF file format provides the option of creating interlaced images. You must select the interlaced option when you create the GIF file; it isn't an option you can invoke in Composer or in the viewer's browser.

# Animated Pictures

Another interesting feature of the GIF file format is the ability to store several images in a single file along with timing instructions to display those images sequentially. The result is a simple animation effect. GIF animations are all the rage on the Web these days now that the popular Web browsers have the built-in capability to display them.

Unlike other, more sophisticated animation techniques, GIF animations can be created quickly and easily using inexpensive shareware utilities. You do not need expensive development tools or programming experience. GIF animations are suitable for small, animated graphics, especially those that can be created by cycling through a few images in a continuous loop. Generally, GIF animations aren't too fancy, but they can provide an eye-catching bit of motion to an otherwise static Web page. For example, the flag at the top of the page shown in Figure 6.7 appears to wave in the breeze.

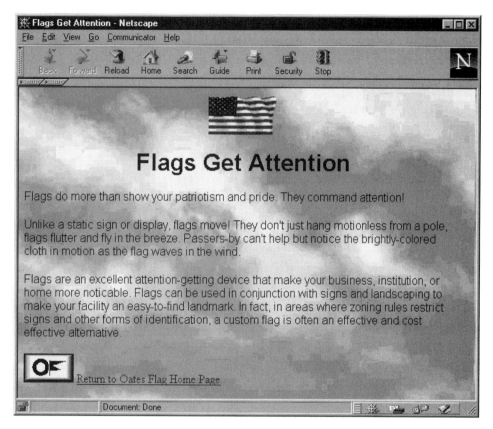

**FIGURE 6.7:**  Although you can't see motion in this illustration, the flag image appears to wave in the breeze when viewed in a Web browser that supports animated GIFs.

## Drop Shadows and Other Cool Stuff

One of the most popular special effects is the drop shadow. In fact, sometimes it seems as though much of what I see on the Web is floating a little above the page background.

Actually, drop shadows aren't a special effect at all. The effect isn't achieved by using any features of a file format or browser. Drop shadows, such as the one behind the logo on the page shown in Figure 6.8, are simply an illustration technique that produces the illusion of depth. It's an attractive effect and, thanks to plug-in filters in some of the popular image editing programs, drop shadows are fairly easy to create. The only problem is that drop shadows have become so popular that they are on the verge of suffering from overexposure.

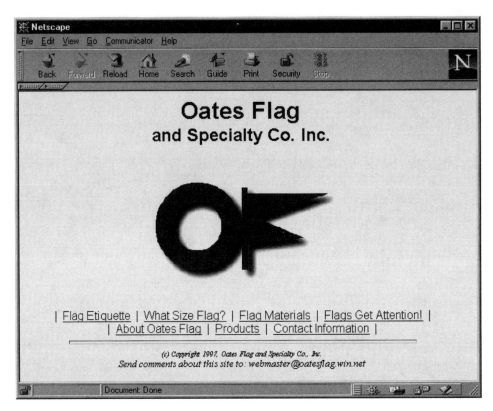

**FIGURE 6.8:** Drop shadows are one of the most popular illustration techniques used to add visual interest to images on Web pages.

There are many other illustration techniques like drop shadows that you can use in your images to create attractive Web pages. There are embossed effects, beveled edges, metallic effects, and much more. Some are popular now, others will gain popularity in the future. But you don't have to follow the popular trends; anything that makes your Web page more attractive and readable is a good choice.

# Chapter 7

# GETTING LINKED UP

Composer

- **Creating links**
- **Links to different types of documents and objects**
- **Using pictures as links**
- **Making the most of link options**
- **Creating a link to your e-mail address**

The previous chapters have covered how to work with text and images on your Web pages. However, although text and images are important components of most Web pages, it's the hypertext links that are the defining characteristic of the World Wide Web. Hypertext links enable you to build relationships between Web pages. You can create links from a location in one Web page to different parts of the same Web page, to other files on your Web site, or to other files on the Internet or an intranet. When a visitor to your Web site views a Web page and clicks a hyperlink, they are transported to another Web address for supplemental information, a continuation of the same topic, or anything else you choose to link to.

Now, without further ado, let's explore how to add hyperlinks to the Web pages you create or edit in Composer.

# Creating Links

The appearance of a hyperlink when it shows up in a Web browser window will differ depending on the browser being used, but usually it'll appear as underlined text in a special color. However, there's much more to a hyperlink than an underline and a distinctive color. When you click the hyperlink, the browser loads the Web page with which the hyperlink is associated (the other end of the link, if you will) and displays it onscreen. Defining the target of the link is the important part of creating a hyperlink in Composer. You don't have to worry about underlining text or changing its color—the browser will take care of that automatically.

## Creating Hyperlinks to Other Files

The most common hyperlink is probably one that links a word or phrase of text to another Web page—either a Web page stored in another file on your Web site or a file located elsewhere on the Internet. To add a hyperlink between text on a Web page you are creating or editing in Composer and an external file, follow these steps:

1. If the text passage that is to contain the hyperlink doesn't already exist in your Web page, type it in using the normal text entry techniques.

2. Select the word or phrase that is to become the hyperlink. You can double-click a word to select it, or you can select a phrase by dragging the mouse pointer across it. It's just like highlighting text for editing or for assigning an attribute such as bold or italic.

3. Begin defining the link by doing one of the following:
   - From the Insert menu, choose Link.

   - Go to the Composer toolbar and click the Insert/Make Link button.
   - Right-click the selected text and choose Create Link Using Selected from the pop-up menu that appears, or Press Ctrl+Shift+L.
   - Any of these actions will open the Character Properties dialog box with the Link tab displayed.

   The selected text appears in the Link Source box near the top of the dialog box. This is the text that will receive the distinctive formatting of a hyperlink when it appears in the Composer editing window and the browser window.

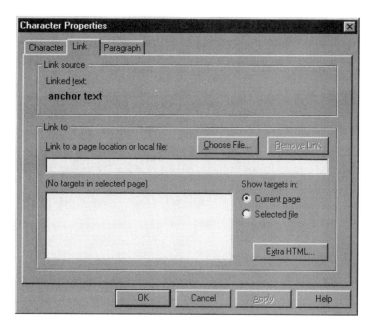

**4.** In the Link To text box, enter the file name or URL for the Web page that you want to be the target of link. This is the file that will be displayed when the user clicks the hyperlink while viewing your Web page. (As an alternative to typing the file name into the Link To text box, you can click the Choose File button to open the Link To File dialog box and then select the target file.) You can enter either a *relative* or *absolute* address for the target. (See the Relatively Absolute Address sidebar.)

**WARNING** You must enter the exact file name and/or URL for the Web page that is the target of the hyperlink. Be sure to type the file name or URL carefully and then double check it for accuracy. A single mistyped character is enough to keep the hyperlink from working properly.

**5.** After you have defined the hyperlink, click OK or Apply to insert the link into your Web page.

Composer formats the hyperlink text on your Web page and, behind the scenes, builds the HTML tag required to define the link between your Web page and the target file.

## Relatively Absolute Address

When you specify an Internet address as the target of a hyperlink, you can use one of two address forms: a *relative* address or an *absolute* address.

Basically, a relative address defines the address relative to the location of the current Web page. You use relative addresses to define hyperlink targets on the same server as the Web page. It's like giving someone directions to a house that's located just down the street. You just give them the house number and point in the right direction. You don't need to include the city and state since they're already in the right area.

- If the file you are linking to is stored in the *same* directory as the Web page containing the hyperlink on your Web site, you would then enter the file name for the target file. For example: **target.html**
- If the file you are linking to is stored in a *different* directory than the Web page containing the hyperlink directory on your Web site, you must enter the correct path (directory names) as well as the file name for the target file. For example: **\subdirectory\target.html.** This is still a relative address.

An *absolute* address leaves nothing to chance; it includes all the information needed to locate the target file including the file name, the directory, the name of the server on which the file is stored, and even the protocol the Web browser will need to use to access the file. An absolute address in the net is like a complete postal address including the apartment number, street address, city, state, and zip code.

You must use an absolute address if the file you are linking to is located elsewhere on the Internet (not on the same Web site as the page containing the hyperlink). However, nothing prevents you from also using absolute addresses for files located on the same server as your Web page.

- For an absolute address, you must enter the full URL for the target file. Be sure to include the protocol (usually `http://` or `ftp://`), the host name (such as `www.sybex.com`), and the path and file name (such as `/~myname/index.html`). For example:
  **http://www.domain.com/directory/target.html**

**NOTE** See the <a href> tag in Appendix B, *An HTML Dictionary.*

You can see this process in action by observing the steps required to create a link from the home page of our sample Web site to another page on the same site. To create the hyperlink, I took the following steps:

1. I opened the home page in the Composer editing window and scrolled down the window to display the text that was to become the hyperlink. (I'd entered the text earlier.)

2. I selected the text for the hyperlink, in this case, Contact Information as shown in Figure 7.1.

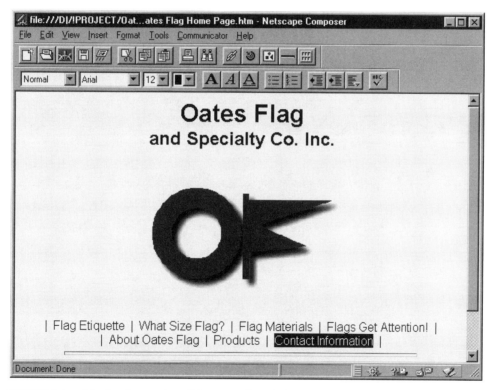

**FIGURE 7.1:** Selecting the text that will become a hyperlink

3. I clicked the Insert/Make Link button to open the Character Properties dialog box. Notice the selected text appears in the dialog box's Link Source box.

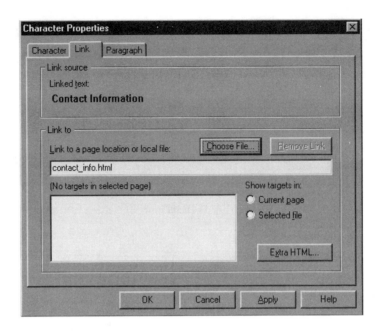

To avoid typing errors when entering file names and URLs, try to cut and paste the entries instead of typing them. Often you can find the URL for the target Web page displayed in the address box of the Web browser while viewing that target page, in the properties sheet for a shortcut to that page, or by editing the target page's entry in your bookmark list. Wherever you find it, highlight the URL for the target Web page and press Ctrl+C to copy it to the Windows clipboard. Then, return to Composer and, with the insertion point positioned in the Link To box of the Character Properties dialog box, click Ctrl+V to paste the URL into the text box.

4. The file I wanted to link to already existed in the same directory as the current Web page, so I simply typed the file name—contact_info.html—into the Link To text box.

5. After defining the hyperlink, I clicked the OK button to close the dialog box. Composer marked the selected text as a hyperlink by changing its color and adding an underline as shown in Figure 7.2.

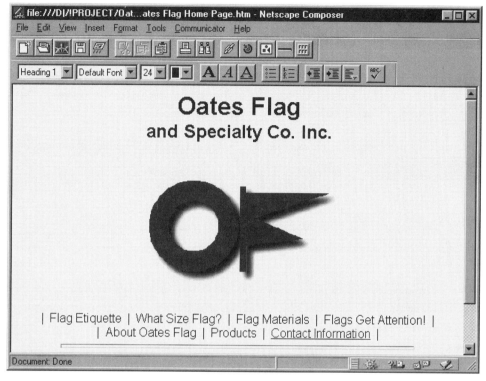

**FIGURE 7.2:** Composer marks the hyperlink with an underline and a different text color (blue).

**TIP**

Here's a quick and easy way to create a hyperlink. You can drag an HTML file icon or a shortcut to a URL from your desktop or Explorer window and drop it on the Composer editing window. Composer will add some text (the file name or URL) to your Web page and automatically define a link between that text and the file or URL.

**TIP**

You can edit an existing hyperlink by right-clicking the link text and choosing Link Properties from the pop-up menu. This will open the Character Properties dialog box with the Link tab displayed. You can change the settings in the dialog box to redefine the link, then click OK to close the dialog box and apply the changes.

## Creating Hyperlinks within a Web Page

In addition to hyperlinks to other Web pages, you can create hyperlinks to locations within the same Web page. You can use this kind of hyperlink to cross-reference two bits of text, or you can create a table of contents for a long Web page document by adding at the top of the page a list of headings that are each linked to the corresponding portion of the document.

> **TIP**
>
> **Creating hyperlinks to targets within a Web page is a good way to give your visitors easy access to the portions of a large document that they may be interested in. The viewer can just click the hyperlink to jump directly to the target area instead of having to scroll through the document to find what they're looking for.**

Creating hyperlinks within a Web page is a simple two-part process—you first create a named target, a hidden HTML tag that Composer places in your Web page, and then you create a hyperlink that is linked to that target.

To create a named target for a hyperlink, follow these steps:

1. Move the insertion point to the location in your Web page where you want to create the target for a hyperlink.

2. From the Insert menu choose Target, or go to the Compose toolbar and click the Insert Target button. Composer will open the Target Properties dialog box.

3. Enter a short name for the target and click OK. Composer closes the Target Properties dialog box and inserts a small target icon into your Web page, as shown in Figure 7.3. Composer also inserts the corresponding tag—

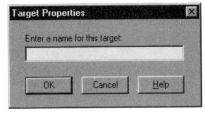

   `<a name="target text">`—into the HTML source code for your Web page.

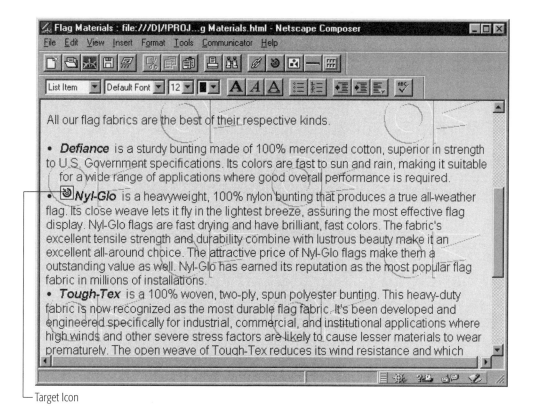

— Target Icon

**FIGURE 7.3:**   The target icon is visible in Composer, but not in a Web browser window.

The target will be invisible when you view the Web page with a browser. The target icon appears in the Composer window so you will have a visual clue to the target's location. The icon also gives you something to select so you can move, add, or delete the target. To help you identify the target, Composer will display the name of the target in a small pop-up box if you place the pointer on the target icon and let it rest there for a couple of seconds.

**NOTE**    See the <a name> tag in Appendix B, *An HTML Dictionary*.

After you create a target in your Web page, you still need to create a hyperlink to that target. To create a hyperlink to another location within the same Web page, follow these steps:

1. Select the text that you want to become the hyperlink.

2. From the Insert menu choose Link, or go to the Compose toolbar and click the Insert/Make Link button. Either action will open the Character Properties dialog box with the Link tab displayed. The selected text of the hyperlink will appear in the dialog box's Link Source text box.

3. In the Link To area, click the Current File radio button and then select a target from the Select a Named Target in Current Page list.

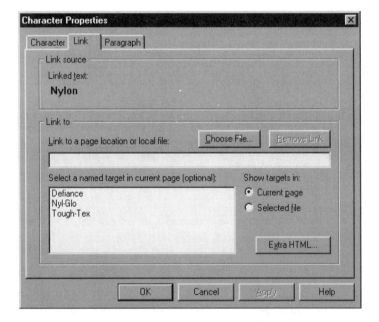

**TIP**

You can link to target locations in other Web pages as well as to targets on the current page. Simply specify the file name or URL for the desired Web page in the Link To text box and then click the Selected File button to display the list of targets defined in that page. Then you can select one of those named targets as the target of your hyperlink.

4. After you have defined the hyperlink, click OK or Apply to insert the link into your Web page.

Composer converts the selected text in your Web page to a hyperlink; it gets the same color and underline treatment of a hyperlink to another Web page. Behind the scenes, Composer builds the HTML tag defining the link between the link text and the target location in your Web page.

**NOTE**  See Appendix B, *An HTML Dictionary*, for an example of the anchor tag `<a href>` linking to a named target.

# Links to Different Types of Documents and Objects

Links to other Web pages and links to named targets within Web pages are, by far, the most common kinds of hyperlinks. However, the target of a hyperlink isn't restricted to HTML files alone. In fact, a hyperlink can point to any file or URL. The target of a hyperlink can be a text file, a sound file, a video clip, or just about anything else. Of course, there are a few practical limitations on what files you can specify as targets of a hyperlink. They are:

- The file must be accessible to the viewer's browser, meaning it must be located on the Web site, downloaded to their local hard drive, or otherwise accessible on the Internet or intranet.
- If you expect to view (or play) the file, it must be one of the file types that is recognized and supported by the browser, by a plug-in, or by other software on the viewer's system.
- The file must be properly identified so that the browser, plug-in, or other playback/display software can recognize the file type and launch the appropriate display program. Usually, that means including the appropriate extension (such as WAV for wave audio files or AVI for Windows video files) in the file name.

When a viewer clicks a hyperlink that links to a different file type instead of a Web page, the browser normally attempts to download the file and open it using the appropriate display or playback software. In some cases, such as text files and standard image files, the target file will be displayed in the browser window. In other cases, the browser must rely on an external program to display the linked file. The software the browser will use for opening each file type is defined in the browser's preferences settings for helper applications.

Creating hyperlinks to sound, video, and animation files is one way to add multimedia effects to your Web pages. I'll cover multimedia in Chapter 9, *Adding Sound and Motion with Multimedia*. In addition to multimedia files, you may occasionally want to create hyperlinks to other file types such as word processor files, spreadsheet files, and so on. The problem with having hyperlinks to non-standard file types is that the typical Web surfing viewer may not have the appropriate software to display the target file. However, creating such links can be very useful when you are posting a Web page on an intranet for use by members of a workgroup. In situations such as that, you can be reasonably sure the viewers will have the necessary software to view (and even edit) the target file.

## Setting Up File Downloads with FTP

Another common use for a hyperlink to a non-HTML file is to create a link for an FTP (File Transfer Protocol) file download. Basically, you simply create a normal hyperlink, specifying the FTP protocol and appropriate URL as the target of the link. When the viewer clicks the hyperlink in your Web page, the browser will initiate a file download using the FTP protocol. (That is, assuming the browser supports FTP downloads—most modern browsers do.)

The details of the process the viewer will go through to download the file will vary slightly, depending on the browser they are using. When a viewer clicks a hyperlink to a FTP file in Navigator, the browser opens the Save As dialog box to give the user an opportunity to specify the location and file name for the downloaded file. After the user clicks the Save button, the browser begins downloading a copy of the target file and displays the status of the process in a message box. After the download is complete, the user can access and manipulate the downloaded file just like any other file on their local hard drive.

To create a hyperlink for an FTP file download, follow these steps:

1. With the Web page open in the Composer editing window, select the word or phrase that is to become the hyperlink.

2. Open the Character Properties dialog box by choosing Link from the Insert menu, clicking the Insert/Make Link button in the toolbar, or right-clicking the selected text and choosing Link Properties from the pop-up menu that

appears. The Character Properties dialog box appears with the Link tab displayed and the selected text listed in the Link Source box.

3.  In the Link To text box, enter the URL for the file you want the user to download. The URL must include the FTP protocol identifier (`ftp://`), the name of the FTP server (such as `ftp.domain.com`), and the full path and file name of the file (such as `\~myname\filename.ext`).

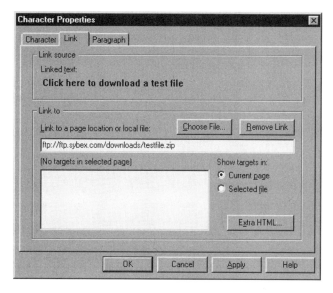

For example, the full URL might look something like this:

```
ftp://ftp.sybex.com/downloads/testfile.zip
```

4.  After you have defined the hyperlink, click OK or Apply to insert the link into your Web page.

As with normal hyperlinks, Composer formats the hyperlink text on your Web page and, behind the scenes, builds the HTML tag required to define the link between your Web page and the target file.

**TIP**   If you need to change the wording of the text that is the anchor for a hyperlink, you can simply edit the text in the Composer edit window.

# Anchoring Hyperlinks to Pictures

The classic hyperlink appears in a browser as underlined text. But images in a Web page can serve as the source of hyperlinks, too. You click a linked image in the browser window, and the browser will load and display the target Web page or file.

In fact, this is the way buttons and many of the other graphical navigation elements you find on Web pages are created. You add an image of a button to your Web page and then create a hyperlink between that image and a page, file, or target that will produce the desired result.

To define a hyperlink for an image, follow these steps:

1. Using the Insert menu or the Insert Image button, insert the image that is to become the hyperlink into your Web page. (See Chapter 6, *Adding Images*, for more instructions on how to insert images if needed.)

2. Select the image by clicking it.

3. From the Insert menu choose Link, or click the Insert/Make Link button on the toolbar. This will open the Image Properties dialog box with the Link tab displayed.

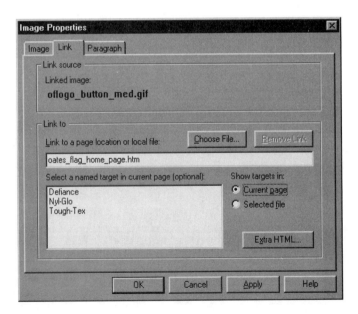

Notice that the Link tab of the Image Properties dialog box is essentially the same as its counterpart in the Character Properties dialog box. The name of the selected image file appears in the Link Source box near the top of the dialog box.

4. In the Link To box, enter a URL or file name for the target file. The target file can be a Web page, an image file, a multimedia file, or anything else you can link to. You can also select a named target as described in the *Creating Hyperlinks Within a Web Page* section earlier in this chapter.

**TIP**

While you have the **Image Properties** dialog box open to create the hyperlink on the **Link** tab, you can also edit other image settings by clicking the **Image** tab. In particular, you may want to edit the **Solid Border** setting or click the **Alt. Text/Low Res.** button to provide an alternate text entry for the image that reflects its status as a hyperlink.

5. After you define the link, click OK or Apply to create the link.

That's all there is to it. Composer makes the necessary changes to the HTML source for your Web page to define the link between the image and the file or URL you specified as the target. When users view your Web page in their browsers, they will be able to click the image and follow the link just like they follow a text hyperlink.

By default, images with links have a border around them and the border is the same color as text links. However, if you want to eliminate the border, you can specify a border width of 0 for the image in the Image Properties dialog box.

**NOTE**

Refer to the `<a href>` tag entry in Appendix B, *An HTML Dictionary*, for an example of the HTML code for an image hyperlink.

# Creating a Link to Your E-Mail Address

There is a special variation on a hyperlink that you can use to make it easy for visitors to your Web page to send e-mail to you (or to anyone else you choose) by creating a hyperlink to an e-mail address. It's called a mailto link. Like any other hyperlink, the mailto link can be linked to any text or image in your Web page. The distinctive part of a mailto link is its target—instead of a file name or URL, the target link is the mailto command followed by an e-mail address.

When a visitor clicks a mailto link, the browser will open a blank e-mail message with the specified address listed as the message recipient. All the visitor needs to do is type a message and click a button or choose a command to send the message on its way.

To create a mailto link, follow these steps:

1. With the Web page open in the Composer editing window, select the text or image you want to become the anchor for the hyperlink.

> **TIP**
>
> **It's a good idea to make the source text for a mailto link the e-mail address to which you want viewers to send mail. That way, if a viewer prints your Web page for future reference or is using a browser that isn't configured to support the mailto feature, the e-mail address will be visible on the printout or screen. Even if the viewer can't conveniently generate an automatic e-mail message to that address, they will still be able to reach you.**

2. From the Insert menu choose Link or click the Insert Link button on the toolbar. This will open the Character Properties dialog box (or, in the case of an image, the Image Properties dialog box) with the Link tab displayed. The selected text or the file name of the selected image will appear in the Link Source box.

3. In the Link To text box, type **mailto:**, followed by the e-mail address, like this: **mailto:name@domain.com**.

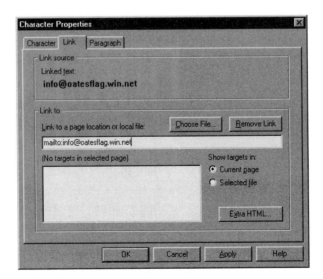

**4.** Click OK to close the dialog box and insert the link into your Web page.

The e-mail link looks just like any other link text on your page. The difference is that when a visitor clicks the link, they will go to their e-mail program instead of another Web page. For instance, Figure 7.4 shows the results of clicking a mailto link on the contacts page of our sample Web site.

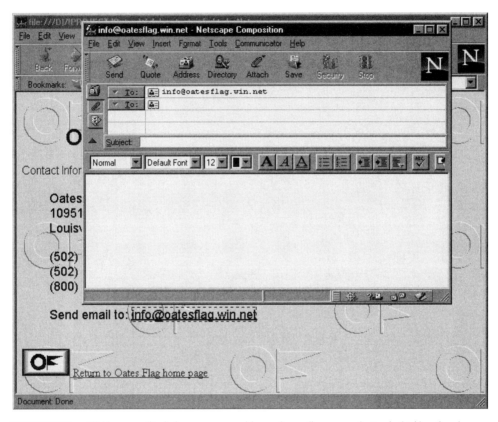

**FIGURE 7.4:** Clicking a mailto link opens a preaddressed e-mail message instead of taking the viewer to another Web page.

**NOTE** See the `<a href>` tag in Appendix B, *An HTML Dictionary*, for an example of a mailto link.

# Chapter 8

# WORKING WITH TABLES

**F E A T U R I N G**

- **Creating a simple table**
- **Adding rows, columns, and cells to a table**
- **Formatting the table**
- **Using cells to span rows and columns**

Tables are a special element on a Web page. They require special handling in order to present information into formatted rows and columns. The standard rules for handling text in HTML documents preclude the possibility of arranging text and numbers in rows and columns. So, special tags had to be developed just to handle tabular matter.

Table tags were not included in the first generation of HTML. But once they were introduced, table tags ushered in a revolutionary change in the appearance of Web pages. It meant Web authors could not only create tables containing formatted text, they could use the same table tags to create Web pages with newspaper-style columns of text.

Composer's WYSIWYG editing environment includes full support for creating and editing tables. As a result, working with tables is simple and straightforward whether you're creating a traditional table or using tables as a page layout tool to control the alignment and positioning of elements on your Web page.

# Using HTML Tables

Tabular matter—text that needs to appear lined up in columns and rows—has always required special handling to get it to look right on the Web. At first, the only option was to use the Formatted paragraph style to format text in a monospaced font and align it into columns by inserting space characters (see Figure 8.1). This solution was crude and ugly, but it worked—sort of.

```
                          Total Widget Sales

                  1st Quarter   2nd Quarter   3rd Quarter   4th Quarter

Gross Sales         234,567       345,678       456,789       567,890

Cost of Goods       123,456       234,567       345,678       456,789

Net Revenue         111,111       111,111       111,111       111,101
```

**FIGURE 8.1:**   Using a monospaced font and multiple space characters provided a crude workaround to the lack of true tables in early HTML.

The advent of HTML table tags has had a major impact on Web page design. Table tags provide a set of powerful and versatile tools for creating richly formatted text in tables. Table tags are ideal for formatting tabular matter such as the table shown in Figure 8.2. Web authors have also realized that the table tags could do far more than just align columns of numbers in a spreadsheet-style table. Table tags can be used on a larger scale as page layout tools. It's table tags that make multicolumn Web page layouts possible. Thanks to tables, Web authors can exercise unprecedented control over the position of text, images, and other elements on a page by defining a large table and then placing the various elements in table cells.

| Total Widget Sales | | | | |
|---|---|---|---|---|
| | 1st Quarter | 2nd Quarter | 3rd Quarter | 4th Quarter |
| Gross Sales | 234,567 | 345,678 | 456,789 | 567,890 |
| Cost of Goods | 123,456 | 234,567 | 345,678 | 456,789 |
| *Net Revenue* | *111,111* | *111,111* | *111,111* | *111,101* |

**FIGURE 8.2:** HTML table tags allow Web authors to create more attractive tables.

Unfortunately, the HTML table tags can be difficult to use in their raw form. Creating a table requires that you work with several different tags and a multitude of parameters and options, all nested together in complex interrelationships. As a result, the HTML source code for a Web page containing a table can be quite intimidating for the uninitiated.

Fortunately, Composer's WYSIWYG editor and table support make it unnecessary for you to deal directly with the HTML table tags. You can create and edit tables entirely within Composer's edit window using a couple of dialog boxes. You won't need to concern yourself with the table tags in the HTML source code for your Web pages.

# Creating a Simple Table

Composer makes it very easy to create and edit tables. To add a table to your Web page, you don't even have to answer a series of questions in a Wizard. You just click a toolbar button or choose a command, check the settings in a single dialog box, and click OK. Presto, you have a table. Then you add text to the table cells, format them as needed, and you're done.

The following sections describe in more detail how to create and edit a table.

## Inserting a Table

To create a new table on the Web page you are editing in Composer, follow these simple steps:

1. Position the cursor on the page where you want to insert the table. (You can always move the table later, if necessary.)

**2.** Click the Insert Table button (at the right end of the Compose toolbar) or choose the Insert ➤ Table ➤ Table command. The New Table Properties dialog box will open.

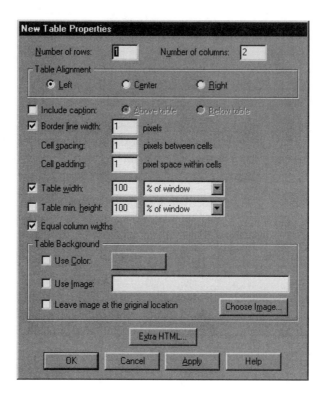

**3.** Enter values in the Number Of Rows and Number Of Columns text boxes to define the initial size of the table. (Don't worry about getting the number of rows and columns correct on the first try. You can add and delete rows and columns later as needed.)

While you have the New Table Properties dialog box open, you can change any of the attributes and table alignment settings, if you know you'll be wanting to change the default values. However, it's not necessary to do so now since you can easily edit the settings later.

**4.** Click OK to close the New Table Properties dialog box. Composer creates an empty table in your Web page.

If you used the default settings for a new table, it will look something like this:

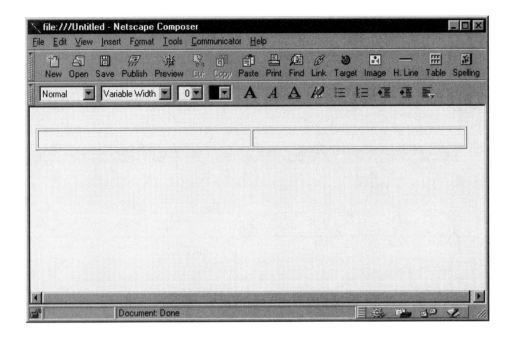

The table starts out with the number of columns and rows you specified in the New Table Properties dialog box. The default table looks pretty useless; because it consists of just a single row. Not to worry, tables and cells in Composer automatically grow as you add data to the table.

# Adding Text to a Table Cell

After you create a table, you'll want to add text and numbers to the table cells. The process couldn't be much simpler; just follow these steps:

1. Click in one of the empty table cells. (You can start anywhere you like.) Composer moves the insertion point to that cell.

2. Enter the text or numbers for the selected cell. As you type, Composer adjusts the size of the cell to accommodate the text. Also, the text will word wrap (automatically break into additional lines) to fit within the cell.

3. Press the Tab key to move the insertion point to the next cell.

**4.** Repeat steps 2 and 3 as needed to fill in the table's remaining cells. When you reach the last cell in the table, you can press Tab and Composer will automatically add another row to the table and move the insertion point to the first cell in that row, so you can continue adding data.

That's all there is to it. Now your table contains the text and numbers that give it a reason to exist. The table may look a little strange because Composer automatically resizes each cell. That's easy to fix with some text formatting and manual adjustment of the cell sizes.

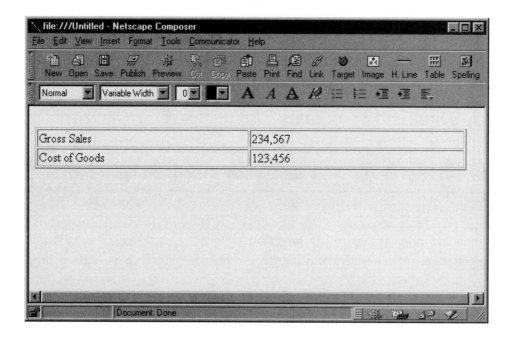

**NOTE** Although in this example only text and numbers were added to a table cell, you're not limited to text entries. A table cell can contain anything. You can insert any combination of text, hyperlinks, images, and even other tables into a table cell.

# Adding Rows, Columns, and Cells to a Table

Often, when you begin working on a table, you don't know exactly how many rows and columns you will need. Fortunately, Composer enables you to add rows, columns, and cells to your table at any time.

## Adding a Row

To add a row to an existing table, follow these steps:

1. Click any cell in the row above where you want Composer to insert the new row into the table.

2. Issue the command to add a row by doing one of the following:
   - Choose Insert ➤ Table ➤ Row
   - Right-click the cell and choose Insert ➤ Row from the pop-up menu that appears.

Composer adds a row of blank cells to the table immediately below the row where the cursor was located when you issued the command. If there are any other rows in the table below the newly added row, Composer moves them down to make room for the new row of cells.

## Adding a Column

You use essentially the same process to add a column to an existing table. Simply follow these steps:

1. Click any cell in the column to the left of where you want Composer to insert the new column into the table.

2. Issue the command to add a column by doing one of the following:
   - Choose Insert ➤ Table ➤ Column
   - Right-click the cell and choose Insert ➤ Column from the pop-up menu that appears.

Composer adds a column of blank cells to the table to the right of the column where the cursor was located when you issued the command. If there are any other columns in the table to the right of the newly added column, Composer will move them over to make room for the new row of cells.

## Adding a Cell

You don't necessarily have to add whole rows or columns of cells to a table. Composer lets you add individual cells one at a time. To add a cell, just follow these steps:

1. Click the cell immediately to the left of where you want the new cell to appear in the table.

2. Issue the command to add a cell by doing one of the following:
   - Choose Insert ➤ Table ➤ Cell
   - Right-click the cell and choose Insert ➤ Cell from the pop-up menu that appears.

Composer adds a blank cell to the table to the right of the cell where the cursor was located when you issued the command. Any remaining cells in the row will be moved one column to the right, creating an extra column if necessary.

Interestingly, a table does not have to contain the same number of cells in each row. By adding a cell to the table you can create a row that contains one or more extra cells compared to other rows in the same table. This gives you a great deal of flexibility in laying out the table—especially when you consider that you can make an individual cell span multiple rows or columns.

### Deleting a Row, Column, or Cell

In addition to adding rows, columns, and cells to a table you might find occasions when you need to delete a row, column, or cell. As you might expect, the process for deleting table elements is very similar to the process for adding them. For example, to delete a row of cells from a table, follow these steps:

1. Click any cell in the row which you want to delete from the table.
2. Issue the command to delete the row by doing one of the following:
   - Choose Edit ➤ Delete Table ➤ Row
   - Right-click the cell and choose Delete ➤ Row from the pop-up menu that appears.

Composer immediately deletes the row of cells—including any text contained in the cells—and moves the rows below the deleted row up to fill in the vacant space.

You can delete a column, an individual cell, or the entire table by following the same steps and substituting Column, Row, or Table, as appropriate, to complete the Delete command.

# Formatting the Table

Perhaps the most impressive thing about tables is the many formatting options they offer the Web page designer. By default, the table is transparent—the page background shows through—and the table cells are surrounded by borders that have the same embossed look as horizontal rules. But you're not stuck with the default table formatting. You can use the various formatting options to define a table with or without borders, change the thickness of those borders, and change the background colors in table cells. You can specify the size of the table and the cells within it. You can also set some alignment and formatting defaults for text in a table.

But that's not all. You can use all the normal text formatting tools on the text in a table. You can apply paragraph styles, text attributes (such as font, size, color, bold and italic), and alignment options (such as left, center, or right). (The alignment options will affect alignment of the text within each cell instead of the alignment on the whole page.)

## Selecting a Table

Composer gives you full and direct access to the cells of a table and the text (or other objects) those cells contain. Clicking a table cell moves the insertion point to that cell. You can use the text editing tools to edit the text in that cell or use the table editing tools to edit that cell of the table. You can even drag the pointer across several cells to select several cells or text blocks for editing as a group. Normally, that's exactly what you want to do. However, sometimes you will need to select the table as a whole. Clicking the table won't do it (that selects an individual cell). Instead, you must drag the pointer across the entire table to highlight it. This selects all the cells or text within the table and also allows you to cut, copy, and paste the table as a whole. Selecting the table this way can be tricky. Fortunately, you can accomplish the same thing more reliably by clicking any cell of the table and then choosing Edit ➤ Select Table.

## Resizing a Table

When you create a new table and don't define a size, it starts out very small—each cell is just a few pixels wide. As you add text to the table cells the table quickly goes to the other extreme, expanding to the full width of your Web page. You don't have to remain at the mercy of Composer's automatic table sizing. You can resize the table yourself.

The fastest and simplest way to resize a table is to size it interactively in Composer's edit window by dragging the table border to make the table larger or smaller. Simply move the pointer over the left or right table border. When the pointer changes to a double-headed arrow, you can drag the border left or right to reduce or increase the width of the table.

By default, the table width is defined as a percent of the Web page width. For example, if the table width remains set to the default 100%, the table will occupy the entire width of the Web page. If you adjust the table width to 50%, it'll occupy half the page width. Sizing the table size as a percent of the page width means the table will always occupy the specified portion of the Web page width, but the actual width of the table will vary depending on the size of the browser window in which the Web page is viewed.

Dragging the border of a table is a fast and easy way to resize the table, but it isn't very precise. You can exercise more precise control over the table size by following these steps:

1. Right-click the table to open the pop-up menu, then choose Table Properties. This will open the Table Properties dialog box.

2. Click the Table tab.

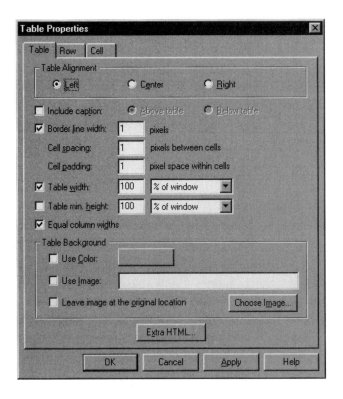

3. Click the Table Width checkbox, then enter a value in the text box and choose Pixels or % of Window from the drop-down list.

   By default, the table width is defined as a percent of the Web page width. For example, if you adjust the table width to 50%, it'll occupy half the page width regardless of changes in the page size, due to changes in the size of the browser window where the Web page is viewed.

   Normally, you'll want to stick with table widths specified as a percent of the Web page window. Specifying the table width in pixels seems more precise, but it could produce unexpected results when viewed in a browser window that is unusually large or small.

4. If you need to specify the minimum height of the table, click the Table Min. Height checkbox, then enter a value in the text box and choose Pixels or % of Window from the drop down list.

   Note that you can specify the minimum but not the maximum height of the table. The HTML table tags allow you to reserve a certain minimum vertical space for the table, even if it contains no text. You can't specify a maximum height because the browser will always expand the table vertically to make room for the contents.

5. Click OK to close the Table Properties dialog box and record the settings. Composer applies the settings to the table.

These options let you control the width of table as a whole. To control the width of the columns within the table, you must adjust the width of the cells (see the section on *Formatting a Cell*, later in this chapter).

# Changing the Table Properties

We've already experimented with some table properties—Table Width and Table Minimum Height. You can control other aspects of the table's appearance as well. To adjust table properties such as border width, cell spacing, and a background color for the table, follow these steps:

1. Right-click the table to open the pop-up menu, then choose Table Properties. This will open the Table Properties dialog box.

2. In the dialog box, click the Table tab to select it.

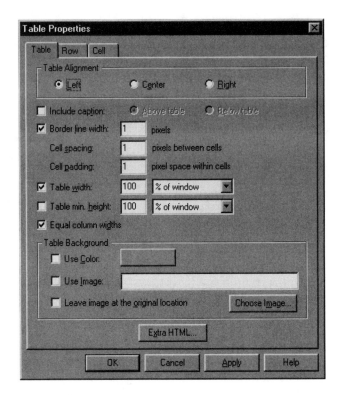

**3.** Adjust the following settings as needed:

**Table Alignment:** In the Table Alignment section, click the Left, Center, or Right radio button to specify how the table should be aligned on the Web page.

**Border Line Width:** In the text box, enter a number to specify the thickness (in pixels) of the borders around the outside edges of the table. Entering a value of 0 will cause the borders to disappear.

**Cell Spacing:** In the text box, enter a number to specify the thickness (in pixels) of the space between cells within the table.

**Cell Padding:** In the text box, enter a number to specify the thickness (in pixels) of the space between the edges of each cell and the text or other objects within the cell.

**Table Background:** To set a background color for all the cells in the table, click the Use Color checkbox. Clearing the checkbox makes the table background transparent. If you elect to specify a table background color, click the color button to open the color selector box. Click a color sample in the color selector box to record your color selection. You can also specify a background image to appear in each cell of the table. The table background image works like the background image for the entire Web page, except that it is confined to the table cells. You have the same options for defining a table background, that you do for a page background. To define a background image for the table, click the Use Image checkbox and then enter the file name of the background image in the text box. As an alternative to typing the file name, you can click the Choose Image button to open the Choose Image File dialog box. From here, select the image file. Click the Leave Image At the Original Location checkbox to instruct Composer to do just that. Otherwise, Composer will save a copy of the image in the same folder as you Web page the next time you save the page.

4. Click OK to close the Table Properties dialog box and record the settings. Composer applies the settings to the table.

**WARNING**

To control the alignment of the table on the Web page you must use the Table Alignment setting in the Table Properties dialog box. Contrary to what you might guess, selecting the table and choosing one of the Format ➤ Align commands or clicking the alignment button in the toolbar affects the alignment of text within the table cells, not the alignment of the table on the Web page.

# Formatting a Row

Composer enables you to change the text alignment and the background color for a row of cells. To adjust the settings, follow these steps:

1. Right-click any cell in the row you want to change. When the pop-up menu appears, choose Table Properties. This will open the now familiar Table Properties dialog box.

2. In the dialog box, click the Row tab to select it.

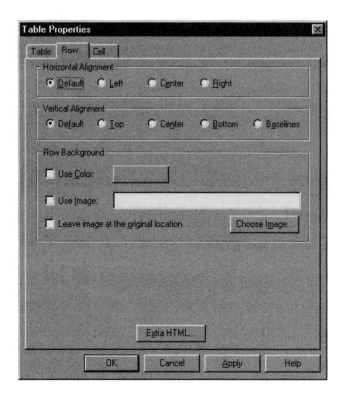

3. Adjust the following settings as needed:

**Horizontal Alignment:** To specify the horizontal alignment of text within the cells in the row, click the Default, Left, Center, or Right radio button.

**Vertical Alignment:** To specify the vertical alignment of text within the cells in the row, click the Default, Top, Center, Bottom, or Baselines radio button.

**Row Background:** To set a background color for all the cells in the row, click the Use Color checkbox. Clearing the checkbox makes the cell backgrounds transparent. If you elect to specify a row color, click the color button to open the color selector box. Click a color sample in the color selector box to record your selection. In addition to the background color, you can also specify a background image to appear in each cell of the row. To define a background image for the row, click the Use Image checkbox and then enter the background image's file name in the text box. As an alternative to typing the file name, you can click the Choose Image button to open the Choose Image File dialog box where you can select the image file. Click the Leave Image At the Original Location checkbox to instruct Composer to do just that. Otherwise, Composer will save a copy of the image in the same folder as your Web page the next time you save the page. This setting will override the Table Background setting on the Table tab.

4. Click OK to close the Table Properties dialog box and record the settings. Composer applies the settings to table.

Actually, you'll rarely use these row settings. It's just as easy to select all the cells in a row and apply cell formatting settings. When you use cell formatting, you'll have all the same options you can apply to rows—and more.

# Formatting a Cell

You can select one or more cells in a table by dragging the pointer across the cells you want to format. Then, you can choose from an assortment of formatting options such as text alignment, cell height and width, and the color of the background of the cell. To format table cells, follow these steps:

1. Select one or more cells in a table and right-click that area. A pop-up menu will open. Choose Table Properties to open the Table Properties dialog box.

2. In the dialog box, click the Cell tab to select it.

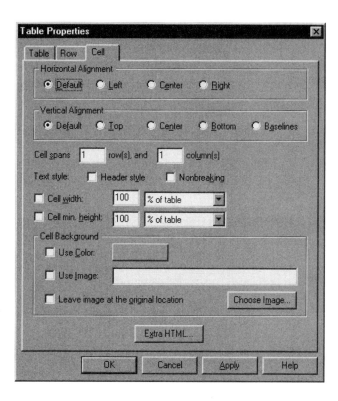

**3.** Adjust the following settings as needed:

**Horizontal Alignment:** To specify the horizontal alignment of text within the selected cells, click the Default, Left, Center, or Right radio button.

**Vertical Alignment:** To specify the vertical alignment of text within the cells, click the Default, Top, Center, Bottom, or Baselines radio button.

**Text Style:** Click the Header Style checkbox to apply a special Table Header paragraph style to the text in the selected cells. The Header style centers the text in the cell and makes it bold. Click the Nonbreaking checkbox to disable the normal word wrapping that breaks lines of text to fit within the width of a cell. Even if you check the Nonbreaking checkbox, Composer and the browser will wrap long lines of text to fit within the cell. The difference is, if the Nonbreaking checkbox is checked, the browser will try to resize the cell to minimize the line breaks in the text if possible.

**Cell Width:** To specify the width of the selected cells, click the checkbox, then enter a value in the text box and choose Pixels or % of Table from the drop-down list.

> **TIP**
>
> Normally, you'll want to specify cell widths as a percentage of the table. Defining the cell width in pixels can create problems if the table width is set to be a percentage of the window, and the window is sized too small to allow room in the table for cells of the specified sizes.

**Cell Min. Height:** If you need to specify the minimum height of the selected cells, click the Cell Min. Height checkbox, then enter a value in the text box and choose Pixels or % of Window from the drop-down list. As with setting the height of the table, this option affects the minimum height of a cell, even if it contains no text. You can't specify a maximum height because the browser will always expand the cell vertically to make room for the contents.

**Cell Background:** To set a background color for the selected cells, click the Use Color checkbox. Clearing the checkbox makes the cell backgrounds transparent. If you elect to specify a cell color, click the color button to open the color selector box. Click a color sample in the color selector box to record the color selection. You can specify a background image to appear in each of the selected cells, just as you can for the table and for rows. To define a background image for the selected cells, click the Use Image checkbox and then enter the background image 's file name in the text box. As an alternative to typing the file name, you can click the Choose Image button to open the Choose Image File dialog box where you can select the image file. Click the Leave Image At the Original Location checkbox unless you want Composer to save a copy of the image in the same folder as your Web page, the next time you save the page. This setting will override the Table Color and Row Color settings.

**4.** Click OK to close the Table Properties dialog box and record the settings. Composer applies the settings to the table.

# Formatting Text in a Table

One of the great things about HTML tables is the richly formatted text you can use in the table. You saw some of the options for formatting text in the *Formatting a Cell* section above. The Cell tab of the Table Properties dialog box includes options that allow you to specify horizontal and vertical alignment, assign a table header style to the text, and minimize or maximize word wrap within a cell.

But the table-specific text formatting we've covered barely scratches the surface of the possibilities. You can also apply all the standard text formatting options to text in tables. The fact that the text is contained within a table cell makes no difference. You can select text in a table cell and apply any, or all, of the following formatting:

- Paragraph styles such as headings and lists
- Font selections
- Text size
- Bold, italic, and other attributes
- Indents (The indentations will be relative to the cell in which the text resides instead of being relative to the browser window.)
- Alignment (Choosing one of the Format ➤ Align commands or clicking an alignment button from the toolbar has the same effect as choosing the horizontal text alignment on the Cell tab of the Table Properties dialog box.)

All of these formatting options work exactly the same on table text as they do on regular text. See Chapter 5, *Working with Text,* for more information on using these formatting options.

# Adding a Table Caption

You can add a caption to your table when the table serves as a figure or illustration in your Web document. The caption is a text block attached to the top or bottom of the table. It stays with the table as it is resized and shifts position on the Web page in response to changes in browser window dimensions.

To create a caption for a table, follow these steps:

1. Right-click the table and choose Table Properties from the pop-up menu that appears. This opens the Table Properties dialog box.

2. In the dialog box, click the Table tab to select it.

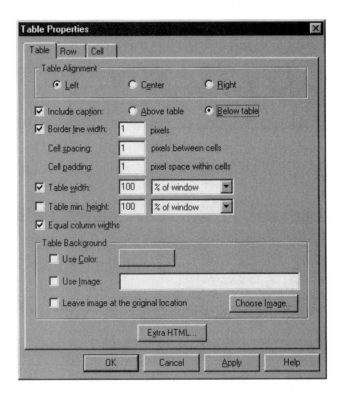

3. Click the Include Caption checkbox and choose either the Above Table or Below Table radio button.

4. Click OK and the Table Properties dialog box will close. Composer adds a caption box to the top or bottom of the table. In the edit window, the caption box is indicated by a dashed line.

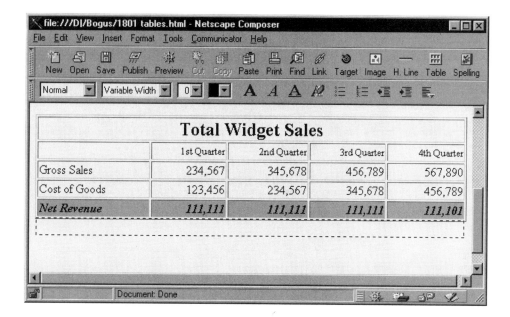

5. Click in the caption box and type the caption you would like to add.

Composer adds the caption text directly to the page as you type.

By default, the caption is assigned normal text attributes and center alignment within the caption box. If you prefer different formatting, you can format the caption any way you like using the same tools you use to format other text on your Web page.

# Defining Cells That Span Rows and Columns

Often, a heading or other element needs to extend across more than one column. For those situations, Composer lets you define table cells that span multiple columns and rows. Just follow these steps:

1. Right-click the table cell that needs to span multiple columns or rows, and a pop-up menu will appear. Choose Table Properties and the now familiar Table Properties dialog box will appear.

2. In the dialog box, click the Cell tab to select it.

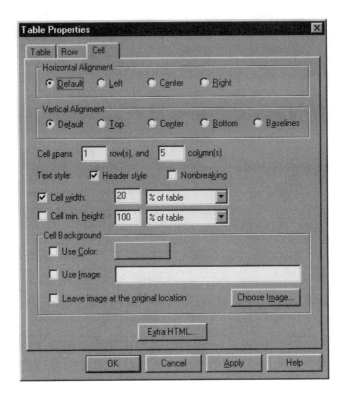

3. To define the size of the expanded cell, enter values in the Cell Spans *x* Row(s) and *x* Column(s) text boxes.

4. Click OK to close the Table Properties dialog box and record your settings. Composer redraws your table with the expanded cell spanning as many columns and rows as you specified. Adjacent cells are pushed to the right or down to make room for the expanded cell.

5. If creating the enlarged cell displaces other cells and pushes them out beyond the previous table width, you'll probably want to delete those excess cells. Select the displaced cells, and choose Edit ➤ Delete Table ➤ Cell. Composer will delete the selected cells.

The result is a table with a single cell that spans several columns or rows, such as the heading in Figure 8.3.

A cell that spans multiple columns or rows is typically used to add a header that extends across the top of a table. There are many other possible applications of this feature, such as a consolidated totals at the bottom of a table, or comments and labels that apply to several rows.

| Total Widget Sales | | | | |
|---|---|---|---|---|
|  | 1st Quarter | 2nd Quarter | 3rd Quarter | 4th Quarter |
| Gross Sales | 234,567 | 345,678 | 456,789 | 567,890 |
| Cost of Goods | 123,456 | 234,567 | 345,678 | 456,789 |
| *Net Revenue* | *111,111* | *111,111* | *111,111* | *111,101* |

**FIGURE 8.3:**  Cells that span multiple columns or rows enable you to create effects such as the heading for this table.

# Part 3

# Using Advanced Design Tools

# Chapter 9

# ADDING SOUND AND MOTION WITH MULTIMEDIA

FEATURING

- **Where does multimedia come from?**
- **The dirty secrets of multimedia**
- **Adding sounds to your Web page**
- **Adding movies and video clips**
- **Adding movement with animation**

Sound! Camera! Action!—Multimedia!!!

These days, Web sites can be composed of much more than text and static images. Web pages can include sounds, video clips, and animation effects. Collectively, these elements are called multimedia, and they are the source of some of the way cool effects that wow and impress Web surfers.

When used judiciously, multimedia effects can be very effective communication tools, and they can become essential elements of a Web site's content. Typically, however, multimedia effects are added to a Web page to give it a little dazzle or a touch of pizzazz. While no amount of multimedia magic can elevate a Web site from awful to awesome, some well-chosen multimedia embellishments can be a nice finishing touch—rather like decorations on cake.

Composer is not a multimedia Web-site-development tool; but that doesn't mean you can't use some multimedia effects in the Web pages you create with Composer. This chapter will present a brief overview of some of the multimedia options that are available and show you how to work with them in Composer.

# Where Does Multimedia Come From?

First of all, you need to be aware that multimedia is a catch-all term. It includes any presentation of audio, video, or animation effects. Multimedia encompasses a variety of effects achieved by an assortment of methods. Many different techniques are needed to incorporate those effects into a Web page.

Multimedia elements can be divided into three general categories:

- Sound effects
- Video or movies
- Animation effects

In each of these categories, several different formats and technologies are available to deliver content from a Web server and display or play it on a viewer's computer. There are also many different multimedia content sources that are suitable for use on a Web page. Collections of prerecorded sounds, videos, and animations are readily available. Like clip art images, you can find multimedia content for sale on CD-ROM and available for download on the Internet. In addition, there are a multitude of programs you can use to create your own multimedia content. Some of them are inexpensive and easy to use, while others have a steep price tab and a steeper learning curve. I won't attempt to explore the assortment of multimedia-creation programs in this book. Instead, when discussing how to work with multimedia elements in Composer, I'll assume that you have a multimedia file in hand (from a clip art collection or professional multimedia producer) and just need to add it to your Web page.

Depending on what format the multimedia content is delivered in, the Web browser may be able to display the effect using its built-in capabilities, some system software, a plug-in program, or other helper application. In some cases, the only way to display multimedia content is to use the Web browser to download the multimedia file to your hard drive and then manually launch a separate application to load and play the newly downloaded file. (Fortunately, this last scenario is increasingly less common as plug-ins become available to handle most of the popular multimedia file formats.)

## Push, Pull, What's the Difference?

You've probably heard the terms push and pull used to describe ways to disseminate information on the Web. For example, Netcaster is widely referred to as an example of push because the channels of information are automatically pushed out from the server at timed intervals. Navigator, on the other hand, is usually cast in the role of pulling data from the server to fulfill a viewer request; for instance, when entering a URL or clicking a hyperlink. The complementary concepts of push and pull also come into play when handling multimedia Web elements.

Some effects are created by simply downloading a file to the viewer's computer, where the Web browser (or a helper application) takes care of displaying the effect. This is an example of pull—and it's similar to the way images are downloaded and displayed. Examples of pulled multimedia are: standard audio and video files, GIF animation, and Java or JavaScript applets—all of which are interpreted and displayed by the Web browser or its helper applications.

When the server begins processing the data for a multimedia effect (as opposed to simply delivering requested files), that's push. Examples of pushed multimedia are some kinds of CGI scripts and streaming audio such as RealAudio. You don't really need to know the nitty-gritty details of how these push effects work; you just need to be aware that they require special support from the server and you'll need to coordinate with the administrator of the Web server hosting your site before you use them.

# The Dirty Secrets of Multimedia

Multimedia is very cool. It's exciting, it's interesting, and it's very effective at engaging the viewer. But despite all the good things you can say about it, multimedia has its dark side.

One very annoying aspect of multimedia on the Web is the confusing assortment of incompatible file formats used for multimedia content. Images for Web pages have been standardized on two file formats—GIF and JPEG—that are universally supported by all the major Web browsers. But standardization of multimedia file formats has not reached a similar level. In many cases, there are several competing file formats for delivery of the same kind of information.

Web browsers do not have built-in support for most of the disparate multimedia file formats. Although that deficiency can be overcome by downloading and installing a plug-in or a helper application, it can be a real hassle to install a separate helper application for each multimedia file format. Often, it's just not worth the effort to acquire and install another plug-in just to be able to experience some multimedia effect. As a result, many viewers may not see your carefully crafted multimedia effect.

## Bandwidth Busters

Text files (and therefore, HTML documents) are usually small and can be transmitted over the Internet quickly and efficiently. Image files are much larger. They consume more storage space on a Web server and take much longer to transfer from the server to the Web browser. The size of image files pales, however, when compared to multimedia files, such as those for sounds and video clips. Multimedia files can gobble up Internet bandwidth at an alarming rate.

The sheer size of some multimedia files is enough to severely restrict their use—especially when viewers will be accessing a Web page over a dial-up Internet connection. Some multimedia file formats are more compact and efficient than others, and many multimedia effects can be accomplished with files that are not much larger than a decent image file. But all multimedia effects must be carefully analyzed and their contribution to the Web page balanced against the impact they will have on the time it takes for the Web page to appear in the browser window.

## Security Risks

As if numerous incompatible file formats and excessive bandwidth requirements weren't problematic enough, some multimedia files can be dangerous to your health (or at least, to the health of your computer).

Java applets (and ActiveX controls) are actually miniature programs that, after being downloaded, run automatically on the viewer's system. Normally, these applets perform benign tasks such as generating animation effects onscreen. However, there is a highly publicized potential for them to engage in more sinister activities, such as deleting files and disrupting the viewer's system.

Netscape has implemented some security strategies that help protect against the dangers of allowing Java applets and ActiveX controls to run on viewers' machines. Still, some viewers disable their browser's ability to display those effects. Again, the result is that many of the multimedia effects you work so hard to incorporate into your Web page may not be seen and appreciated by your intended audience.

# Adding Sounds to Your Web Page

Navigator, and most other browsers, supports several kinds of sound files, either directly, or through plug-ins, or through the sound support built into the operating system. Of course, in order to play sound files of any description, the viewer must have a sound card and speakers installed on their system. But given the prevalence of multimedia-equipped computers, that doesn't disenfranchise many Web surfers.

Sound file formats such as WAV and MIDI enjoy widespread support, and other formats are available as well. The WAV file format used on Web pages is the same Wave audio format commonly used for system sounds on Windows systems. The popularity of the Windows platform means that most Web surfers' systems will be able to play WAV sound files and playback utilities that are available for other platforms. Unfortunately, WAV files aren't very efficient, and files that contain more than a few seconds of audio tend to be very large. MIDI files are much more efficient because they don't attempt to store digitized sounds—just the instructions for a synthesizer to play the sound.

Adding a sound to your Web page is as simple as adding a hyperlink. You create a link to the sound file, then, when a viewer clicks that link, the browser will download and play the sound. Adding a link to a sound file is just like adding any other link in Composer. You will need some descriptive text or an image on the Web page to serve as the anchor for the hyperlink. To define the link, just follow these steps:

1. Select the text or image for the hyperlink anchor and click the Insert Link button on the toolbar or choose the Insert ➤ Link command from the menu. Depending on whether the hyperlink anchor is text or an image, the Image Properties or the Character Properties dialog box will open.

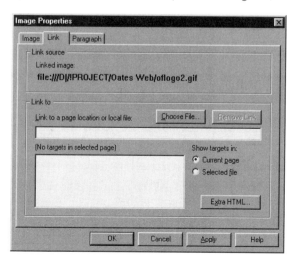

2. From the Properties dialog box, choose the Link tab. Then go to the Link To text box and enter the file name of the sound file. If you choose to click the Choose File button and browse for the file in the Link to File dialog box, you'll find that, by default, only HTML files are listed. However, you can select one of the common sound file formats from the Files of Type drop-down list box to display sound files for your selection.

3. After you specify the file name for the link, click OK to close the Properties dialog box. The text or image that serves as the link source for the sound file will appear in the Composer window with the characteristic formatting of a hyperlink. Composer adds the hyperlink to the HTML source code for your Web page.

You won't be able to preview the sound in Composer. Instead, the hyperlink to the sound will work when you browse the Web page in Navigator or another browser. Clicking the hyperlink in the browser window will cause the browser to download the file and activate the appropriate plug-in or other resource to handle playback.

## Streaming Audio

Streaming audio is a technology that allows some sound files to begin playback even before the entire file is downloaded. Programs such as RealAudio can dramatically reduce the time between clicking a link and hearing the sound. The first part of a sound file begins to play as the subsequent portions of the sound file are being downloaded. Because the Web page visitor isn't forced to wait for the entire file to be downloaded, streaming audio makes it practical to deliver longer sound selections. To perform this magic, you need special software to run on the Web server and a plug-in for the viewer's browser. As a result, using some types of streaming audio may be more complicated than embedding a simple link to a WAV file in your Web page. At the very least, you will need to check with the administrator of your Web server to make sure streaming audio support is available.

## Background Sounds

Sounds that you insert into your Web page with hyperlinks aren't the only sounds that can be associated with Web pages. It's possible to embed a sound in a Web page so the browser downloads and plays the sound automatically when a viewer loads the page. It happens in the background, kind of like background images.

To have a sound automatically start playing shortly after a Web page appears is an interesting effect. But it's not without its drawbacks. The effect is available only for Web surfers using recent versions of the most popular browsers. The time required to download the sound file can create a significant delay between the time the page appears and the sound starts to play, which dilutes the effect. Also, a sound that is interesting to a Web surfer visiting your site for the first time can become annoying to repeat visitors.

**TIP**
You can use the <embed> tag to do more than create background sounds. You can also use it to embed sounds, video clips, and other objects in your Web page. An embedded object is like an automatic link that is downloaded and displayed automatically without the viewer clicking it. Also, the video clip or the playback sound control panel for an embedded object appears on your Web page, instead of in a separate window.

Perhaps the biggest problem with embedded background sounds is that, unlike hyperlinked sounds, you can't conveniently manipulate them with Composer. There is no button, command, or dialog box setting for background sounds. If you want to add background sounds to a Web page, you'll have to do it by manually adding the required HTML tags, using either the HTML Tag dialog box or an external HTML editor.

**NOTE**
See Appendix B, *HTML Dictionary*, for information on the <embed> tag.

# Adding Movies and Video Clips

Just as Navigator and other browsers support the playback of sounds, the popular browsers support movies and video as well—usually via an operating-system-level add-in. The most popular video formats are Video for Windows (AVI) and QuickTime movies (MOV), but MPEG is becoming increasingly common. Like adding sounds to your Web page, you create a link to a video file and, when a viewer clicks that link, the browser will download and play the video clip. Depending on the file format and the support software installed on the viewer's system, the video may appear in its own window or in the browser window.

In Composer, you can create a link to a video file just like you do with any other hyperlink. You will need some descriptive text or an image on the Web page to serve as the link source, because Composer (and Navigator) can't display the video file on your Web page. To add the hyperlink, follow these steps:

1.  Select the text or image for the hyperlink anchor and click the Insert Link button or choose the Insert ➤ Link command. This action will open either the Image Properties or Character Properties dialog box, depending on whether the selected anchor is an image or text.

2.  From the dialog box's Link tab, go to the Link To text box and enter the file name of the video file. Alternatively, you can click the Choose File button and browse for the file in the Link to File dialog box. From the Files of Type drop-down list box, you can select the Video for Windows or QuickTime formats to display video files for that selection.

3.  After you specify the file name for the link, click OK to close the Properties dialog box. As with adding a link to a sound file, Composer formats the text or image that serves as the hyperlink anchor with the characteristic formatting of a hyperlink. Behind the scenes, Composer adds the hyperlink to the HTML source code for your Web page.

**NOTE**    If you don't select text or an image to be the link source when you start to define a link, you'll have the option of entering some text in the Link Source text box in the Properties dialog box. If you leave that field blank, Composer will use the file name of the linked file as your link source.

# Adding Movement with Animation

Adding sounds and video clips to a Web page is a fairly straightforward proposition. There are several different file formats available, but you can use essentially the same techniques to add any of them to your Web page. Animation, on the other hand, is a different story. There are different kinds of animation produced with a variety of techniques and technologies, and, as such, you'll need to work with them in assorted ways.

# Including Animated GIFs

Perhaps the simplest way to add animation effects to a Web page is to use animated GIFs. This is a variation on the standard GIF image file. Instead of a single image, a GIF animation stores several images in the same file along with instructions to display those images one after the other in sequence.

Simple animation effects such as flashing lights, spinning globes, and tumbling logos are relatively easy to create as animated GIFs. You can create the necessary component images using any suitable image-editing program. Then you can use a program, such as GIF Construction Set, to assemble the images into a single file and add timing information to create the animation.

Adding an animated GIF to your Web page is just like adding a regular image. Composer makes no distinction between an animated GIF and a run-of-the-mill GIF file containing a single image. Inserting the image simply creates a reference to the GIF file in the HTML source code for your page. Composer then displays the animation in the editing window. When viewers visit your Web page, they will see the animation effect in Navigator and other late-model browsers, as soon as the GIF file is downloaded. Because it is composed of several individual images, an animated GIF file is larger than a GIF file containing a single image of a similar size, and it takes proportionally longer to download and display initially. One of the neat things about an animated GIF is that the effect can continue running automatically without continued support from the Web server.

# Getting Shocked or Astounded

There are a number of programs that are capable of producing animations suitable for use on a Web page. Perhaps the best-known programs are MacroMedia Director and Astound. These programs can produce anything from simple animations, such as scrolling text and rotating logos, to animations where images appear to move along complex paths.

After an animation is created, it is saved in a proprietary file format. To view the animation, the Web surfer must first download and install a plug-in or other helper application. (The plug-in for playing MacroMedia Director animations is called ShockWave.)

To use the animation on your Web page, you need to create a hyperlink to the animation file—just like creating a hyperlink to a sound or video file. When the viewer clicks the hyperlink on your Web page, the browser downloads the animation file and displays it (with the assistance of the helper application).

# Server-Side Animation and CGI

One way to produce animation effects on the Web is to use CGI scripts—mini programs that run on the Web server and create effects that are then sent out to the Web browser. (Other programming languages and techniques can also provide similar effects by running programs on the server, generating pages and special effects that show up in the Web browser window. However, CGI scripts are probably the most common form of server-side Web programming.) CGI scripts and other server-side programming can produce animation effects, image maps, and whole Web pages. CGI is seldom used for simple animation effects anymore because other, simpler techniques have become available. However, CGI is used extensively for online shopping-cart systems and other database-driven Web sites. This is the realm of professional developers and computer programmers! You're not likely to deal with CGI and other push or server-side technologies as you work with Web pages in Composer. However, you can use the HTML Tag dialog box to manually insert a tag into your page that will run a pre-existing CGI script that resides on the Web server. You'll need to check with the Web server administrator to see if there are any scripts available for your use and get instructions on exactly which tags and codes you need to add to your page's HTML source in order to use the scripts.

# Java and JavaScript Animations

Java and JavaScript are two variations of a programming language that has been developed for the Internet and the World Wide Web. The major Web browsers have built-in support for Java, meaning that the browser can detect Java or JavaScript programming codes in an HTML document, interpret the commands, and execute the instructions. Using Java or JavaScript, a programmer can create anything from a small applet (mini application) that produces an animation effect to full-fledged applications such as word processors.

Composer has no built-in support for Java or JavaScript. However, you can insert Java and JavaScript code into your Web page with either the HTML Tag dialog box or an external HTML editor. Composer will simply display a generic HTML tag icon to mark the location of the Java code in your Web page. Then, after you save your Web page, you'll be able to view it in your Web browser and see the effect of the Java applet there.

> **NOTE** See Chapter 11, *Getting Your Hands Dirty: Editing HTML*, for instructions on using the HTML Tag dialog box and external HTML editor.

The specifics of Java and JavaScript are beyond the scope of this book. Java programming is another area that is best left to computer professionals that specialize in such things. (If you'd like to try your hand at learning JavaScript programming, a good place to start is by reading *ABCs of JavaScript* by Lee Purcell and Mary Jane Mara, also published by Sybex.) However, you might be able to use some Java and JavaScript effects on your Web pages, even if you don't learn to write Java programs yourself. Preprogrammed Java applets that perform a variety of functions and effects are available for purchase or download from a number of sources.

You don't have to know how to program in Java to paste one of these preprogrammed effects into your page. Typically, all you need to do is copy some files into the same directory as your Web pages and then copy some codes and paste them into your page as a series of HTML tags. You may need to edit the codes to fill in adjustable settings, such as the location of files on your system. Then you will have a Java animation on your Web page.

> **NOTE** If you're looking for Java applets, check out the Gamelan site at http://www.gamelan.com/.

# Chapter 10

# CREATING MULTICOLUMN LAYOUTS WITH TABLES

- **Designing a layout grid**
- **Creating a layout grid with a table**
- **Filling the columns**

There has been a quantum leap in Web page design, now that tables can be used as a page layout tool!

The HTML table tags are, in reality, a system for positioning elements on a Web page. Although the feature was developed to create spreadsheet-style tables, its applications are not confined to traditional tables alone. In fact, some of the most exciting applications of tables don't look like tables at all.

Shortly after the table tags were introduced, some innovative Web developers started using table tags as page layout tools. A large, page-sized table becomes a layout grid where you can place text, images, and smaller tables. The Web page designer has much more control over text and other elements when they are placed into a cell which can then be positioned relative to the other cells in the table. If you specify a transparent table background and 0-width borders, the table itself becomes invisible except for the effect it has on the page layout.

Suddenly, multicolumn magazine-style layouts are not only possible, they're practical and even relatively easy to achieve.

# Designing a Layout Grid

When graphic designers develop a page design for a magazine or other publishing medium, they typically work on a layout grid that breaks the page into multiple columns. Not surprisingly, one of key features of desktop publishing programs is the ability to define the page as a series of columns. Then, the designer positions text, images, and so on in those columns. The columns are the designer's principal tool for organizing information and positioning elements on the page.

Web authors too can define columns on a page—by using tables. If a table fills the Web page, the table columns effectively become page layout columns (See Figure 10.1). Unlike tables in some word processors, any kind of content can be placed in a table cell in an HTML document. Cells in a Web page table automatically expand vertically to make room for any amount of text, images, and other content.

Tables on a Web page can simulate the columns used as a layout design tool by graphic artists. About the only thing Web page columns can't do is automatically continue text from the bottom of one column to the top of the next. But that's not really a problem because, unlike pages of printed material, Web pages don't have a fixed page length, so columns aren't forced to break at some arbitrary measure.

Multicolumn Web pages are usually fairly simple, two- or three-column layouts. Two or three columns offer versatility without cluttering up the relatively small computer display by breaking it into too many small sections.

It is quite simple to create a table that serves as a page layout grid for a two- or three-column page. Often, the table can consist of a single row with the appropriate number of columns. Because the table and the individual cells expand vertically, they can accommodate whatever you place in them; a single table cell can easily hold and define an entire column that runs the full height of your Web page. Occasionally, in the page layout table you may want to add a separate row as a header, above the body copy, and perhaps another row as a footer or something else that needs separate alignment controls, below the body copy. You'll seldom need more that three rows in the table that defines your page layout grid.

Although page layout tables are usually simple two- or three-column affairs, you can get more adventurous, if you so desire. You can create multicolumn page layouts, and you can define cells that span multiple rows and columns to create complex page layouts. You are only limited by your imagination and ingenuity.

**FIGURE 10.1:**   In an HTML table you can create a multicolumn grid to use for page layout.

## Answering the Size Question

One potentially troublesome part of creating a table to serve as a page layout grid is defining the correct size for the table and its component cells. Obviously, for the table to function as a page layout tool, the table needs to fill the Web page. But how big is a Web page? That's hard to say because the dimensions of the Web page change to fit into each viewer's Web browser window.

You can define table and cell sizes two ways:

- by specifying a fixed size in pixels
- by using relative (percentage) sizes (you specify the size of the table relative to the page, and the size of a cell relative to the size of the table)

Using fixed sizes gives you more control over the appearance of the table. You will know exactly how big a column will be, how much text it will hold, and how an image will fit. However, if you define a table that is larger than the viewer's browser window, the viewer may need to scroll horizontally as well as vertically to see all of the page. On the other hand, if the viewer's browser window is larger than you anticipated, your Web page content may not fill the browser window.

Using relative sizing allows the table to automatically adapt to the browser window size. This way, your multicolumn page acts more like a regular Web page. The downside is that text and images may not display as expected on very large or small screens. Cell spacing and sizing may be distorted if they contain images and other elements that can't be resized. It's the same problem that occurs with regular, single-column pages, but now it happens simultaneously in each column.

Choosing between fixed and relative sizing is a matter of weighing the advantages and disadvantages of each, deciding what the impact is on the content and design of the page you're working on, and then choosing between them.

Actually, the choice between fixed and relative sizing isn't an all or nothing proposition. It's possible to combine the two techniques in the same table.

Sometimes, a combination approach allows you to have the best of both worlds. For example, (as you will see in the sample page later in this chapter) you could define a table to be 100% of the width of page, then specify a fixed width for the left column and allow the right column to fill the rest of the table width. As a result, the first column has a fixed size, but the right column will still expand and contract with changes in the size of the Web browser window.

> **TIP**
>
> A tip from the pros: Start with a table defined as 100% of the width of the window. For maximum control over the appearance of your page, define two or three columns with fixed widths, but make sure they total less than 550 pixels, so they will fit in a browser window on a small screen with a little room to spare. Then define one more column on the right with no specified width. This column will expand and contract as needed to fill the rest of the width of the table when the page is viewed in larger browser windows.

Combining fixed and relative sizes sometimes leads to problems. For example, if you define the table size relative to the page and then use fixed sizes for the columns within the table, the table (and, therefore, your Web page columns) may not display properly if the sum of the column widths don't match the width of the table. If the table is wider than the cells, it's not too bad; the real problems occur when the table is too narrow for all the columns to fit.

# Creating a Layout Grid with a Table

Using tables as layout tools is limited only by your imagination. The possibilities are so vast that they are beyond the scope of this book. Instead, I'll summarize the generic steps and then demonstrate a simple example of how to use a table to create a two-column page layout. From there, you can explore and experiment on your own.

The process of creating a two-column page layout in Composer might go something like this:

**1.** Create the page headline and other elements at the top of the page as appropriate. Then position the cursor where the multicolumn layout should begin.

**2.** Next, you need to insert a new table into the page to provide the structure for your multicolumn page layout. Choose Insert ➤ Table ➤ Table or click the Table button on the toolbar. This will open the New Table Properties dialog box.

**New Table Properties**

Number of rows: 1    Number of columns: 2

Table Alignment
- ⦿ Left    ○ Center    ○ Right

☐ Include caption:    ⦿ Above table    ○ Below table
☑ Border line width: 1    pixels
Cell spacing: 1    pixels between cells
Cell padding: 1    pixel space within cells

☑ Table width: 100    % of window
☐ Table min. height: 100    % of window
☑ Equal column widths

Table Background
☐ Use Color:
☐ Use Image:
☐ Leave image at the original location    Choose Image...

Extra HTML...

OK    Cancel    Apply    Help

3. Adjust the settings in the New Table Properties dialog box to define the initial characteristics of the table. The exact settings you use will depend on your page layout and the effect you want to achieve, but the following settings are typical:

- In the Number of Rows and Number of Columns text boxes enter the number of rows and columns you will need in the table. For a simple, two-column layout, you'll probably need only 1 row and 2 columns. To create a page layout with more columns, simply increase number in the column setting accordingly.
- You can leave the Table Alignment option set at its default value of Left. Because a table that is used for page layout purposes almost always spans the full width of the page, the horizontal alignment makes no difference.
- Check the Border Line Width checkbox and enter **0** in the text box. This reduces the width of the border lines around the table and cells to nothing—effectively making them disappear.

**TIP**

**Simply leaving the Border Line Width checkbox blank is sufficient to get rid of the lines around table cells when you view your page with Navigator. However, to ensure that the effect is the same with all browsers, it's a good idea to explicitly specify a Border Line Width of 0.**

- Adjust the values in the Cell Spacing and Cell Padding text boxes to separate the columns the desired amount. Setting the Cell Spacing to 0 pixels will eliminate the space between the cells of the table. And setting Cell Padding to 12 pixels will establish a 12-pixel margin within each cell by adding space between the edges of the table cells and whatever you place in them. This creates an effect within each cell that is similar to the margin around the Web page as a whole. You may want to increase or decrease the Cell Padding number to achieve the spacing you like between the columns.
- Check the Table Width checkbox and make sure the width is set to be **100** % of Window. This setting will allow the table to automatically expand or contract to occupy the full width of the Web browser window.
- Usually, you will want to clear the Table Min. Height checkbox so that the table can expand or contract vertically to accommodate the text and other items you place in the table cells. This leaves room for headings and other elements above and below the table.

Alternatively, you can check the Table Min. Height checkbox and set the height to **100** % of Window to force the page layout table to fill the entire page.

- If you want all the columns to be the same width, check the Equal Column Widths checkbox. If, on the other hand, you want to control column widths individually, leave this option unchecked and adjust the cells separately after you create the table.
- In the Table Background box, clear the Use Color and Use Image checkboxes. This will disable the background color and background image displays for the table and allow the page background to show through.

4. Click OK to close the New Table Properties dialog box. Composer will create a blank table according to your specifications.

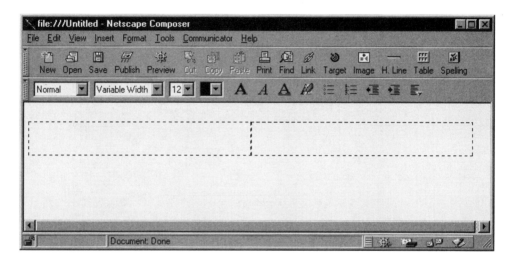

At this point, you should have a basic table on your Web page. Because the table cells are empty and the table has no background or borders, it would be invisible if Composer didn't display dashed lines to indicate the edges of the table cells. These dashed lines are just there to help you work with the table in Composer; they won't show up when you view the page with a Web browser.

You could immediately begin using the table as a page layout tool by adding text and graphics into the table cells. However, you'll probably find that this is a convenient time to adjust a few of the table's cell formatting options before you begin inserting anything into those cells.

Continue setting up your table by following these steps:

**5.** Select one or both cells of the table by dragging the pointer across the cell or cells, then right-click the selected cell. (You can select individual cells and adjust the cell formatting separately or select multiple cells to apply the same cell formatting to all the selected cells.) When the pop-up menu appears, choose Table Properties. This opens the Table Properties dialog box.

**6.** Click the Cell tab to adjust the cell attributes of the selected cells. Again, the settings you choose will depend on the effect you want to achieve with your page layout, but the following settings are typical:

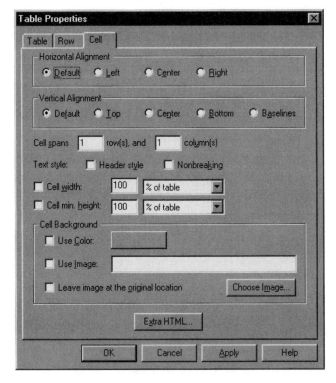

- In the Horizontal Alignment box, click Left, and in the Vertical Alignment box, click Top. You could leave these options set at their default values, but choosing Left and Top alignment ensures that any text or other items you add to the cells will start out positioned in the top-left corner of the cell; just as anything you add to the Web page starts out in the top-left corner of the page. If you keep the default settings, anything you add to a table cell will start out aligned with the left side of the cell and centered vertically in the cell.

- Most of the time, you'll leave the Cell Spans options set at the default values of **1** Row[s] and **1** Column[s]. However, the ability to define cells that span multiple rows and columns creates opportunities for some interesting effects in more complex page layouts.

**NOTE**  See Chapter 8, *Working with Tables*, for a discussion of cells that span rows and columns.

- Make sure both Text Style options (Header Style and Nonbreaking) are cleared. You'll want to use regular text formatting for the text you place in a column, not these table styles. The exception to this rule is if a cell is empty—then you'll want to check the Nonbreaking option to force Composer to give the cell its allotted space, instead of automatically reducing the size of the empty cell.
- If you need to adjust the individual column width, click the Cell Width checkbox. Define the width by entering an appropriate value in the text box and selecting either % of Table or Pixels from the drop-down list. Typically, you will define cell widths as a percent of the table and allow the Web browser to resize the table, and the cells, as needed to fit in the browser window. If you define column widths in pixels, you run the risk of having the fixed-width columns fit poorly in the viewer's browser window.

**NOTE**  If you did not elect to activate the Equal Column Widths option when you defined the table, be sure you specify column widths for the cells with the Cell Width option. If you leave both options unchecked, Composer will constantly resize the column widths as you insert text and other elements, which can be very disconcerting and can disrupt your planned page layout.

- Usually, you would leave the Cell Min. Height checkbox unchecked but you can, if necessary, define the minimum height of the column in pixels or as a percent of the height of the table.
- In the Cell Background area, make sure the Use Color and Use Image checkboxes are unchecked to allow the page background to show through.

**7.** Click OK to close the Table Properties dialog box and apply the settings to the table.

**8.** If necessary, repeat steps 5 through 7 for the remaining table cells.

After making the changes in the cell formatting settings, the table probably still looks the same as before (unless you changed the width of one or more columns). However, if you used the suggested settings, the table will behave a little differently than it would otherwise. The column widths won't change as you insert text and other elements into them, and anything you enter into a column will be aligned with the top-left corner of the cell.

This is a very basic example. You could have defined more columns and rows, if needed. In fact, you can create layout grids that are as complicated as you want. Tables can consist of several columns and rows, and you can add and delete cells, and set cells to span columns and rows to create a complex jigsaw-puzzle pattern.

## A Real-Life Example of a Two-Column Layout

Sometimes, it's difficult to visualize how you can apply a technique such as using a table to create a multicolumn page layout. So, in the rest of this chapter, I'll show you, step by step, how to apply this technique to a real-life situation. You should be able to adapt this technique to your own situations easily. If you'd like to try duplicating the steps described here, you'll find the background graphic and text (as well as the finished page) available for download from this book's Web page on the Sybex Web site. (For details about how to navigate around the Sybex Web site, see the *Sybex* section in Appendix C.)

**The situation**    For this example, I'll return to the recurring sample: the Oates Flag Web site. On the company history page, we'd like to use a colorful flag bunting as the background effect that runs down the left side of the page. The background is eye-catching and appropriate for the topic of the page. However, the bunting is too bright and contrasty to make a good background for text. If we just add text to the page in the usual way, it extends over the bunting as shown in Figure 10.2, making the text difficult to read.

As you can see, there is ample room for text on the plain background to the right of the bunting. The challenge is to find a way to push the text to the right. A two-column page layout is the answer. One column will fit over the bunting and the other column will encompass the rest of the page. Then the left column can remain empty to avoid conflicts with the bunting background and the text can be placed in the right column.

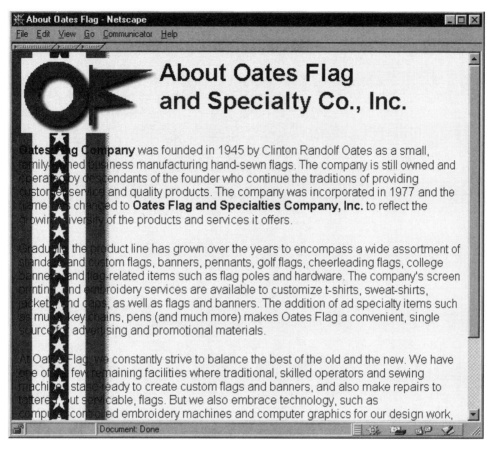

**FIGURE 10.2:** A two-column layout will solve the problem of text extending over an incompatible background.

**Creating the Table**    To duplicate the process of defining a two-column page layout, you would follow these steps:

1. Create the page and add the flag bunting background image. Then, position the cursor at the top of the page in the upper left corner.

2. Choose Insert ➤ Table ➤ Table or click the Table button on the toolbar. This will open the New Table Properties dialog box.

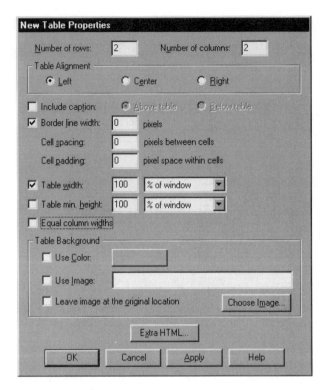

3. In the Number of Rows text box, enter **2** and then go to the Number of Columns text box and enter **2**. (In this case, I created separate rows for the headline and body text.)

4. Check the Border Line Width checkbox and enter **0** in the text box.

5. In the Cell Spacing and Cell Padding text boxes, enter **0**. (There isn't going to be anything in the left column, so there's no need to define the spacing between the columns.)

6. Check the Table Width checkbox and make sure the width is set to be **100** % of Window. Make sure the Table Min. Height checkbox is cleared.

7. Clear the Equal Column Widths checkbox. (You'll define separate column widths for each column when you adjust the cell formatting a little later.)

8. In the Table Background box, clear the Use Color and Use Image checkboxes.

9. Click OK to close the New Table Properties dialog box. Composer will create a blank table that runs the full width of the page and is two columns wide, by two rows deep.

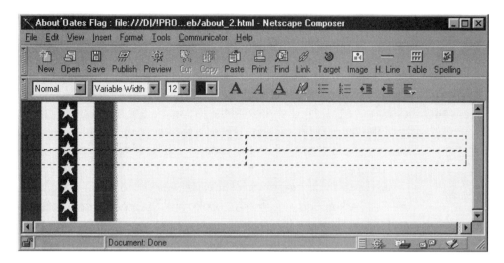

After you create the basic table, you can adjust the settings for the cells. Continue setting up your table by following these steps:

**10.** Right-click the top-left cell of the table. When the pop-up menu appears, choose Table Properties. This will open the Table Properties dialog box.

**11.** Click the Cell tab to begin adjusting the cell attributes of the selected cell.

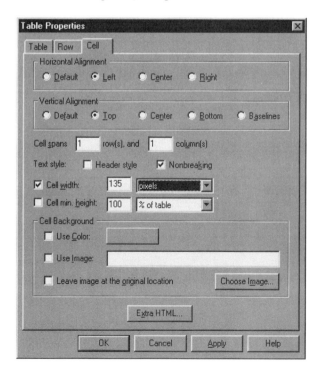

12. In the Horizontal Alignment box, click Left, and in the Vertical Alignment box, click Top.

13. Leave the Cell Spans options set at the default values of **1** Row[s] and **1** Column[s]. In the Text Style options, clear the Header Style checkbox, but check the Nonbreaking checkbox.

14. Click the Cell Width checkbox, enter **135** in the text box and select Pixels from the drop-down list. This defines a minimum width for the left column that is just a little more than the width of the bunting stripes in the background image.

15. Leave the Cell Min. Height checkbox unchecked and also make sure that, in the Cell Background area, the Use Color and Use Image checkboxes are unchecked.

16. Click OK to close the Table Properties dialog box and apply the settings to the left column of the table.

Composer redraws the table cells with an exaggerated left column and a tiny right column. The columns are temporarily out of balance because you have defined a minimum size for the left column but not for the right. Don't worry, the right column will expand to its correct size as soon as you enter a line of text.

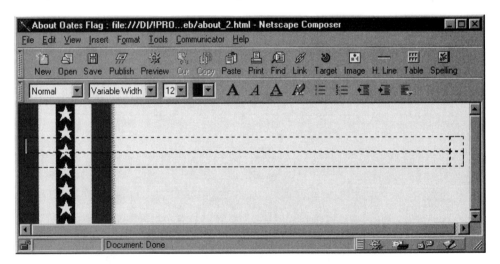

To continue formatting the table cells, follow these steps:

**17.** Right-click the top-right table cell, and when the pop-up menu appears, choose Table Properties. This will open the Table Properties dialog box again.

**18.** Repeat steps 11 through 16, but this time, leave the Cell Width checkbox unchecked. By not defining a width for the right column, you allow Composer to resize the column to occupy any or all of the remaining width of the table that isn't occupied by the left column

**19.** Repeat the formatting on the cells in the second row, applying the same settings you used for the corresponding columns of the top row.

After adjusting the cell formatting settings, the table is ready to use.

# Filling the Columns

Now that the table is defined, it's time to start adding text and other elements to your multicolumn page layout. Remember, just about anything you can usually add to your page can go into a table cell as well. That includes text, images, hyperlinks and targets, horizontal lines, and even tables.

All the typical formatting options are also available and they behave just as they do outside of the table. One notable exception is the alignment options. When you specify left, center, or right paragraph alignment, Composer will align the paragraph to the margins of its cell instead of aligning it to the page margins. The same thing applies to the alignment options for images and other elements inserted into a table cell.

Basically, each table cell acts like a mini-page. To add text to a column, just click the table cell to move the insertion point cursor into the cell and start typing—just as you would type text on the main Web page outside the table. Similarly, you can add and edit images, hyperlinks, HTML tags, and everything else.

**Continuing the Example: Adding Text and Images**  To complete the company history page example, you need to add an image of the company logo, a headline, and several paragraphs of text to the page. The logo and all the text need to go into the right column. In this case, the left column will remain empty, allowing the flag-stripe background to show through without conflicting with any text. The logo and headline will go into a separate row from the body text so that the image and headline can be aligned with each other without affecting the body text.

To add text and images into the column layout of the example, you would follow these steps:

1. Click in the lower-right table cell to move the insertion point cursor into that cell.
2. Type the text into the column just like you would type text onto the Web page outside of a table.
   - Before you begin typing, select your desired font from the drop-down list in the formatting toolbar.
   - Enter the text.

   - Add boldface to some text by dragging the pointer across the text and then clicking the Bold button.
   - Edit the text and add any other necessary paragraph or character formatting.
     As you add text to the right table cell, it will expand from its previous diminutive size and the left column will shrink until it reaches the size you defined (135 pixels). When the lower-right cell reaches its maximum width, it begins expanding vertically to accommodate the text you have entered. The other cells of the table are resized accordingly.
3. Click the upper-right table cell to move the insertion point cursor to that cell.
4. Type the headline.
5. Select the headline text and format it, changing the font, size, and other attributes to suit your fancy.
6. Click at the beginning of the headline text to move the insertion point in front of the first letter.
7. Insert the image of the logo and choose left alignment with text wrapping around the image.

That's all there is to it. Composer will display the results in the editing window (see Figure 10.3). The text and image you entered into the table cells appear in the right column of the two-column page layout. The left column remains empty, acting as a spacer to make room for the flag-stripe background image.

There are a couple of anomalies to be aware of in the Composer display. The table cells are indicated by dashed lines even though the cell borders are defined as zero width to make them invisible. Also, Composer can't properly display how the headline text will wrap around the logo image. To see the full effect, you'll need to view the page in a Web browser.

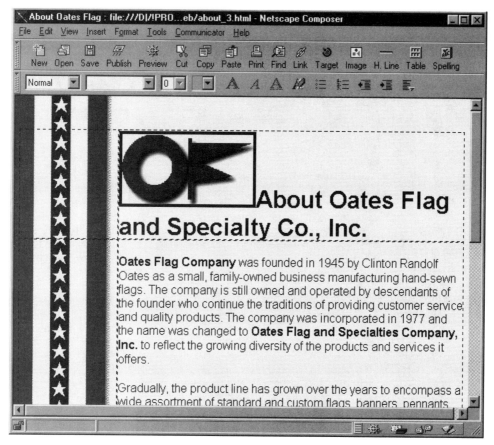

**FIGURE 10.3:** A two-column layout resolves the conflict between the text and the flag-stripe background image.

To view your newly completed page in Navigator, choose File ➤ Browse Page, or click the Preview button. If you haven't already saved the page, Composer will prompt you to do so. Then, after your page is saved to a file, it will appear in a Navigator window as shown in Figure 10.4. Now you can see how it will appear to viewers on the Web. The table cells disappear completely, leaving the text and images aligned in a column offset to the right, which makes room for the flag-stripe background image.

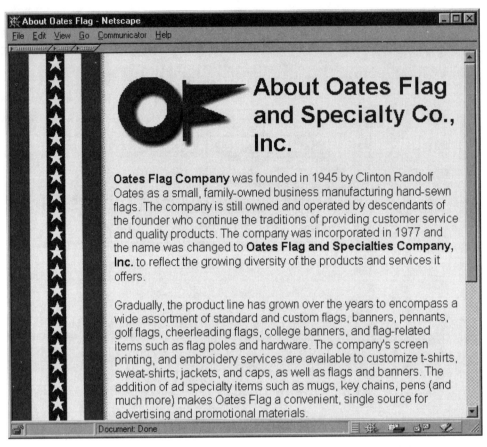

**FIGURE 10.4:** The grid lines completely disappear when you view the page in a Web browser.

# Chapter 11

# GETTING YOUR HANDS DIRTY: EDITING HTML

**Composer**

- **Entering raw HTML code in Composer**
- **Editing HTML source code with an external editor**
- **Tweaking a page manually**
- **Checking the results**

Composer provides a WYSIWYG editing environment where you can create and edit your Web pages. Composer effectively shields you from any direct interaction with the HTML tags that produce the effects you see on your Web page. You probably realize that Composer is building an HTML document—a text document with special HTML tags embedded in it to control formatting, hyperlinks, and such—that will be interpreted by the Web browser software, but you don't need to work directly with that HTML document and its arcane codes to create most Web pages.

However, Composer doesn't support every possible HTML tag and every effect you can create on a Web page. There are some things that you just can't do in Composer. For example, if you want to create a page that uses frames or includes online forms, you won't find a convenient command for those features in Composer. If you want a form on your Web page, you have no choice but to develop an intimate relationship with the HTML tags that produce the effects you desire.

For those times, Composer provides you with convenient access to the HTML code for your page. You can view the page source at any time to see what HTML tags Composer has inserted into the HTML document that defines your page. You can manually enter HTML tags for individual effects. Or you can open an external HTML editor to handle more extensive work with the HTML document.

# Getting Down to the Nitty Gritty: Entering Raw HTML Code in Composer

Composer usually lets you type text, click buttons, and drag images around onscreen to create a Web page without being concerned about what's happening to the HTML source code that defines that page. However, you may occasionally need to manually enter HTML codes into your Web page to achieve an effect for which Composer doesn't have a command or button. Composer provides a convenient dialog box where you can type a single HTML tag. Then, Composer will place the tag into your page at the insertion point.

**NOTE** See Appendix B, *An HTML Dictionary*, for examples of some of the HTML tags you can enter in the HTML Tag dialog box.

## Entering an HTML tag

To enter HTML codes using the dialog box, follow these steps:

1. From the Insert menu, choose HTML Tag. This will open the HTML Tag dialog box.

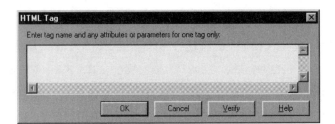

2.  Type an HTML tag into the dialog box. You must be careful to type the HTML tag properly, including the correct tag name, parameters, and punctuation (such as the quotes around some parameters and the angle brackets that surround the tag itself). You should enter only a single HTML tag and its parameters. For instance, in the case of paired opening and closing tags, you would enter only the opening or closing tag—not both.

3.  Click Verify and Composer will check the contents of the dialog box to see if it follows the format of a valid HTML tag. For example, Composer will verify that you have entered only a single tag and that the tag is properly enclosed in angle brackets. If Composer detects a problem, an error message appears. (You can skip this step. Composer will perform the verification automatically before inserting the HTML code into your document. But verifying the entry yourself avoids surprises.)

4.  Click OK to close the dialog box and insert the HTML tag into your Web page.

Composer inserts the HTML tag into your Web page. In the Composer edit window, you'll see an icon indicating the location of each HTML tag entered with the HTML Tag dialog box. Usually, you'll enter HTML tags in pairs—one before the affected text and one after—and Composer will display slightly different icons for beginning and ending tags.

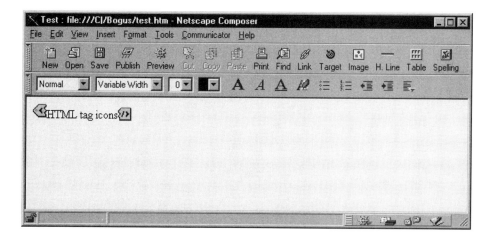

Composer doesn't attempt to interpret the HTML tags you enter in the HTML Tag dialog box or display the results in the edit window. Even if those HTML tags are for basic features commonly used in Composer, the program simply displays a generic icon to indicate the location of each tag and ignores any effect that tag would have on the appearance of the page you are editing. However, if you save and then re-open the Web page, Composer will interpret any HTML tags it understands and display the results in the edit window in place of the HTML tag icons. Any tags Composer doesn't recognize will continue to be displayed as icons.

# Editing HTML Source Code with an External Editor

The HTML Tag dialog box enables you to insert one HTML tag at a time into your Web page but there may be times that inserting tags one-by-one is too cumbersome. You may need to define a larger block of HTML code, or review and edit the HTML codes in an entire file. Composer's WYSIWYG editing environment isn't suited to such use. So, Composer allows you to select an external HTML editor and use it to edit the HTML source code for your page. After you define what HTML editor you prefer, Composer makes it easy to launch that program and load the HTML code for the page you are editing. Then, after you complete your HTML editing, you can return to Composer by simply saving the file and closing the HTML editor program.

Remember that HTML files are really plain ASCII text files. Unlike word processing files, these ASCII text files include no formatting, and they employ no fancy fonts or attributes such as **bold** or *italics*. All the special effects that you see in a Web document—**bold**, *italic*, <u>links</u> to other documents—are represented in the ASCII text files with HTML tags, and those are also are made up of plain text characters.

Since an HTML document is composed of nothing but ASCII text, you can use any program that is capable of editing ASCII text files to edit your HTML source code. You can use a word processor such as Word for Windows or WordPerfect, a text editor such as DOS Edit or Windows Notepad, or a program that is designed specifically for editing HTML documents such as HoTMetaL or Arachnophilia. (If you use a word processor, you'll need to use its HTML editing mode, or at least make sure you can save the document as plain ASCII text instead of the normal word processing file format.)

A special HTML editor program isn't necessary—you can get the job done with a simple text editor such as Notepad. But there are certain advantages to using a program that is designed to make working with HTML codes easier. The latest versions of the popular word processors all include some sort of HTML editing mode that helps automate the task of entering HTML tags. The current crop of HTML editors go even further. They typically provide menu access to a comprehensive list of HTML tags plus the ability to verify that the HTML codes you enter are in the proper form and syntax. As a result, you can be confident that the Web browsers will be able to interpret and display your page properly.

## Finding an HTML Editor

HTML editors come in a variety of flavors and most of them are available to download from the Internet. Some are free or low-cost shareware programs. Others are full-fledged commercial programs with price tags to match. A few of the popular programs are: HotDog, available at `http://www.sausage.com`, WebEdit, available at `http://www.nesbitt.com` or `http://www.sandiego.com/webedit/`, and HoTMetaL PRO for Windows, available at `http://www.sq.com`.

# Setting Up an External Editor

Before you can use an external HTML editor from within Composer, you must tell Composer which program you want to use. After you record your preference, Composer will launch that program when you choose the Edit ➤ HTML Source command to begin editing the HTML source code.

To set the HTML editor preference, follow these steps:

1. From Composer's Edit menu, choose Preferences. This will open the Preferences dialog box. (If necessary, select Composer from the Category list.)

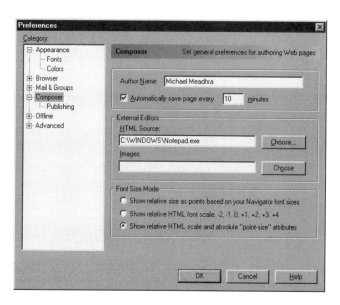

2. In the HTML Source text box located in the External Editors area, type the file name of the editing program you want to use. This can be a word processor such as Word for Windows (winword.exe), a simple text editor such as Notepad (notepad.exe), or a program designed specifically for editing HTML files.

As an alternative to typing the file name of the editor you want to use, you can click the Choose button to open the Choose an HTML Editor Application dialog box where you can browse for the program file. It functions like a standard File Open dialog box. Locate and select the file and then click the Open button to insert the file name into the HTML Source text box in the Preferences dialog box.

> **TIP**
>
> Unless you choose a program such as Notepad that resides in your Windows directory, you'll need to include the full path (drive and directory), along with the file name of the program you select to edit HTML source files. For example: `c:\htmledit\htmledit.exe`

3. Click the OK button to record your preference.

Now Composer knows what external editing program to use when you choose the Edit ➤ HTML Source command.

## Using an External Editor

After you set your preference for an external HTML editor, you can use that editor to edit the HTML source code you are working on in Composer. You'll rarely (if ever) use an external editor for the things you can do more easily in Composer's editing window. You may need to use an external editor to create effects that Composer doesn't support, such as forms. You can also use an external editor to revise the HTML codes entered by Composer when you need a bit more control over some effect. For instance, Composer allows you to specify any font on your system for your text, but you'll need to manually edit the `<font>` tag to specify alternate fonts that a browser should use, if the font you selected in Composer isn't available on the viewer's system.

To use an external editor to edit the HTML source code for your Web page, follow these steps:

1. With your page open in the Composer editing window, choose the Edit ➤ HTML Source command.

2. Unless you have just saved your page, Composer will display a dialog box prompting you to save your page before continuing. Click the Yes button to save the page. (If you have not previously saved the page, Composer will display the Save New Page dialog box instead.

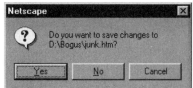

Click Save to open a standard Save As dialog box, where you can specify the path and file name for the page. Click the Save button to save the file and then supply a title for the page when prompted in another dialog box.) After your page is saved, Composer will launch your chosen HTML editing program and load the source code for the current page.

3. Edit the HTML source code in the HTML editor window. You can manually add HTML tags for features not supported by Composer or do any other editing you need to do. At this point you are working in the external editor and Composer is no longer in control of the page. You can use the features of the external editor just as if you had launched it independently.

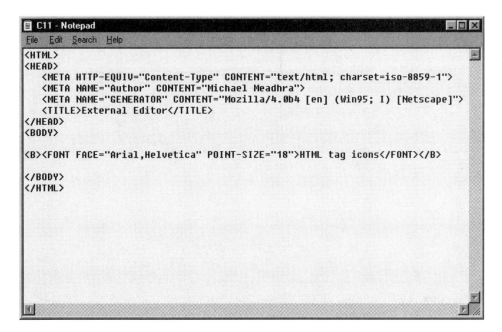

```
C11 - Notepad
File  Edit  Search  Help
<HTML>
<HEAD>
   <META HTTP-EQUIV="Content-Type" CONTENT="text/html; charset=iso-8859-1">
   <META NAME="Author" CONTENT="Michael Meadhra">
   <META NAME="GENERATOR" CONTENT="Mozilla/4.0b4 [en] (Win95; I) [Netscape]">
   <TITLE>External Editor</TITLE>
</HEAD>
<BODY>

<B><FONT FACE="Arial,Helvetica" POINT-SIZE="18">HTML tag icons</FONT></B>

</BODY>
</HTML>
```

4. After editing your HTML file in the external editor, save the file using the external editor's File ➤ Save command (or whatever command or options the editor provides for saving your work). Then exit the external editor or return to Composer by using the Windows taskbar or clicking in the Composer window.

**5.** When you return to Composer after modifying the current page in an external editor, Composer displays the Reload Page dialog box. Click the Yes button to refresh the Web page in the Composer window.

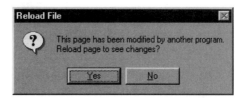

When your page reappears in the Composer window, you can resume editing it with Composer. Depending on what changes you made in the HTML file with the external editor, Composer may, or may not, be able to display your page in a way that accurately previews how the page will appear in a browser.

If you used the HTML tags Composer supports, Composer will be able to display the page correctly. (But if you are going to use HTML tags Composer supports, why use the external editor to enter them?) It's more likely that you used the external editor to enter HTML tags that aren't supported by Composer, in which case, Composer will display the unrecognized HTML tags as generic icons (see Figure 11.1).

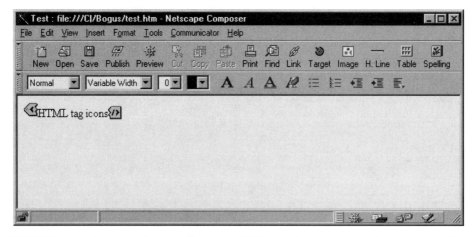

**FIGURE 11.1:** Composer displays unrecognized HTML tags that were entered in an external editor as icons.

**TIP**

To get a quick preview of the HTML code behind an icon, let the mouse pointer rest on an icon for a few seconds. Composer will open a pop-up tip, similar to the tips that describe the function of the toolbar buttons, that shows the contents to the HTML tag.

You can cut, copy, and paste the HTML tag icons. You can delete them and drag them to new locations on your page. You can even edit individual tags in the HTML Tag dialog box (right-click the icon and choose HTML Tag Properties from the pop-up menu that appears). What you can't do is edit the icons directly in the Composer editing window and get an instant preview of how the effect will appear in a browser. Sometimes this is only a minor nuisance, other times it becomes almost impossible to visualize what the page will look like.

**NOTE**

See Chapter 12, *Beyond the Limits of Composer*, for examples of HTML features you may want to incorporate into your page when you use an external editor to enter the required HTML codes.

# Checking the Results

Composer will be unable to properly display the results of HTML tags for features the program doesn't support. If you use an external HTML editor or the HTML Tag dialog box to enter such foreign HTML codes, Composer will display an icon in the editing window in place of the usual WYSIWYG simulation of the way your page will appear when viewed in a browser.

The icons give you limited editing capabilities in Composer (you can move, copy, paste, or delete them), but you can't see what your finished Web page will look like. For that, you must view the page in a browser such as Navigator.

To view your current page in a browser, follow these steps:

1. Save your page. You can save the current page in Composer by choosing File ➤ Save. (If you fail to save your page before attempting to view it in your browser, Composer will prompt you to save it before you can move on.

**2.** Choose File ➤ Browse Page. Composer will launch your default browser (presumably, that will be Navigator) and load your page into the browser window for viewing.

That's all there is to it. You can view the local HTML file for your page in the browser window. Composer will remain open, and you can return to the Composer window to continue editing your page at any time. To return to Composer, simply exit the browser.

**WARNING**
After viewing a page in your browser, be sure you return to your original Composer window to continue editing your page. You can do so by closing the browser window or switching back to the Composer window with the Windows taskbar. Don't use the File ➤ Edit Page command in Navigator. That will open another Composer window with the same page loaded. This can lead to confusion about which Composer window contains the most current copy of your page.

# Chapter 12

# GOING BEYOND THE LIMITS OF COMPOSER

- **What Composer can't do**
- **Getting feedback with forms**
- **Organizing content in frames**
- **Layers and absolute positioning**
- **Using style sheets**
- **Inserting a preprogrammed Java applet**

Although Composer is convenient and easy-to-use for creating Web pages, it isn't capable of producing the full range of effects that can appear on a Web page. Composer can handle most of your Web page publishing needs; but there are some features and effects that can be defined with HTML tags and displayed in the newer Web browsers for which no corresponding commands, buttons, or dialog box options exist.

If you want to use any of the HTML features that are not supported by Composer, you're on your own. You'll have to manually insert the HTML tags for those features into the HTML source code.

Because this is a book about using Composer, I won't go into great detail about how to do things outside of the program. However, because this is also a book about publishing Web pages, it seems appropriate to at least include a brief survey of the Web design options available outside of Composer.

# What Composer Can't Do

Composer can meet the vast majority of your day-to-day Web page creation needs, and does so using its convenient built-in tools and WYSIWYG editing environment. However, there are a few things the program just can't do.

Some of Composer's limitations are relatively small. For example, there isn't an option that enables you to embed a background sound into your page so that it will begin playing automatically when the page is viewed. Also, when you select a specific font (such as Ariel) for some text, Composer will automatically list alternate fonts (such as Helvetica) in addition to your selection—but there is no provision for changing the alternate font or even determining what alternate font Composer listed.

These small limitations are pretty easy to overcome. To do it, you'll have to edit the HTML source code for your Web page manually, but the required edits are simple. For instance, each of the two examples above can be handled by adding or editing a single HTML tag.

In addition to an assortment of small details, there are some larger issues in how Composer supports the Web page design features of HTML. It's these areas that concern Web authors because they limit the kinds of Web pages that can be produced with the program. Some of the significant features of Web pages that Composer does not support are as follows:

- Forms
- Frames
- Layers
- HTML Style Sheets
- Java and JavaScript

If you want to use any of these features, you must edit the HTML source code for your page manually. Also, unlike embedding a background sound in a Web page, adding a form or a style sheet involves doing some fairly extensive manual HTML editing. Attempting to add the numerous required tags one-at-a-time to produce these effects using the HTML Tag dialog box isn't very practical, so you have no choice but to use an external HTML editor.

Furthermore, when you load a Web page containing unsupported features into Composer, the program will not recognize the HTML tags for these features and cannot properly display the page in its editing window. Those tags will appear as generic HTML tag icons, as shown in Figure 12.1.

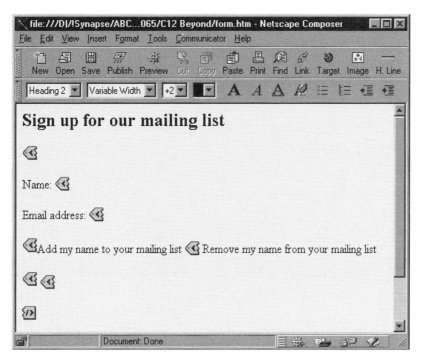

**FIGURE 12.1:**   Composer displays unrecognized HTML tags as icons.

# Getting Feedback with Forms

The HTML language includes provisions for creating onscreen forms to solicit feedback and information from visitors to your Web site. You can create a Web page with text boxes, list boxes, checkboxes, and radio buttons similar to those you find in dialog boxes and database applications. A visitor viewing the Web page can fill in the blanks and select options, then click a Submit button to send the information to the e-mail address you've specified.

For example, Figure 12.2 shows a very simple form that enables visitors to submit their names and e-mail addresses, and request to be added to, or removed from, a mailing list. Figure 12.3 shows the HTML source code for this simple form.

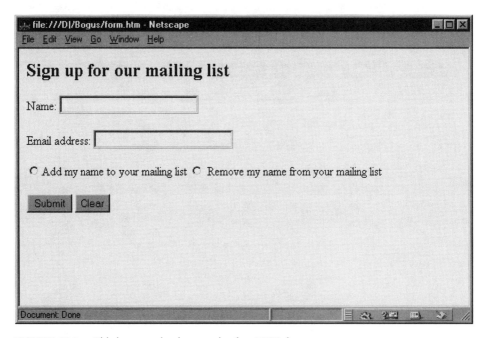

**FIGURE 12.2:**   This is a very simple example of an HTML form.

Because Composer does not include support for creating or working with forms, you will need to create HTML forms using an external HTML editor and entering the HTML codes to define a form manually. Or you can use an HTML editor that includes form creation tools. For instance, the Internet Assistant add-in for Microsoft Word for Windows (version 6 or 7) includes forms support. The new Word 97 has HTML forms capability built in. In addition, there are programs such as WebForms that are designed especially for creating HTML forms.

Onscreen label
Instructions for handling submitted information
Beginning of form

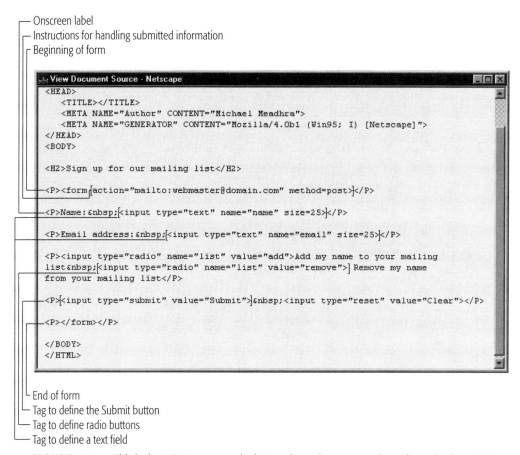

```
View Document Source - Netscape                                    _ □ X
<HEAD>
    <TITLE></TITLE>
    <META NAME="Author" CONTENT="Michael Meadhra">
    <META NAME="GENERATOR" CONTENT="Mozilla/4.0b1 (Win95; I) [Netscape]">
</HEAD>
<BODY>

<H2>Sign up for our mailing list</H2>

<P><form action="mailto:webmaster@domain.com" method=post></P>

<P>Name: <input type="text" name="name" size=25></P>

<P>Email address: <input type="text" name="email" size=25></P>

<P><input type="radio" name="list" value="add">Add my name to your mailing
list <input type="radio" name="list" value="remove"> Remove my name
from your mailing list</P>

<P><input type="submit" value="Submit"> <input type="reset" value="Clear"></P>

<P></form></P>

</BODY>
</HTML>
```

End of form
Tag to define the Submit button
Tag to define radio buttons
Tag to define a text field

**FIGURE 12.3:**   This is the HTML source code that produces the onscreen form shown in Figure 12.2.

**WARNING**   Successfully processing forms submissions and forwarding the information to an e-mail address requires special software that runs on your Web server. Many servers provide this service, but some don't. Be sure to check with your Web server administrator before attempting to set up a form on your Web site.

**NOTE**   If you decide to try your hand at creating HTML forms from scratch, you can find a good reference on HTML tags for forms at http://www.stars.com/Vlib/Authoring/Forms.html.

# Organizing Content in Frames

Frames enable the Web page author to divide the browser window into smaller segments and control the contents of each frame independently. Each frame becomes a separately scrollable area—a separate window within the browser window.

The Netscape Page Wizard shown in Figure 12.4 is one example of how frames are used. The wizard consists of three frames. The left frame contains the instructions, the bottom frame contains the data entry form, and the right frame contains a preview of the Web page being constructed.

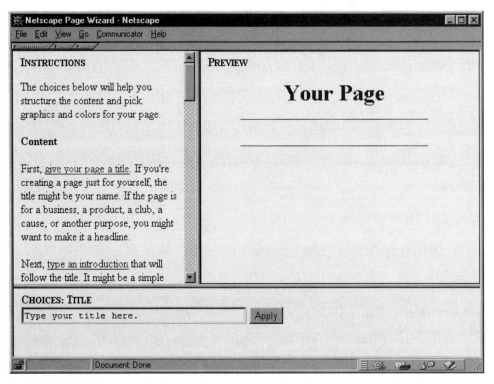

**FIGURE 12.4:**  It's easy to see the three separate frames that make up the Netscape Page Wizard window.

Another common use of frames is to place navigation buttons or links in a small frame along the top or one side of the browser window. By placing the navigation links in a separate frame from the rest of the Web page, the Web page designer can make sure they remain available at all times—they don't scroll off the screen as the user scrolls through the page (see Figure 12.5).

**FIGURE 12.5:** Placing navigation links in a separate frame ensures that they are always available.

# When Not to Use Frames

Frames have their uses, but they definitely have some real drawbacks.

The biggest problem with frames is that they are expensive in terms of how much available space they consume in a browser window. Adding frames reduces the space available for the main portion of the Web page. It's not too much of a problem for users viewing a page on a large, high-resolution monitor with the Web browser window maximized. In a large browser window, there's ample room for a frame of navigation buttons and a good-sized frame for the usual Web page content. However, a frame of navigation buttons will take up nearly as much space in a smaller browser window—as would be the case with a user who views the Web page on a smaller, lower-resolution monitor. On a smaller screen, the frame of buttons leaves precious little space for the rest of the Web page, making it look crowded and hard to read. Furthermore, frames are not supported by some older browser software that is still in fairly wide use.

Frames have other problems as well. Unlike the simple HTML tags used for formatting text, frames are much more complicated to set up. The complex HTML tags used for defining frames (see Figure 12.6) can be intimidating to a Web author who lacks experience with programming languages. And, because Composer doesn't support frames in its WYSIWYG editing environment, there is no practical alternative to defining frames by manually entering the necessary HTML tags into the HTML source file.

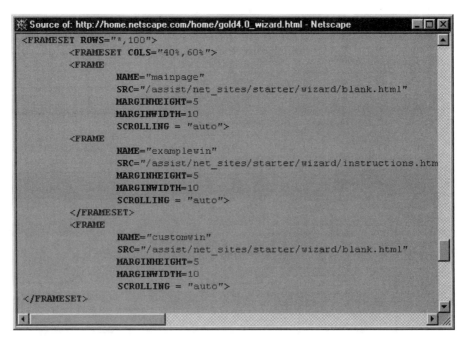

**FIGURE 12.6:**  The HTML tags for defining frames can be intimidating for the uninitiated.

# Layers and Absolute Positioning

Layers are a revolutionary new concept in Web page design. Typically, the content of a Web page (mainly the text) adapts to fit the width of the Web browser window being used to display the page. Lines of text re-wrap, and images move around on the page to fit the available space. But layers change all that. Using layers, the Web author can define a working area of an exact size and put elements in that area. The positions of text and images placed on layers remain fixed, and the relationships between the elements can be precisely controlled. Not only that, images and text on one layer can overlap (appear in front of or behind) elements on another layer, and the Web author can control the order in which elements appear on the page. It's a whole new approach to designing Web pages.

The kind of absolute positioning offered by using layers is a mixed blessing. Having the ability to predict a page size and control where (and when) elements will appear on that page gives Web authors an unprecedented level of control over the appearance of the Web pages they create. However, it also means that the Web page is locked to that predefined size and shape. As a result, using layers sacrifices the Web browser's ability to reformat the Web page to deliver information in a presentable form regardless of the platform it's on, or the size of the browser window.

The tags for defining layers are some of the newest extensions to HTML. The latest version of Navigator (Navigator 4.0—the one introduced in the Communicator suite) is the first to support layers. Other browsers will undoubtedly soon follow suit, but older browsers can't properly display a Web page that uses layers.

In its current incarnation, Composer does not support layers. The program doesn't include any provisions for defining and working with layers and it can't properly display a page that includes HTML tags for layers. The layer-related tags aren't confined to an isolated portion of the HTML source code; so, it's not very practical to attempt to do most of your page creation in Composer and use an external HTML editor to add layers to the existing page. If you decide that you must work with layers on a Web page, you'll probably need to do it outside of Composer.

# Using Style Sheets

Style sheets are another new extension to HTML. They hold the promise of being real time-savers for Web authors who create numerous heavily formatted text pages.

By now, you're no doubt familiar with the standard HTML paragraph tags for the various heading levels and lists. By applying a paragraph style to a paragraph of text on your Web page, you can apply a predefined set of formatting attributes without having to set each of the formatting characteristics (such as font, size, boldface, indents, and alignment) individually.

Style sheets enable you to redefine the standard HTML paragraph styles and define your own custom variations on those paragraph styles. Then you can apply those styles to paragraphs of text on your Web page. Applying a custom style from a style sheet creates the same general effect as applying one of the standard HTML paragraph styles—it applies all of the formatting attributes defined for that style to the selected paragraph. By creating and using your own customized styles, you can ensure that the formatting for the text is consistent throughout your page and throughout your whole Web site.

To use style sheets, you define the styles you plan to use on a page by adding the appropriate tags to the header area at the top of the HTML source code. Each style consists of a name and a set of formatting attributes. You can define the styles in the header of the page where they are used, or put all the style definitions in a separate file and simply refer to that file in a style sheet tag. To apply a style to a paragraph of text, you simply add an HTML tag to the beginning of the paragraph that references the desired style by name.

**NOTE** See Appendix B, *An HTML Dictionary*, for the HTML tags that you need to use to define style sheets.

If you use the same set of formatting attributes repeatedly throughout a document, using a named style from a style sheet can save you some time. However, the big timesavings comes when you need to change some aspect of the formatting in all those paragraphs. Without style sheets, you'd need to go through your entire Web page making changes to each paragraph individually. But if you used a custom style from a style sheet on all those paragraphs, you could change the formatting of all the paragraphs at once by simply editing the style definition in the style sheet.

Saving all that time reformatting paragraphs is a pleasant prospect, but it gets better! Because you can store a style sheet in a separate file and reference it from many different Web pages, you could make a formatting change one place—in the style sheet—and have it automatically apply to all the paragraphs using that style, on all the pages throughout your Web site.

Because style sheets are relatively new, they are not yet supported by Composer or most older Web browsers. The custom style formatting will simply be ignored and your text will be displayed with the default formatting. (Composer will display a generic HTML tag icon in place of the unrecognized style tags.) Even though Composer doesn't display the results of style sheets and custom styles properly, you can add those tags to your Web pages manually by using the HTML Tag dialog box or an external HTML editor. If you work with a lot of heavily formatted text or need to maintain consistent styles across numerous pages, it may be worth the trouble to do some manual HTML editing in order to use style sheets.

# Inserting a Preprogrammed Java Applet

Java is an object-oriented programming language developed by Sun Microsystems for cross-platform use on the Internet and the World Wide Web. Although it's possible to develop full-fledged applications in Java, Web authors are more likely to encounter Java applets—mini-applications that can be embedded in the HTML source code for a Web page. JavaScript is the subset of Java that Netscape has developed for use with its browser. When it loads a Web page containing Java or JavaScript code, a Java-enabled browser (such as Navigator) can execute the Java programming instructions to perform various functions, such as producing animation effects and interactive Web page elements.

It's probably safe to assume that readers of this book have neither the desire nor the programming expertise needed to attempt to develop Java or JavaScript programming. Fortunately, it isn't necessary to be a Java programmer to reap the benefits of Java applets. You can find preprogrammed applets available to perform a wide variety of useful tasks.

**NOTE** **You'll find an extensive selection of Java applets at the Gamelan Web site at** http://www.gamelan.com/

To add a Java applet or JavaScript script to your Web page, you'll need to use an external HTML editor because Composer doesn't have facilities for entering Java code from its WYSIWYG editing environment. Usually, when you acquire a Java applet, it will come with instructions for adding the applet to your Web page. The process typically entails copying one or more Java program files to your Web site directory and adding several lines of code to the HTML source for your Web page. You can usually copy the necessary code from a file supplied by the Java programmer and paste it into your HTML file. Often, you'll need to edit some of the parameters in the Java code to refer to the correct file names, directories, and URLs on your Web site.

Because Composer does not support Java or JavaScript you won't be able to preview the effect of the applet in the Composer editing window. Instead, Composer will display a series of HTML tag icons to indicate the location of the Java applet code. You should be able to see the effect of the Java applet when you view your Web page in Navigator.

# Part 4

# Publishing Your Web Site

# Chapter 13

# POSTING YOUR PAGES ON THE WEB

**FEATURING**

- **Finding a Web server**
- **Using Composer's Publish feature**
- **Maintaining your Web site**

After you've invested your time in creating a set of Web pages, you won't want to just leave them sitting on your hard disk. After all, the World Wide Web exists to make your Web pages available to the world (or at least to your coworkers connected to an intranet). For that, you must copy your Web pages to a Web server—a computer that is designated to store Web pages and respond to requests from Web surfers who want to view those pages.

You will likely post your Web pages on a Web server maintained by your Internet service provider or your corporate intranet administrator. Composer includes a special Publish feature that automates much of the task of copying Web pages to such a server. You can also manually copy Web pages using a standard FTP utility program. This chapter will show you how to do both.

After you post your Web site on a server, don't forget to keep it up-to-date. You'll need to devote some maintenance time to your Web site in order to keep the content fresh and all the links working properly.

# Finding a Web Server

A Web server needs to be available around the clock to handle requests for Web pages 24-hours a day, 7-days a week. It isn't practical for a typical computer with a dial-up connection to the Internet be a Web server. Even if you have a full-time Internet connection through a local area network, you probably wouldn't want to use the resources of your personal computer as a Web server. So, the solution is a separate computer with a reliable, full-time Internet connection dedicated to the role of a Web server. This solution is prohibitively expensive for most people and companies to set up on their own. Fortunately, there's no shortage of convenient and inexpensive alternatives.

Most Internet service providers maintain a Web server and offer Web hosting services to their clients for a small monthly fee. A Web site on an Internet service provider's server may even be included as part of the regular cost of your Internet access account. In some cases, you might want to consider contracting with one Internet service provider for your regular Internet access and choose a different provider to host your Web site. In addition to Internet service providers, there are a growing number of local, regional, and national companies that specialize in Web hosting services. Many corporations are able to maintain their own Web servers. In fact, some corporations have one or more Web servers for internal users on an intranet, and separate Web servers for the broader World Wide Web on the Internet.

When you use a Web hosting service (whether it's provided by your Internet service provider, a Web hosting company, or your corporate network services department), you are basically renting space for your site on a Web server. You will get a Web address and an allotment of storage space on the server's hard disk where you can put your Web pages, images, and other files. To set your Web site up on a server, copy your Web files into the assigned directory on the server. The server will then use those files when responding to requests addressed to your Web site's URL. The Internet service provider or Web hosting service will take care of all the technical issues involved in maintaining the Web server and keeping it operational around the clock. Your Web site will be available even when your own computer is offline or shut down.

Naturally, you'll need to know the URL that the Web hosting service assigns to your Web site. You'll want to know how to access your site yourself and how to tell others how to find it. But the URL alone isn't usually enough information about your Web site to enable you to post your pages and other files on the server. In addition to the URL, you'll need to know the protocol (FTP or HTTP) to use for uploads, and the directory assigned to your site. In most cases, you'll also need a user name and password to gain access to your site. (This ensures that you are the only one allowed to make changes to your site.) You can get all this information from the system administrator for the Web server when you set up your site. In fact, it's typically included in the welcome message you will receive when you sign up for the service.

> **TIP**
>
> **Make careful note of the access information (URL, directory, user name, password) for your Web site. You'll need it to publish pages on your Web site whether you use Composer's Publish feature or copy files manually.**

# Using Composer's Publish Feature

So, you've made arrangements to use the facilities of an Internet service provider or Web hosting service to publish your Web site. Now, your next task is to get your Web pages transferred from your local hard disk to the Web server where they will be available to a wider potential audience.

Composer includes a Publish feature that makes the process of transferring your files from your system to the Web server as easy and painless as possible. Composer can transfer files using either the HTTP or FTP protocols. Composer's one-button publishing automatically copies image files and other linked files along with the HTML file that defines the Web page itself.

The first time you use Composer to publish a Web page, you'll need to enter some detailed information such as the server address, the user ID, and the password you will use to gain access to the system. Later, when you publish subsequent pages to the same server, you won't need to re-enter all this information. In fact, after everything is set up, you can publish the page you are editing in Composer with just a couple of mouse clicks.

## Setting Composer's Publishing Preferences

Before you use Composer to publish Web pages, you must supply some information about where your Web site is located. The best way to do this is to fill in the Preferences dialog box. Or you can skip this setup procedure and just supply the information in the

Publish dialog box when you get ready to publish your first Web page. However, if you're like me, you'll find that it's easier to look up and enter stuff like the directory name, user name, and password for your Web site ahead of time. Then, when you're ready to publish a Web page, those details are taken care of and the publishing process is faster and simpler.

To set Composer's publishing preferences, follow these steps:

1. Choose Edit ➤ Preferences. This will open the Preferences dialog box.

2. In the Category list, under the Composer category, select Publishing. (If the Publishing category is not visible, click the plus sign beside the Composer item.) The Publishing options will appear in the Preferences dialog box.

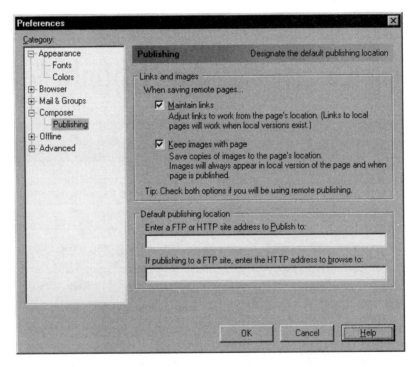

3. In the Links and Images area, you have two options that enable you to instruct Composer in how you want the program to handle the hyperlinks and Images in the Web pages you publish. Usually, you'll want to make sure both options are checked. Click the checkbox for an option to toggle that option on or off.

**Maintain Links:** If this option is checked, Composer will automatically modify the hyperlinks on your Web page that point to files on your local hard disk so instead they point to copies of those files which presumably will exist on the Web server.

**Keep Images with Page:** If this option is checked, Composer will automatically copy image files (and other hyperlink targets) that are included on your Web page from your hard drive to the Web server.

4.  Click the top text box in the Default Publishing Location area—the one labeled Enter a FTP or HTTP Site Address to Publish To. Enter the address for the location of your Web site on the Web server. Be sure to enter the *complete* address where you were told to post your Web site files. Include the protocol (usually FTP, but sometimes HTTP), the server name, and the directory. For example, the site address might look something like this:

    `ftp://webserver.com/userwebs/~yourname/`

**WARNING** Make sure you include the slash at the end of the final directory name in the Web site address. If you omit the final slash, Composer can confuse the directory name with a file name.

5.  Click the bottom text box in the Default Publishing Location area—the one labeled If Publishing to a FTP Site, Enter the HTTP Address to Browse To. Enter the full Web address (URL) for your Web site. This is your regular Web site address—the one you enter into a browser to view your site. Be sure to enter the protocol (`http://`), the server name (such as `www.server.com`), and the path (`/~yourname/`), but omit any specific filename (such as `home.html`).

    Actually, you can leave this text box blank if it would be the same as the Publish to address. However, in most cases, you'll need to fill in both addresses.

**NOTE** Usually, the Web site address where you publish your Web pages will be a little different from the address you use to access the Web site. It may start with the FTP protocol instead of HTTP, the server name may be slightly different, and there may be a couple of extra directories in the path.

**6.** Click the OK button to record your settings and close the Preferences dialog box.

Composer will record your publishing preferences and they will appear as the defaults in the Publish dialog box when you publish your Web pages.

# Publishing Pages

Copying completed Web pages from your local hard disk to the Web server is easy with Composer. You can publish the page you're working on in the Composer window with just a few mouse clicks.

One of the problems Web authors must face when manually publishing Web pages is making sure all the referenced images on a given page get copied to the Web server along with the HTML file for the page itself. File management for a site that uses lots of images can be a nightmare. Composer helps you manage your Web site files by identifying the image files referenced in a Web page and giving you the option to copy those files to the server along with the Web page.

Composer even gives you the option to select and copy to the Web server all the files in the folder with the current Web page in one operation. This makes it easy to publish an entire multipage Web site at once.

## Publishing Web Pages on Your Own

You aren't restricted to using Composer's built-in publishing feature to publish your Web pages. You can always manually copy Web pages and other files from your local hard disk to a Web server.

To copy files to a Web server at an Internet service provider or Web hosting service, you can use an Internet file transfer utility program (FTP) such as WS_FTP or FTP Explorer. On an intranet, you may use other techniques to copy files across the local-area network. If you choose to go this route, you're on your own when it comes to gathering up all the images and other files associated with each Web page and making sure that they are transferred to the server along with the HTML file for the page.

Despite the inconveniences, there are some situations in which you might want to manually publish your Web site. For example, if you are publishing to a Web server on a corporate intranet, you may not be able to use the FTP or HTTP protocols Composer offers to copy your files. Instead, you may need to use the

## Publishing Web Pages On Your Own (continued)

same techniques you use to copy files to another network drive. You might also want to manually publish your pages if you have a large Web site that is organized into separate sub folders. Composer's publish feature doesn't do a good job of transferring a directory structure from your local disk to the Web server.

To publish your current Web page to a Web server, follow these steps:

1. Save the current Web page you are editing in the Composer window. (Choose File ➤ Save and supply a file name and a page title for the page if you haven't already done so.)
2. Choose File ➤ Publish or click the Upload button located in the Compose toolbar. This opens the Publish dialog box.

Publish

**Publish: C:\Bogus\bogus.html**

| Page Title: | Publishing Test Page | e.g.: "My Web Page" |
| HTML Filename: | bogus.html | e.g.: "mypage.htm" |

HTTP or FTP Location to publish to:

| User name: | | Use Default Location |
| Password: | | ☐ Save password |

Other files to include

⦿ Files associated with this page    ◯ All files in page's folder

Select None      file:///C|/Bogus/oflogo.gif
Select All        file:///C|/Bogus/oflogo_button_med.gif

OK      Cancel      Help

The Page Title and HTML Filename text boxes contain the file information you entered when you saved the page. The rest of the dialog box fields are empty the first time you use the publish feature.

3. Edit the Page Title and HTML Filename text boxes if necessary. Then, click the Use Default Location button to enter the Web server address you defined in the Publishing preferences dialog box into the HTTP or FTP Location to Publish to text box. If you need to publish this page to a different server address, type the full address of the Web server in the text box. Be sure to enter the complete address where you were told to post your Web site files. Include the protocol (usually FTP, but sometimes HTTP), the server name, and the directory. (For example: `ftp://server.com/userwebs/~yourname/`)

**TIP**

Composer remembers the server addresses to which you have published pages. To publish a page to one of your recently used server addresses, click the down arrow at the right end of the HTTP or FTP Location to Publish To box and select the address from the drop-down list. You won't have to retype the whole address again.

4. In the User Name text box, type the user ID to log onto the Web server and gain access to your Web site.
5. In the Password text box, enter your password for the Web server (asterisks appear as you type the password). Also, check the Save Password option to instruct Composer to save this information so you won't have to re-enter it next time.

**WARNING**

Instructing Composer to remember your password can save time by eliminating the need to retype the password each time you publish a page, but it also eliminates the security the password provides. This means that anyone who has access to your computer will be able to use Composer to make changes to your Web site without needing to know the password. If you're concerned about Web site security, leave the Save Password option unchecked.

**6.** The list in the Other Files to Include area enables you to determine what other files Composer will copy to the Web server along with the HTML file for your current page. You can choose what files appear in the list by selecting one of the following options:

**Files Associated with this Page:** If you select this option, Composer will analyze the current page and list all the images and other local files that are the targets of hyperlinks in the page. (Note: This does not list hyperlink targets that point to URLs elsewhere on the Internet. The list will contain only files stored on the local computer. The option is greyed out if your page doesn't contain any hyperlinks to other files.)

**All Files in Page's Folder:** Selecting this option causes Composer to list all the files in the same folder as the current page. This option is handy when you want to publish an entire Web site.

Composer will publish the highlighted files in the list. You can click the Select All or Select None buttons to select all or none of the listed files. Click the individual filenames in the list to toggle the highlight for that file on or off.

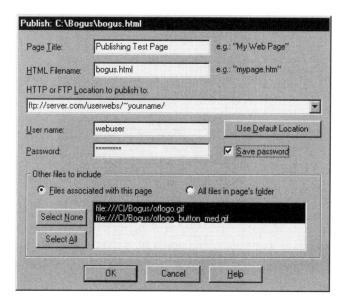

**7.** After you have selected the files to publish, click the OK button to start the file transfer.

> **NOTE** Any files that you copy to the Web server with Composer's Publish feature will replace existing files of the same name. This enables you to easily update existing files with newly edited versions. However, you must be careful to avoid assigning the same file name to different pages.

**8.** If necessary, click Connect or take any other steps to establish an Internet connection to your Internet service provider so the file transfer can proceed. Composer automatically handles the file transfer of the selected files to the Web server. It usually takes just a few seconds and Composer will display a status message to keep you informed of its progress.

**9.** When the file transfer is complete, Composer displays a message to that effect. Click the OK button to close the message box.

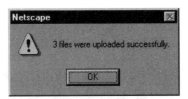

Your newly created (or modified) Web page is now published on the Web server, and ready to be viewed by the world. You can use Navigator to load the Web page from the Web server and check it out.

## Editing Web Pages on the Server

The typical Web publishing process assumes that you will create and save your Web pages on your local hard disk and then publish them on the Web server when they are finished. To update a page, you would make changes to the copy on your local hard disk and then publish the updated pages, replacing the older copies of those pages on the Web server.

However, if you need to make some quick edits to a Web page that is already posted on a server, you can skip a couple of steps by following this procedure:

1. Use Navigator to browse to the page you want to modify.
2. When the page is displayed in the Navigator window, choose File ➤ Edit Page. A Composer window will open displaying the Web page for you to edit.
3. Edit or revise the page as needed. There is no need to save the changes to your local hard disk.
4. When you've completed your edits in Composer, choose File ➤ Publish. The Publish dialog box appears.
5. Adjust the settings in the Publish dialog box as needed. For instance, you may need to change the Publish To location from the HTTP address you use for browsing to the FTP address you use to publish pages. Enter your user name and password. If you're simply editing the HTML file for your Web page, you'll probably want to deselect the files listed in the Other Files list because they aren't likely to need updating.
6. Click the OK button to publish the edited page.
7. When the file transfer is complete, Composer displays a message box. Click the OK button to close the message box. You can also close the Composer window you used to edit the page.

That's all there is to it. Your Web page is now updated on the server.

## Maintaining Your Web Site

After you create all your pages and publish them to the Web server, your task is done, right? Wrong! In some ways, publishing a Web site is just the beginning of a long-term commitment.

First, you must check and recheck each and every page of your Web site by viewing it from the server using Navigator. Although Composer does a good job of locating the images and other files associated with your Web pages and transferring those files from your hard disk to the server, a few glitches are still possible. If everything checks out with Navigator, try viewing your site with another browser. It's also a good idea to ask some friends and colleagues to try accessing your Web site from different locations on the Internet or intranet. They might spot problems that your own testing didn't uncover. Only after you've checked your site thoroughly and fixed any problem you find, is it time to announce your site to the world and invite visitors to view it.

Even after your site passes its initial tests, you can't sit back and rest on your laurels. Your site is likely to require regular maintenance to keep it in top shape. After all, a Web site is (or should be) a dynamic thing—constantly growing, evolving, and being refreshed with updated information.

At the very least, you must be vigilant to prevent creeping link rot from eroding your pages. You must check your Web site regularly for broken links (hyperlinks that point to pages that have been moved, changed, or withdrawn) and replace or update those hyperlinks. Also, you should remove or replace any outdated information that appears on your site.

> **TIP**
>
> **Put an e-mail address on your Web page where visitors can send comments about your site. Then, respond to the feedback you receive. Comments from visitors can be invaluable in locating problems and suggesting new directions for your site. (Just try not to take the inevitable sharp-tongued criticisms personally.)**

If you really want to have a top-notch Web site, you'll need to add new material constantly to keep visitors coming back again and again. Also, you'll want to give your site a fresh appearance from time to time with new colors, backgrounds, and layouts.

# Chapter 14

# PUBLICIZING YOUR SITE

Composer

- **Submitting your site to directories and search engines**
- **Extending the Web with backlinks**
- **Promoting your site online**
- **Using traditional media to support your online efforts**

"Build it and they will come." That may work for dream baseball fields, but not for Web sites. If no one knows about your site, no one will visit it. It's not like opening a storefront on a busy street; potential visitors aren't going to notice your site as they walk by on their way to somewhere else. If you want Web surfers to visit your site, you'll need to do the electronic equivalent of passing out flyers, getting a listing in the yellow pages, and other advertising and public relations efforts.

**NOTE**

This chapter assumes that you want to use your Web site to share your particular vision with interested people from all over the Internet. To do so, you must do some publicity. On the other hand, if you are preparing Web pages for publication to a limited community of users on an intranet, you may not want to publicize the site. In fact, your audience—the other members of your workgroup—may be hounding you with messages wondering when the information will be ready for viewing. If you belong to this latter group, you'll probably want to skip this chapter and get back to work creating your Web pages.

The World Wide Web thrives on hyperlinks! Therefore, the most effective way to build traffic for your site is to get others to create links to your site. If there are no links to your page, you won't get any hits. This is a fundamental principal of the way the Web works. Web surfers follow links from page to page and site to site—they don't want to type in addresses for individual Web pages if they can avoid it.

To build traffic to your Web site, you want many entry points to your site, and lots for people to do and see once they get there. Most visitors will come to your Web site by following links from other sites or from one of the directories or search engines. Therefore, you will want to encourage other Web authors to create links to your site, and you'll want to get your site listed in the popular directory listings and search engine databases.

In addition to getting others to create hyperlinks to your site, you can do a number of other things to get your site the attention it deserves. The Internet affords unique opportunities to promote your site. Many of the traditional methods of promoting a business or idea can help to publicize your Web site as well.

Of course, for your Web site to be effective, it must make a favorable impression on the Web surfers that find it. You want them to stay at your site long enough to get your message, to return to it often, and recommend it to their friends. To do that, your site must present interesting content in an appropriate manner. Good content and good design coupled with style, wit, and originality is the recipe for a winning Web site.

# Submitting Your Site to Directories and Search Engines

When a typical Web user needs to find something in the vast expanse of the World Wide Web, they usually start with a search in one of the big Web directories or search engines such as Yahoo, Excite, or Infoseek. (For simplicity, I'll just call them all search engines from here on out.) These search engines maintain huge indexed databases listing millions of Web sites. A user simply enters a key word into a form on the service's Web page, and the search engine will return a page of links to the Web sites that match the search criteria.

If you're serious about building traffic on your Web site, you'll want to make sure Web surfers can find it by using the popular search engines. In fact, getting your site listed in the major search engines is probably the single most effective thing you can do, if your goal is to promote your site to a large and diverse audience.

Getting your Web site listed in a search engines isn't difficult. Usually, the process involves going to the search engine's site and filling out an onscreen form to submit your site's URL. You may also need to supply some contact information, a description of your site, and perhaps a category or list of key words.

> **NOTE**  On most of the popular search engine sites it is easy to locate the page where you submit your Web site to be included in the database. Look for a link such as Add URL on the opening page (usually near the bottom) of the search engine's Web site.

After you submit your Web site to a search engine, the search engine's automated software (often called a spider or crawler) will visit your site and gather information for your listing. The different search engines gather and index slightly different information. All the search engines include the title of your Web page and at least some text. Some search engines look farther into your Web site than others. Some look at only the first few lines of text on each page they index, while others index all the text on a page. Some examine only the first page of a site, while others follow links to explore all the linked pages at your site. Some search engines will include information you place in special meta tags in your listing, while others will ignore the meta tag entries. Once the automated spider completes its information gathering, the data will be compiled, indexed, and added to the search engine's database. But be patient, it may take anywhere from a few a days to several weeks for your new site to show up in searches of the search engines.

**NOTE** Some search engines, such as HotBot at `http://www.hotbot.com/addurl.html` ask only for the URL of the site you are submitting and your e-mail address. Others, such as Excite at `http://www.excite.com/Info/add_url.html` require you to supply more information. You can also submit your site to the WebCrawler at `http://Webcrawler.com/WebCrawler/SubmitURLS.html`. Submitting a site to Yahoo! (perhaps the best-known of the major Web search engines) is a little different. Since the search engine is organized into categories, you must surf to the appropriate category first, then click the Add URL link to add your Web site to that category. See the instructions at `http://add.yahoo.com/fast/add`.

Sometimes just getting listed on a search engine isn't enough. A search for a popular keyword can return a list of thousands of Web sites. If you want to attract visitors to your site, you must find a way to stand out from the crowd by getting your site to appear near the top of the list or ranked as highly relevant. Your efforts should start with careful consideration of the title, description, and keywords you list for your site. The next few pages of this chapter will show you how add titles, descriptions, and keywords to your Web pages, in a way that many of the search engines can find and use to index your site. The way you use these and other techniques to enhance your site's search engine listings is up to you. Some research into the various search engines and how they operate can pay dividends in better placement.

**TIP** Want to learn more about promoting your Web site? An informative place to visit is the VirtualPROMOTE site at `http://www.virtualpromote.com/`.

## Providing Text for the Search Engine to Index

Since the search engines all include Web page titles and some text from the body of your page, it's important to provide a title for them to index. Make sure you give every Web page a title—preferably one that incorporates key words that Web surfers are likely to use when searching for the topic of your site. To add a title: from the Format menu choose Page Colors and Properties, and the Page Properties dialog box (shown in Figure 14.1) will appear. If necessary, click the General tab, then type the title in the Title text box.

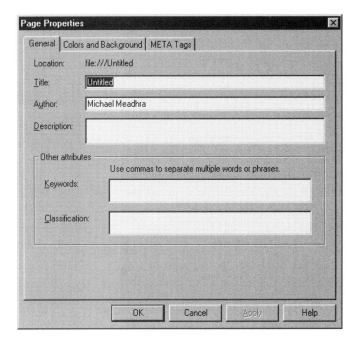

**FIGURE 14.1:**
The settings in this dialog box help define how your page is indexed in the big Web search engines.

Also, make sure each page includes some text relating to the content of the site. A page consisting of just an image map and a few navigational links won't be indexed properly by the search engines.

## Using Meta Tags to Control How Search Engines List Your Site

Most automated Web indexing programs attempt to index the text on your Web page and use the first few lines of that text as a description. That may not result in a very useful description or list of keywords to serve as the basis of searches.

Digital's Alta Vista directory, along with Yahoo, CNET's Search.Com, and others using the Alta Vista search engine, can use the contents of a Meta tag (an HTML tag that can be placed in the Head area of a Web page to describe and document the page without being displayed by a Web browser) to aid in indexing Web sites in their database. You can use this fact to control the description and the keywords associated with your site in these databases.

To control the description and keywords for your site in the Alta Vista database, you need to add two Meta tags into your Web page, one for the description and one for the keywords. You can define the description and keyword Meta tags by opening the Format menu and choosing Page. When the Page Properties dialog box appears, choose the General tab, as shown in Figure 14.1. Enter a short description of your site in the Description text box and a series of keywords for searches in the Keywords text box. Keywords can be words or phrases separated by commas.

Alta Vista's Web Spider will pick up those keywords and use them to index your site in the database. Using Meta tags can be very helpful to get you site listed in the way you want. Your clever selection of keywords can result in your site appearing higher on the list of results when a Web surfer institutes a search on those keywords. But be careful; don't just repeat the same keyword over and over in order to increase the number of hits on that word. The Web spider will ignore any keywords that are repeated more than a certain number of times. (The limit is rumored to be seven repetitions.)

> **TIP**
>
> You can see the Meta tag and the other HTML codes that make up a Web page by opening the View menu and choosing Source. Composer will open a separate window to display the ASCII text file that contains the codes defining your Web page. You'll find the Meta tags for keyword and description near the top of the file, between the <Head> and </Head> tags.

Some Web developers have resorted to sneaky tricks designed to increase the likelihood that their Web page will be near the top of the list of links when a search engine does its thing. Tricks such as repeated use of popular keywords and multiple submissions of the same URL have worked in the past. However, the managers of the directories have been quick to adopt defensive measures such as ignoring any keyword that appears more than a certain number of times.

**WARNING** Don't try to spam the search engine with multiple submissions of the same URL or other tricks. You're efforts will probably be wasted and might cause the directory to reject your Web site.

## Using Submission Services to Post Your Web Site

Submitting your Web site to a single directory takes just a few minutes. However, there are about a dozen major search engines and hundreds of minor search engines, announcement lists, and other sites where you might want to promote your Web site. Submitting your site to more than a few of them can be a tedious and time-consuming chore. So, it isn't surprising that some enterprising folks have come up with some tools to make the task easier. There are services that enable you to submit your URL once and have it posted automatically to a number of directories, search engines, and announcement sites. Some of them are free and others charge a fee for the service. You can also find software that will automate the submission process to various directories.

**NOTE** Want to try using one of the submission services? Check out Submit It! at http://www.submit-it.com/ or Easy-Submit at http://www.ohiocars.com/submit/main.html.

# Extending the Web with Hyperlinks

One of the great things about the Web is the ability to create hyperlinks from one page to related information on another page—or another Web site. Web surfers delight in following links from site to site in a stream-of-consciousness style of exploration and discovery. It's the very essence of the Web that Web pages aren't stand-alone entities, but are part of the interconnected fabric of the whole World Wide Web.

Given the nature of the Web, you can expect that many people will visit your Web site by way of links from other Web sites. But how do you establish such links? Obviously, you cannot create them yourself because the hyperlinks are part of another

Web site under the control of another Webmaster. You're Web site is just the target of the link. Therefore, in order to generate hyperlinks to your site, you'll need to spread the word about your site to other Webmasters. After all, you're probably not the only one with a Web site about your chosen topic, whether it's collecting pocket protectors or discussing the technological predictions in science fiction stories.

Start by searching for a Web site with a topic that relates to yours—one that will appeal to the same visitors you hope to attract to your site. Then locate the e-mail address of the Webmaster (you can usually find an e-mail address or an e-mail link at the bottom of the site's home page). Send a message to the Webmaster of that site, requesting a link from that site to yours. Most Webmasters are more than willing to provide links from their sites to other sites on related topics—especially if you are willing to reciprocate with a link from your site to theirs. After all, the crosslinks will benefit both parties by bringing in interested Web surfers. As long as your site is of good quality and doesn't promote a competing product or service, the chances are good that you'll get the requested link to your site.

Having links to your Web site from other sites not only provides Web surfers with additional ways to reach your site, it also makes your site more visible to Web search engines. Many of the Web spiders follow links from site to site and the more often your site shows up, the higher it will be rated in the database.

# Promoting Your Site Online

Getting listed with Web search engines and getting other Webmasters to create hyperlinks to your site aren't the only ways you can publicize your Web site. You can use a variety of other methods to get the word out to people who might be interested in your site. And, since the World Wide Web is an online medium, many of the best promotional opportunities are available online.

## Making News on the What's New Lists

There are several Web sites that exist to provide a forum for announcing new Web sites. A surprising number of people check these What's New sites regularly, just so they can be the first to find an interesting new site. So it's a good place to post a birth announcement for your new creation. Some What's New-type sites are very choosy about what sites they include in their lists; others accept all comers. To submit a listing to a What's New-type Web site, just follow the instructions posted on the site. Often, you can submit your site for consideration by simply filling out an onscreen form.

When the Web was relatively new, these What's New sites were very popular. Everyone was anxious to check out any new additions to the club. Now the sheer size of the Web and the volume of new sites that come online every day make it less appealing to try to keep track of all the newcomers. Still, a What's New announcement can be a nice start for your promotional efforts.

## Purchasing Advertising on Other Web Sites

If you've surfed the Web at all, you've seen those colorful banner ads at the top of search engine pages and some other Web sites. This is an example of pure commercial advertising, like billboards on the roadside. The advertiser paid a fee to place an ad on a popular Web site where it will be seen by many people. A Web ad has a distinct advantage over a billboard or an ad in a magazine because clicking the Web ad takes you to, guess what, another Web site. That's another way to get hyperlinks to a Web site—buy 'em.

Generally, purchasing ad space on a high-volume Web site is an option only for those with big budgets for promoting high-profile products and Web sites. Placing an ad on one of the major search engines or Netscape's site might cost many thousands of dollars. However, with millions of visitors seeing your ad each month, it might be worth the cost. On the other hand, a Web site with fewer visitors might charge a more modest fee for an ad. You'll need to weigh the costs and potential return of advertising on the Web just as you do when you advertise in other media.

To inquire about advertising your page or product on a site, simply send an e-mail requesting information to the Webmaster of a site where you'd like to place an ad. Some of the big sites even provide links to information for advertisers, right on the pages where your ad will appear.

## Making Announcements in Newsgroups and Mailing Lists

There are newsgroups and mailing lists on almost every topic imaginable. There's a very good chance that you can find several newsgroups and mailing lists that relate to your Web site, and you may be able to promote your site there. Posting an announcement on a newsgroup or mailing list can be an efficient way to get your message out to people with similar interests. This seems like such an easy and obvious way to publicize your site that you may be tempted to post an announcement on every newsgroup and list you can find. But be forewarned, if you are overzealous in your promotional efforts, they may backfire on you.

Direct mail is an accepted marketing method in the real world. Although few people claim to like finding a bunch of ads in their postal mail boxes, most people don't object strenuously. They just look at the ads for the cool stuff and toss the junk mail in the trash. The advertiser bears the cost of printing and mailing the ads, so most people don't object to getting direct mail, as long as they don't have to actually read the stuff.

This is not so on the Internet! Unsolicited ads are called spam and any message considered spam can earn the sender the ire of every recipient—definitely not the effect you had in mind! This adverse reaction to spam stems, in part, from the non-commercial roots of the Net. That attitude is changing as commercialism creeps on the Net and becomes an acknowledged fact of life. Another part of the objection to unsolicited ads is that Net users, or their companies, must pay for the privilege of downloading messages. As a result, they object to spending time and money to handle unwanted ads. That's not likely to change anytime soon.

This doesn't mean you shouldn't use newsgroups, mailing lists, and e-mail to promote your Web site. But you must be very discreet to avoid being labeled as a spammer. The accompanying sidebar explains some steps you can take to ensure that your promotional efforts are perceived as tasteful and informative rather than blatant advertising or spam. Basically, you must make sure your announcement is timely, relevant, to the point, and respectful of the particular culture of the newsgroup or mailing list where you are posting it.

## How to Avoid Spamming and Still Get Your Message Out

Spamming—sending unwanted e-mail messages to multiple recipients—is the electronic counterpart to junk mail. Indiscriminately sending duplicate messages to every newsgroup and mailing list you can find is considered very bad form. Your Web site will not be well received if your promotional efforts are perceived as spam. But this doesn't mean you shouldn't promote your site. You just need to use judgment and discretion in your electronic promotions.

- Be selective. Post announcements only on newsgroups and mailing lists where the members are likely to have a genuine interest in your site.
- Before posting an announcement of your Web site on a Usenet newsgroup or a mailing list, monitor the group to get a feel for its tone and culture. Then, tailor your announcement to the group.
- Check and respect the rules of the newsgroup or mailing list on which you plan to post an announcement. Some allow brief announcements, others explicitly forbid them. There is usually a FAQ file or charter available that spells out the rules for a given list or newsgroup.
- Be brief. Keep any announcements short and to the point and give your message an appropriate subject that identifies its purpose.
- Include your Web site URL in a short signature at the bottom of each e-mail message you send. This subtle form of promotion is generally accepted most places on the Net.
- Participate in relevant newsgroups and mailing lists. A little low-key self promotion by a regular group member is often accepted when the same behavior by a newcomer would be met with a barrage of flames—angry e-mail messages.
- Be helpful. An excellent way to get the word out is to answer a question or suggest a solution to a problem being discussed on a mailing list or newsgroup and refer the reader to your Web site for more information.

# Using E-Mail to Promote Your Site

There are a couple of ways you can use e-mail to promote your Web site. First of all, it's customary to place a small block of text at the end of e-mail messages to identify the sender. In addition to your name, this signature block (called a *sig*) usually contains your e-mail address and company or institution affiliations. This sig is the e-mail counterpart to your business card or the logo and address on your stationary. Adding your Web page URL to your e-mail sig is a subtle but effective way to get let anyone with whom you correspond know you have a Web site.

You can also create an e-mail mailing list of Net contacts that are interested in your Web site. (This is a different kind of mailing list than the discussion groups and news updates that are handled by automated list-management programs called mailbots.) Netscape Communicator (and many other e-mail programs) provides a way to define groups of e-mail addresses so that you can send a message to all the addresses in the group.

If you put your URL in an e-mail message, recipients reading the message in the e-mail component of Netscape Communicator (or with some other popular e-mail programs) will be able to click the URL in the e-mail message to launch their Web browser and load your page. This feature allows you to send out announcements to interested parties when you launch or update your page. If you're careful to include only those people who have expressed an interest in you, your company or topic, or your Web site, you can be very forthright in your announcement without the risk of being labeled as a spammer.

## Setting Up a Mailing List

One interesting way to build traffic for your Web site is to sponsor an e-mail mailing list. Mailing lists can take two forms: a distribution list for announcements, or an e-mail discussion group on a particular topic. Either way, subscribers to your mailing list will all get copies of any messages distributed to the list. A distribution list-style mailing lists is a one-way affair with announcements going out from the mailing list owner (you) to the list of subscribers. A discussion group list, on the other hand, provides a forum for lively discussions among list subscribers by allowing anyone on the list to send messages (and replies to messages) to a special e-mail address where specialized software will automatically forward the messages to all members of the list.

### Setting Up a Mailing List (continued)

One good way to learn more about setting up a mailing list is to check out the article, *How to Set Up and Run Your Own Internet Mailing List*. You can find it in the how-to section on the popular CNET site (`http://www.cnet.com`).

Setting up a mailing list takes a fair amount of work and requires an ongoing commitment to administer the list as well. Consequently, you shouldn't set up a mailing list solely to promote your Web site. But, if you decide that running a mailing list is something you want to do, it will provide ample opportunities to discreetly direct list subscribers to your Web site and vice versa. A mailing list and a Web site can be very complimentary.

# Using Traditional Media to Support Your Online Efforts

Of course, all your promotional efforts for your Web site don't have to be confined to the Internet. You can use any and all the traditional, promotional media at your disposal as well. For example, you can send out press releases about your new Web site, mail an announcement to your regular customers, add a page to your catalog telling shoppers they can find you on the Web, or use any other methods that make sense for your business.

A good way to promote your Web site is to leverage your other promotional efforts. For instance, you can add your Web site's URL to your business card, your stationery, or in ads, flyers, and brochures. Basically, you can add your Web site address to almost any communication between you and your clients, prospects, and colleagues.

Not too long ago, if a URL appeared on a business card or letterhead, it was a novelty and many viewers might not have even recognized the strange looking string of characters punctuated with periods. Initially, URLs were just status symbols—a way of cashing in on the glamour of the growing Internet. No one really expected a visit to a Web site as a result of someone finding the site's URL on a business card or in an ad.

Now, Web site addresses are almost universally recognized and are becoming commonplace on many business (and some personal) communications. In addition to business cards, stationary, brochures, and other printed pieces, URLs are showing up regularly in magazine ads and on TV commercials. I've even heard announcements for Web site addresses while waiting on hold on a telephone call.

> **TIP**
>
> In some areas, you can get your Web address listed in the telephone book. It costs about the same as getting an additional listing. Also, if you have a display ad in the Yellow Pages, you'll probably want to include your Web address there as well.

Essentially, you can and should treat your Web site URL as part of your extended address—much like your telephone and fax numbers. Any place where you list contact information is a potential place to promote your Web site as well. Web users can, and often do, make note of these URLs so that they can follow up with a visit to the Web sites of companies that interest them.

# Part 5

# Appendices

# Appendix A

# COMPOSER'S OTHER ROLE IN THE COMMUNICATOR SUITE

Composer's primary reason for existence is to enable you to create and publish your own Web pages. Composer is the complement to Navigator that allows you to become a contributor to the World Wide Web as well as a viewer, letting you create the pages that you and others view with Navigator and other Web browsers.

Composer provides an easy-to-use WYSIWYG editing environment in which you can create Web pages in much the same way you create printed documents in a word processor. Behind its WYSIWYG façade, Composer is an HTML editor designed to create and edit documents formatted with HTML, the standard language of the World Wide Web. The program shields you from the gritty details of creating an HTML source document for the page you are working on. After you create a Web page in Composer, you can use the one-button publishing feature to load the finished HTML document onto a Web server, where it can be accessed by World Wide Web surfers.

Although Composer's obvious application is to create and publish Web pages for use on the Internet's World Wide Web, the program is equally suited to creating pages for use on a corporate intranet, in a stand-alone presentation, or in an interactive terminal. You can use Composer to create pages for any purpose or situation where HTML documents are viewed by a browser.

Composer is also used in other parts of the Communicator suite: The message composition windows in Messenger and Collabra are really thinly disguised versions of the Composer editing window.

## Using Composer to Create Messages

Netscape Messenger, the e-mail component of Netscape Communicator, supports e-mail messages in HTML as well as in plain text. Collabra, Communicator's newsgroup and collaboration component, provides the same HTML capabilities for messages you post on newsgroups and collaboration workgroups; this means your e-mail and newsgroup messages can be as richly formatted as a Web page. The days of drab text-only e-mail are history. Now your messages can contain text formatting (fonts, sizes, colors, and formatting attributes such as italic and boldface), images, hyperlinks, and tables, just like Web pages. Messenger and Collabra can handle both incoming and outgoing messages with rich HTML formatting; the programs can even display your messages in their own viewing windows with all the formatting, images, and hyperlinks intact—in other words, there's no need to view HTML-formatted messages in an external viewer.

For creating outgoing e-mail messages, Messenger and Collabra rely on a version of Composer. When you choose File ➤ New ➤ Message in either Messenger or Collabra, the Composition window shown in Figure A.1 will open. A quick examination of the Composition window reveals the similarities to the Composer editing window shown in Figure A.2. (If your Composition window doesn't have these formatting buttons, choose View ➤ Show Formatting Toolbar.)

Of course, the two windows are not exactly the same. The Composition window must include message-specific features, such as the address and subject lines and buttons for message-handling tasks (quoting other messages, attaching files, and sending the message). The formatting toolbars in both windows are nearly identical. As a Composer user, you'll recognize the drop-down lists for paragraph styles, fonts, text sizes, and text colors. Then come the familiar buttons for bold, italics, underline, remove all styles, bulleted lists, numbered lists, increase indent, decrease indent, and the drop-down button for paragraph alignment. All these buttons and lists perform exactly the same function they do in the regular Composer window. You'll find many of the menu commands in the Composition window equally familiar.

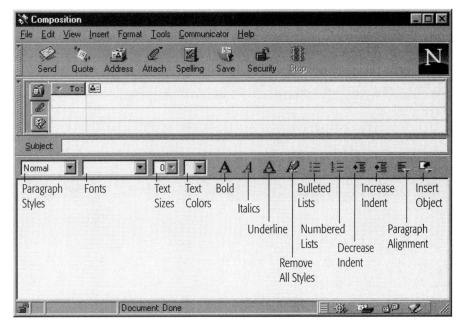

**FIGURE A.1:** The Composition window gives you the tools you need to add HTML formatting to your e-mail messages.

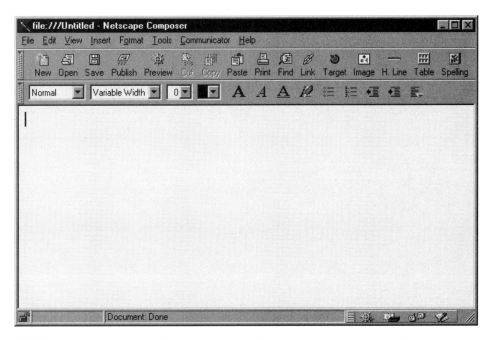

**FIGURE A.2:** Many of the buttons and commands in the Composition window are borrowed from the Composer window.

The only stranger on the Composition window's formatting toolbar is the Insert Object button on the right. Clicking the Insert Object button causes a drop-down list of buttons to appear. Again, the buttons and their functions will be familiar to a Composer user. The buttons enable you to insert into your message hyperlinks, link targets, images, horizontal lines, and tables.

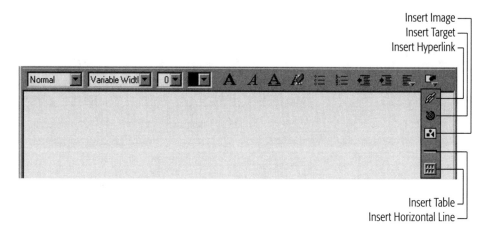

Insert Image

Insert Target

Insert Hyperlink

Insert Table

Insert Horizontal Line

# Appendix B

# HTML
# DICTIONARY

In this appendix, you'll find a listing of the HTML tags you're likely to encounter in the HTML source code for your Web pages. You'll find that each tag is listed with a brief description of the effect it has on your page. Where applicable, I've also included cross references to the Composer feature or command that you use to generate or edit the tag.

The purpose of this HTML dictionary is to help you decipher the HTML code you see when you view the HTML source for a page you are creating or editing in Composer. It isn't meant to be a programmer's reference for generating HTML code manually; and it certainly isn't a comprehensive listing of the available HTML codes.

If you're intent on hand-coding HTML, you'll need to consult other references. There are a number of good Sybex books on the subject, such as *Mastering HTML* by Eric Ray and *HTML: No Experience Required* by Stephen Mack and Janan Platt (both are due out in Fall 1997). You can also check out these online resources: `http://www.w3.org/hypertext/WWW/MarkUp/MarkUp.html` and `http://www.sandia.gov/sci_compute/html_ref.html`.

# Anatomy of an HTML Tag

HTML tags are the coded instructions that tell the viewer's Web browser how to display your page. The tags are enclosed in angle brackets (less than and greater than symbols <...>) to distinguish them from the normal text of your Web page.

```
<TITLE>This is your page title</TITLE>
```

HTML tags normally come in pairs. An opening tag—such as <TITLE>—preceeds the text to which it will apply. A closing tag—such as </TITLE>—follows the affected text and serves as a sort of off switch marking the end of the effect. The closing tag is easy to recognize; it's the tag name with a slash (/) in front of it. Some HTML tags stand alone, without the need for a closing tag.

Some HTML tags include one or more parameters or commands in addition to the tag name, all appearing within the angle brackets of the opening tag. For example, a horizontal rule tag—<HR>—might include parameters like this:

```
<HR WIDTH=250 ALIGN=CENTER>
```

to define the width of the rule as 250 pixels and specify that it be centered in the browser window. HTML tag parameters often include file names for image files and hyperlink targets.

HTML tags are not case sensitive. It makes no difference whether the tag itself appears as <TITLE> or <title>. However, on some computer systems, filenames are case sensitive, so be sure that the capitalization of any file names you enter or edit, match the way those files appear on the computer systems where they reside.

Line breaks and extra spaces within an HTML tag are ignored. As a result, you may encounter HTML source code with long tags containing many parameters broken into several lines. This changes nothing; everything between the angle brackets is still part of the same tag and the Web browser will execute the instruction the same whether the tag appears on one line or several. Sometimes the strange line breaks happen as a result of word wrapping in the viewing window. Sometimes programmers add line breaks to long tags deliberately, to make the tags easier for mere mortals to read.

# Page Tags

### &lt;HTML&gt;...&lt;/HTML&gt;
Defines the beginning and end of the HTML document. Normally, the &lt;HTML&gt; tag is the very first thing at the top of the file, and the &lt;/HTML&gt; tag is the very last thing at the bottom. Composer adds these tags automatically when you create a new page.

### &lt;HEAD&gt;...&lt;/HEAD&gt;
Defines the beginning and end of the header area of the HTML document. It always appears at the top of the file, above the information for the page itself. The header is where some descriptive information about your page, such as the page title, is stored. Composer adds these tags automatically when you create a new page.

### &lt;META NAME="Author" CONTENT="name"&gt;
### &lt;META NAME="GENERATOR" CONTENT="Mozilla/4.0–(Win95; I) [Netscape]"&gt;
### &lt;META NAME="KeyWords" CONTENT="keyword1,keyword2"&gt;
### &lt;META NAME="Description" CONTENT="description"&gt;
These tags appear in the header area of the HTML document and record reference information about your Web page, such as who created it and the software you used. The KeyWords and Description meta tags are used by some search engines to index your Web page in their databases. Composer adds these tags automatically using information from the General tab of the Page Properties dialog box.

### &lt;TITLE&gt;...&lt;/TITLE&gt;
The text between the &lt;TITLE&gt; and &lt;/TITLE&gt; tags is the title of your Web page. This is the title that appears in the title bar of the Web browser window when your page is being viewed. Composer adds these tags to the header area of your page automatically. You're prompted to enter the title text when you save your page the first time. You can edit the title on the General tab of the Page Properties dialog box.

### &lt;BODY&gt;...&lt;/BODY&gt;
Marks the beginning and end of the body of the Web page. The &lt;BODY&gt; tag always appears just after the &lt;/HEAD&gt; tag near the top of the HTML file. Then all the text and

HTML tags that make up your Web page itself fit between the <BODY> tag and the </BODY> tag, which appears just ahead of the </HTML> tag at the bottom of the file.

The <BODY> tag can include several parameters that define the appearance of the Web page. For example, in this tag:

```
<BODY BACKGROUND="background.gif" TEXT="#0000FF"
BGCOLOR="#0000FF" LINK="#00000" VLINK="#FF0000" ALINK="#FF6666">
```

the BACKGROUND= parameter defines a background image (background.gif) for the page. The TEXT= parameter defines the default text color. The BGCOLOR= parameter defines the page's background color. And the LINK=, VLINK=, and ALINK= parameters define the colors for regular hyperlinks, visited links, and active links.

**NOTE**   Most colors are recorded in HTML tags with six-digit, hexadecimal numbers (actually three pairs of hexadecimal numbers) that define the red, green, and blue components of the color. (A few common colors, such as red, black, and white, are predefined and referenced by name.) The numbers are hard to decipher, but back in Composer, you'll be able to select colors from an onscreen color palette.

# Paragraph Styles and Tags

### <P>

Traditionally, this tag defines the beginning of a paragraph. Web browsers will automatically insert a blank line preceding a paragraph marked with this tag. Composer doesn't normally use the <P> tag every time you press the Enter key, but it does show up sometimes to set off images and other paragraphs. The <P> tag often includes an alignment parameter such as ALIGN=RIGHT. The </P> closing tag is optional and it's seldom used.

### <BR>

Defines a line break in a text paragraph without generating a blank line between paragraphs as with the <P> tag. This is the tag Composer normally inserts into the

HTML source for your page when you press Enter in the editing window. There is no companion, closing tag to go with the <BR> tag.

### <NOBR>...</NOBR>

Marks a block of text that must appear on one line and not be broken by the Web browser when wrapping text to fit within the width of the browser window. To add this tag to text in Composer, select the text and then choose Format ➤ Style ➤ Nonbreaking.

### <BLOCKQUOTE>...</BLOCKQUOTE>

Marks a paragraph of text to be indented from both the left and right margins—the traditional formatting for a large block of quoted text. To apply this paragraph style to text in Composer, select the paragraph and then choose Format ➤ Paragraph ➤ Block Quote.

### <CENTER>...</CENTER>

Centers the text paragraph (or object) horizontally in the browser window. To Use this tag in Composer, select the paragraph, image, or object, and then choose Format ➤ Align ➤ Center.

### <H1>...</H1>
### <H2>...</H2>
### <H3>...</H3>
### <H4>...</H4>
### <H5>...</H5>
### <H6>...</H6>

These are the heading paragraph styles. <H1> is the largest, most prominent heading and <H6> is the least prominent. To apply heading styles to paragraphs in Composer, go to the formatting toolbar and select a heading from the paragraph style drop-down list or choose Format ➤ Heading and choose the heading number.

### <PRE>...</PRE>

This is the Preformatted paragraph style. The browser will display paragraphs formatted with this style in a monospaced font and will display the text with multiple spaces exactly as typed in the source code. To apply the <PRE> tag to a paragraph in Composer, select the paragraph of text and then go to the toolbar and select Preformatted from the paragraph styles drop-down list or choose Format ➤ Paragraph ➤ Formatted.

**<ADDRESS>...</ADDRESS>**

The address paragraph style is normally displayed as italic text in a slightly smaller size that the normal body text. To apply the <ADDRESS> tag to a paragraph in Composer, select the paragraph of text and then go to the toolbar and select Address from the paragraph style drop-down list or choose Format ➤ Paragraph ➤ Address.

# Character Formatting

**<FONT SIZE=1>...</FONT>**
**<FONT POINT SIZE=22>...</FONT>**

Specifies the size of the text between the tags. The tag uses the <FONT SIZE=n> format when you select one of the standard relative sizes. If you select a specific point size for the text, the tag appears in the form <FONT POINT SIZE=n>. To set the size of text in Composer, select the text you want to resize and then go to the formatting toolbar and select a size from the text size drop-down list or choose Format ➤ Size and choose the text size.

**<FONT COLOR="#FF0000">...</FONT>**

Specifies the color of the text between the tags. To apply a color to text in Composer, select the text and then go to the formatting toolbar, click the color drop-down list, and select a color from the color palette that appears. You can also open the color palette by choosing Format ➤ Color.

**<FONT FACE="Fontname, Alternate Font">...</FONT>**

Specifies the font the browser should use to display the text between the tags. The FACE="fontname" parameter instructs the browser to use the font name enclosed in quotes to display the text. The face command can accept more than one font name, each separated by commas (as in the example above). The browser will display the text using the first font in the list that is available on the user's system. This lets you (or Composer) specify alternate fonts to use if the first choice isn't available. For instance, if you select the Arial font, Composer automatically lists Helvetica as an alternate font. Helvetica is roughly equivalent to Arial and it's more commonly available on Macintosh systems. If the browser finds none of the listed fonts, it will display the text in the default font.

To specify a font for text in Composer, select the text and then go to the formatting toolbar and select a font from the Fonts drop-down list or choose Format ➤ Font and choose a font from the menu. If you select a common font, Composer will automatically supply a list of alternates. If you select an uncommon font, only the one you selected will appear in the <FONT FACE="fontname"> tag. If you want to define alternate font selections, you'll need to edit the HTML source manually.

### <B>...<B>

Adds the **Boldface** attribute to the text enclosed by the tags. To add the bold attribute to text in Composer, select the text and then go to the formatting toolbar and click the Bold button or choose Format ➤ Style ➤ Bold.

### <I>...</I>

Adds the *Italic* attribute to the text enclosed by the tags. To add the italic attribute to text in Composer, select the text and then go to the formatting toolbar and click the Italic button or choose Format ➤ Style ➤ Italic.

### <U>...</U>

Adds the Underline attribute to the text enclosed by the tags. To add the underline attribute to text in Composer, select the text and then go to the formatting toolbar and click the Underline button or choose Format ➤ Style ➤ Underline.

### <TT>...</TT>

Marks the text enclosed in the tags to be displayed in a monospaced font simulating an old-style typewriter. To apply the typewriter style to text in Composer, select the text you want to format, then go to the formatting toolbar and select Fixed Font from the Font drop-down  list or choose Format ➤ Font ➤ Fixed Font.

### <STRIKE>...</STRIKE>

Applies the ~~strikethrough~~ attribute to the text enclosed by the tags. To apply the strikethrough attribute to text in Composer, select the text and choose Format ➤ Style ➤ Strikethrough.

### <SUP>...</SUP>

Applies the superscript attribute to the text enclosed by the tags. To apply superscript to text in Composer, select the text and then choose Format ➤ Style ➤ Superscript.

### <SUB>...</SUB>

Applies the subscript attribute to the text enclosed by the tags. To apply subscript to text in Composer, select the text and then choose Format ➤ Style ➤ Subscript.

### <BLINK>...</BLINK>

The infamous <BLINK> attribute causes the text enclosed by the tags to blink off and on. To apply the blink attribute to text in Composer (if you insist), select the text and choose Format ➤ Style ➤ Blinking.

### <BIG>...</BIG>

Makes the text between the tags larger than normal text. This is a logical attribute that will be interpreted by the viewer's browser to determine how much larger the text will be. This tag isn't used by Composer.

### <SMALL>...</SMALL>

Makes the text between the tags smaller than normal text. This is a logical attribute that will be interpreted by the viewer's browser to determine how much smaller the text will be. This tag isn't used by Composer.

### <EM>... </EM>

Gives the text between the tags emphasis compared to normal text. This is a logical attribute that will be interpreted by the viewer's browser to determine how to emphasize the text—usually, the text is italicized. This tag isn't used by Composer.

### <STRONG>...</STRONG>

Gives the text between the tags strong emphasis compared to normal text. This is a logical attribute that will be interpreted by the viewer's browser to determine how to emphasize the text—usually, the text is boldfaced. This tag isn't used by Composer.

# List Tags

### <UL>...</UL>

Defines the beginning and end of a unordered list, better known as a bulleted list. The list items appear between these two tags and are marked with the <LI> tag. To designate text as a bulleted list in Composer, select the text and choose Format ➤ List ➤ Bulleted.

By default, Navigator uses solid discs as bullets for each item in a bulleted list. See the *Changing Bullet Shapes* section in Chapter 5 for instructions on how to change bullet shapes in Composer. If you select an optional bullet style, Composer will embed a `type` command in your opening `<ul>` tag, like this:

<ul type=square>

All bullets in your list will be neat, solid squares.

The following commands specify the bullet styles for bulleted lists:

| The Command | Will Produce |
|---|---|
| type=disk | Solid Circle |
| type=circle | Open Circle |
| type=square | Solid Square |

## <OL>...</OL>

Defines the beginning and end of an ordered list—better known as a numbered list. The list items appear between these two tags and are marked with the `<LI>` tag. To designate text as a numbered list in Composer, select the text and choose Format ➤ List ➤ Numbered.

The default numbering is Arabic numerals starting with 1. See the *Changing the Numbering Style* section in Chapter 5 for instructions on how to change bullet shapes in Composer. If you choose another numbering scheme, Composer embeds a command in the first `<ol>` tag. For example, if the fruit list looks like this,

```
<ol TYPE=I>
<li>Apple</li>
<li>Orange</li>
<li>Cherry</li>
</ol>
```

Netscape will display it with roman numerals, like this:

      I.    Apple

     II.    Orange

    III.    Cherry

The following commands specify the type of numbering in a numbered list:

| The Command | Will Produce |
| --- | --- |
| type=A | Uppercase letters, starting with A |
| type=a | Lowercase letters, starting with a |
| type=I | Uppercase roman numerals, starting with I |
| type=i | Lowercase roman numerals, starting with i |
| type=1 | Arabic numerals, starting with 1 |

**NOTE** Not all Web browsers "understand" the type options for numbers as Netscape does. If you create a page using these options and someone loads the page using a Web browser that doesn't allow for this, he or she will see the items listed using arabic numerals.

### \<LI>...\</LI>

Defines a list item in a bulleted or numbered list. The text between the tags will appear as one item in the list. The list items should appear between \<UL>...\</UL> or \<OL>...\</OL> tags. (See the example in the \<OL> definition above.) To designate list items in Composer, select the text for one item, then go to the formatting toolbar and select List Item from the paragraph style drop-down list. Adding new paragraphs within a bulleted or numbered list causes Composer to automatically tag those paragraphs as list items. (The closing \</LI> tag is optional.)

### \<DL>...\</DL>

Marks the beginning and end of a description list (also called a definition list or glossary). These tags enclose list items formatted with the \<DT> and \<DD> tags to appear as titles (flush left) and descriptions. To create a description list in Composer, select the text for the list of items and choose Format ➢ List ➢ Description. Then format the list items as either description titles and description text as needed. (See the \<DD> and \<DT> tags below.)

Here is a sample of coding for a description list:

```
<dl>
<dt>Apple
```

```
<dd>A round fruit, often red in color when ripe but sometimes
green or yellow
<dt>Orange
<dd>A round, orange fruit
<dt>Cherry
<dd>A small, round, red fruit
</dl>
```

The result of this sample coding will look like this:

Apple
  A round fruit, often red in color when ripe but sometimes green or yellow
Orange
  A round, orange fruit
Cherry
  A small, round, red fruit

### <DT>

Marks the beginning of a description title in a description list. This tag should appear between <DL> and </DL> tags. To designate a paragraph as a description title in Composer, click the paragraph, then go to the formatting toolbar and select Desc. Title from the paragraph styles drop-down list.

### <DD>

Marks the beginning of a description text (or definition) in a description list. This tag should appear between <DL> and </DL> tags. To designate a paragraph as description text in Composer, click the paragraph, then go to the formatting toolbar and select Desc. Text from the paragraph styles drop-down list.

### <MENU>...</MENU>

Marks the beginning and end of a menu list. Composer doesn't properly display this kind of list, but the program allows you to create one anyway. To do so, select the text for the list in the Composer window and then choose Format ➤ List ➤ Menu.

### <DIR>...</DIR>

Marks the beginning and end of a directory list (like a DOS directory listing). Composer doesn't properly display this kind of list, but the program allows you to create one anyway. To do so, select the text for the list in the Composer window and then choose Format ➤ List ➤ Directory.

# Image Tags

### <IMG SRC="image.gif">

Defines an inline image. This is the HTML tag Composer inserts into the source code for your page when you add an image to your Web page. To add an image to the page in Composer, go to the toolbar and click the Insert Image button or choose Insert ➤ Image from the and then fill in the information and options in the Image Properties dialog box. (See Chapter 6 for more information on how to work with images in Composer.)

The <IMG SRC> tag always includes the filename (or the full URL) of the image file that the browser should display. In addition, the tag can include several optional parameters. For example:

```
<IMG SRC="http://www.sybex.com/sybexlogo.gif" WIDTH="75"
HEIGHT="65" ALIGN=LEFT ALT="View this logo">
```

will cause the image stored in the file `sybexlogo.gif` on the `www.sybex.com` machine to be displayed as part of the Web document. The browser will resize the image to be 75 pixels wide by 65 pixels high. The image will be aligned with the left margin and the text *View this logo* will appear in place of the image while the image is loading or if the viewer has image loading disabled.

# Links Tags

### <a name="anchor_name">... </a>

Defines a named target location in a page to serve as the target for a hyperlink. The opening and closing tags can enclose some text or other page content, or the closing tag can immediately follow the opening tag. To create a target in Composer, click at the location where you want the target and choose Insert ➤ Target or go to the toolbar and click the Insert Target button. Enter a name for the target in the Target Properties dialog box and click OK. Composer displays a target icon to show the location of the target. The target will be invisible when you view the page in a Web browser.

**\<a href="URL">...\</a>**
**\<a href="#anchor_name">....\</a>**
**\<a href="URL#anchor_name">...\</a>**

This tag defines a hyperlink. The target of the hyperlink is specified as the parameter in the `<a href=>` tag. The target can be another Web page, a named target on the current page or another page, or any other Web resource referenced by a URL. The text enclosed between the opening and closing tags will receive the distinctive formatting of a hyperlink in the browser window. When a viewer clicks the hyperlink text, the browser will load and display the target of the link.

Here's an example of how a hyperlink works in HTML: If you created a hyperlink from the word Internet, the HTML code would look like this:

```
<a href="http://www.sybex.com/internet.html">Internet</a>
```

Then, when the document is viewed with any Web browser, such as Netscape, the word *Internet* will appear as a link. When a user clicks it, the file `internet.html` will automatically be transferred from the HTTP server at the `www.sybex.com` host computer.

A hyperlink to named target would look like this:

```
<a href="#bullseye">On target</a>
```

To create a hyperlink in Composer, select the text that will be the anchor for the link and choose Insert ➤ Link or go to the toolbar and click the Insert Link button. In the Character Properties dialog box, specify the link target on the Link tab and click OK. See Chapter 7, *Getting Linked Up*, for more details on working with hyperlinks in Composer.

**\<A HREF="URL"> \<IMG SRC="filename" border=0> \</A>**

Defines a hyperlink from an image. The HTML code for a linked image gets a little long and involved. But it's really not so complicated. It's just a `<a href=>` tag to define the link that has an `<img src=>` tag in place of the text of a typical text hyperlink. For example, this HTML code links an image called `tocatalog.gif` to a Web page named `catalog.html`.

```
<a href="http://www.sybex.com/catalog.html"><img
src="http://www.sybex.com/tocatalog.gif"></img></a>
```

To create a hyperlink from an image in Composer, select the image that will be the anchor for the link and choose Insert ➤ Link or go to the toolbar and click the Insert Link button. In the Image Properties dialog box, specify the link target on the Link tab and click OK. See Chapter 7, *Getting Linked Up*, for more details on working with hyperlinks in Composer.

# Table Tags

### <TABLE BORDER=1 WIDTH=100%>...</TABLE>

Designates the beginning and end of a table. Enclosed between the <TABLE> and </TABLE> tags, you'll find the tags <TR>, <TH>, and <TD> to define individual table rows and cells, plus all the text and other elements contained in those cells Often, there are large quantities of text and other tags between the <TABLE> and </TABLE> tags. Composer adds these tags (and others) to the HTML source for your page when you add a table to the Web page. You can adjust the BORDER=, WIDTH=, and other parameters for the <TABLE> tag by adjusting settings in Composer's Table Properties dialog box. See Chapter 8, *Working with Tables*, for information about working with tables in Composer.

### <TR>...</TR>

Defines the beginning and end of a table row. These tags should fall between the <TABLE> and </TABLE> tags that define the beginning and end of the whole table. The <TR> and </TR> tags, in turn, enclose one or more pairs of <TH> and <TD> tags to define individual cells within the row. Composer automatically generates these tags as needed when you create and edit a table. The <TR> tag can also include parameters such as ALIGN= and VALIGN= which you adjust in Composer by changing the settings on the Row tab of the Table Properties dialog box.

### <TH>...</TH>

Defines a table header cell in a table. The text or other elements between these tags will appear in a table cell, formatted as a header (centered in the cell and formatted in boldface). This pair of tags should appear between <TR> and </TR> tags defining a table row, which should, in turn, appear between <TABLE> and </TABLE> tags defining the table. Composer automatically generates these tags as needed when you create and edit a table. Checking the Header Style checkbox on the Cell tab of the Table Properties dialog box is what distinguishes the <TH> tag from the standard <TD> tag that defines regular table cells. The <TH> tag can also include parameters such as

HEIGHT= and WIDTH= which you adjust in Composer by changing the settings on the Cell tab of the Table Properties dialog box.

### <TD>...</TD>

Defines a regular cell in a table. The text or other elements between these tags will appear in a table cell. This pair of tags should appear between <TR> and </TR> tags defining a table row, which should, in turn, appear between <TABLE> and </TABLE> tags defining the table. Composer automatically generates these tags as needed when you create and edit a table. The <TD> tag can also include parameters such as HEIGHT= and WIDTH= which you adjust in Composer by changing the settings on the Cell tab of the Table Properties dialog box.

### A Simple Table Example

| HTML Code | What it does |
|---|---|
| <TABLE> | (start of table) |
| <TR> | (beginning of first table row) |
| <TH>Program</TH> | (the first cell, a header) |
| <TH>Information</TH> | (the next cell, another header) |
| </TR> | (end of the first row) |
| <TR> | (beginning of the next row) |
| <TD>Netscape Navigator</TD> | (the first cell of the row) |
| <TD>The leading Web browser!</TD> | (the next cell) |
| </TR> | (end of table row) |
| </TABLE> | (end of table) |

And this is how the table will look:

| Program | Information |
|---|---|
| Netscape Navigator | The leading Web browser! |

# Forms

### <FORM ACTION="URL" METHOD=POST>...</FORM>

Defines the beginning and end of a form on a Web page. Between these two tags, there will be text and tags to define form elements and regular Web page elements such as normal text and images. The parameters in the <FORM> tag define how the data gathered by the form will be handled. The ACTION= parameter defines the location of the program that will process the form and the METHOD= parameter specifies the method used to exchange data between the browser and the forms processor.

Composer doesn't support forms, so you can't create or edit forms in Composer's WYSIWYG editing window. You may encounter forms tags in HTML source for Web pages created with other programs. If you want to create forms of your own, you must do it by manually editing the HTML source for your page with an external HTML editor.

### <INPUT TYPE="type" NAME="fieldname" VALUE="value" SIZE="n">

This tag defines an input field where a viewer can enter or select information. The parameters in the <INPUT> tag define kind of input field, its size, and assign it a name and default value.

The TYPE= parameter defines the kind of input field. Valid options for the TYPE= parameter are as follows:

- text—a text box that the viewer can type into
- password—another text box, but this one hides the characters that are entered
- checkbox—like the checkboxes in dialog boxes
- radio—radio buttons like those in dialog boxes allow the viewer to select only one of a series of choices
- submit—defines a button that the viewer can click to send the data from the form for processing
- reset—defines a button that the viewer can click to reset all the form fields to their default values

The NAME= parameter defines a name (such as *address, city*, or *state*) for the form field that will be associated with the data that is submitted from that field. This name is not displayed on Web page. The VALUE= parameter establishes a default value for the input field. The SIZE= parameter establishes the size of the input field.

### <SELECT NAME="fieldname" SIZE="n" MULTIPLE>...</SELECT>

This tag defines a list box of options from which the viewer can choose. These tags define the beginning and end of the list. Between the <SELECT> and </SELECT> tags a series of <OPTION> tags define each of the items in the list—much like the list items in a bulleted list.

The NAME= parameter defines a name for the form field that will be associated with the data that is submitted from that field. This name is not displayed on the Web page. The SIZE= parameter establishes the number of options that will be available. The

MULTIPLE parameter allows the viewer to select multiple options from the list instead of only one.

**<OPTION>**

This tag marks the beginning of an option item in a selection list field. The tag and its associated text must appear between the <SELECT> and </SELECT> tags. A SELECTED parameter added to an <OPTION> tag makes that option the default selection in the list.

**<TEXTAREA NAME="name" ROWS="n" COLS="n">...</TEXTAREA>**

This pair of tags defines a rectangular text entry box where the viewer can type in a multi-line message, such as a comment or description. Unlike the TEXT type of <INPUT> field, the <TEXTAREA> field can be large enough for several lines of text. Any text enclosed between the <TEXTAREA> and </TEXTAREA> tags will appear in the field as default text.

As with the other form fields, the NAME= parameter defines a name for the field that will be associated with the data that is submitted from that field. This name is not displayed on Web page. The ROWS= and COLS= parameters specify the size of the text area field in rows (lines of text) and columns (number of characters wide).

# Frames Tags

**<FRAMESET COLS="*,0">**
**<FRAMESET ROWS="*,70">**
**<FRAME SRC="test2.html" NAME="Main">**
**<FRAME SRC="frame.html" MARGINHEIGHT="1" NORESIZE>**
**</FRAMESET>**
**</FRAMESET>**

These are some of the HTML tags that define frames on a Web page. Composer doesn't support frames so you won't be able to create or edit frames with the program. And it's not practical to provide, in the limited space of this listing, all the information you'd need to work with frames by manually editing HTML source. I've included a few examples of frames tags here so you will be able to recognize them if you encounter frames tags in the HTML source for a Web page created by another program.

# Java Tags

```
<APPLET CODEBASE="/LED/Led" CODE="LED.class" WIDTH=500
HEIGHT=48 ALIGN=CENTER>
  <PARAM NAME="script" VALUE="/LED/scripts/Demo.led">
  <PARAM NAME="border" VALUE="2">
  <PARAM NAME="bordercolor" VALUE="100,130,130">
  <PARAM NAME="spacewidth" VALUE="3">
  <PARAM NAME="wth" VALUE="122">
  <PARAM NAME="font" VALUE="/LED/fonts/default.font">
  <PARAM NAME="ledsize" VALUE="3">
</APPLET>
```

This is an example of the HTML code for embedding a Java applet in a Web page. The <APPLET> and </APPLET> tags mark the beginning and end of the applet. The parameters in the <APPLET> tag tell the browser where to find the program code for the applet and how much space the applet will need on the Web page. The various <PARAM NAME=> tags define adjustable settings to control actions in the applet.

Composer doesn't support Java applets, but you may run across Java applets in Web pages you get from other sources. Also, you can add Java applets to your own Web pages by manually editing the HTML source using an external HTML editor. If you do, be sure you enter the code for the applet exactly as you are instructed by the Java programmer that supplied the applet.

```
<SCRIPT LANGUAGE="JavaScript">
<!-- Hide
document.write("Hi - I'm a JavaScript script!");}
// -->
</SCRIPT>
```

This is an example of the HTML code for embedding a JavaScript programming script in a Web page. The <SCRIPT LANGUAGE=> and </SCRIPT> tags mark the beginning and end of the script. Between those tags is an HTML comment tag containing the script commands. (The script is contained in a comment to prevent it from being displayed on the Web page.)

Like Java applets, Composer doesn't support JavaScript scripts, but you may run across scripts in Web pages you get from other sources, so you should be able to recognize them in the HTML source for a page. Also, you might want to add a JavaScript

script to your own Web pages at some point. You can do so by manually editing the HTML source using an external HTML editor. If you do, be sure you enter the script commands exactly as you are instructed by the JavaScript programmer that supplied the script.

# Miscellaneous Tags

### \<HR SIZE=n WIDTH=n ALIGN=LEFT\>

This is the HTML tag for a horizontal rule. It's not necessary to indicate the end of the rule with a closing tag. Used alone, the \<HR\> tag inserts a shaded, embossed line that crosses your Web page (no matter what size the page appears to be on screen) from the left margin to the right. To add a horizontal rule to your page in Composer, position the insertion point where you want the rule and choose Insert ➤ Horizontal Line or go to the toolbar and click the Insert Horiz. Line button.

The SIZE= parameter specifies the thickness of the rule in pixels. The WIDTH= parameter defines the length of the rule in pixels or as a percent of the width of the browser window. The ALIGN= parameter specifies alignment of the rule with the left or right margin or centered on the page. Changing the settings in the Horizontal Rule Properties dialog box in Composer adds corresponding commands to the \<hr\> tag in the HTML code for your page. See the *Inserting Horizontal Lines* section in Chapter 5 for the details.

### \<!-- This is a comment --\>

This tag allows you to embed comments and information in the HTML source for your Web page that will not appear on the page when it is viewed in a Web browser. Note the format of the tag: The \<!-- and --\> mark the beginning and end of the tag; the text in the middle can be anything you want.

Composer doesn't provide a built-in button or command specifically designed for entering comments, but you can easily enter and edit comments using the HTML Tag dialog box.

### \<EMBED SRC="filename"\>

This tag enables you to embed objects in your Web page. It's typically used to embed sounds and video clips in the page, but you can use it to embed all sorts of things such as spreadsheets and word processing documents. Embedding a sound or other object is similar to creating a link to the file, except that the browser automatically downloads the embedded file instead of waiting for the viewer to click the hyperlink. Also, the control panel for playing the sound or video is incorporated into the Web page instead of appearing in a separate window. You can control several details of the appearance and behavior of the embedded object with the following parameters added to the tag:

> SRC= the filename or URL of the embedded object (this parameter is required)
>
> HEIGHT= and WIDTH= specifies the size of the object or the playback control panel that appears on your Web page
>
> AUTOSTART= add this parameter and the value "true" to have the sound automatically start playing as soon as it's downloaded.
>
> HIDDEN= if this parameter is "true" the embedded object is hidden from view
>
> LOOP= include this parameter and set the value to "true" to have the sound play over and over and over again

Composer doesn't support the <embed> tag so you can't add or edit it in Composer's WYSIWYG editing window and Composer won't display or play embedded objects or their control panels. You can, however, add the <embed> tag to your page manually by using Composer's HTML Tag dialog box or an external HTML editor.

**&lt;STYLE TYPE="text/css"&gt;**
**&lt;!--**
**... style sheet information ...**
**--&gt;**
**&lt;/STYLE&gt;**

The <STYLE> and </STYLE> tags mark the beginning and end of the style sheet definition area. These tags appear in the header of an HTML document between the <HEAD> and </HEAD> tags. In the style sheet area, you can define the attributes of any of the standard paragraph style tags and define your own variations on those tags. The style sheet definitions are enclosed in an HTML comment tag to prevent them from appearing on your page or its title bar.

Using style sheets, you can set text attributes such as font-family, font-style, font-weight, color, size, line height, alignment, indents, margins, and much more. I'd need to add another appendix to this book in order to describe all the options. Style sheets are a new development and they aren't yet supported by Composer or by older Web browsers. Composer won't properly display the formatting specified in style sheets. You can't create or edit style sheet entries in Composer's WYSIWYG editing environment. If you want to use style sheets, you'll have to resort to manually editing the HTML source with an external HTML editor.

If you're interested in pursuing style sheets, you can find reference material in the developer's section of the Netscape site at `http://developer.netscape.com`. Click the Find link and then conduct a search on "style sheet." If you prefer a simpler overview of style sheets, check out `http://www.htmlgoodies.com/ ie_style.html`.

> **TIP**
>
> **Netscape Navigator supports both cascading style sheets and JavaScript style sheets. Of course, Netscape is pushing the JavaScript version because JavaScript is their baby. But cascading style sheets are a little simpler and have the added advantage of being compatible with Microsoft Internet Explorer as well as Navigator.**

# Special Characters

Special characters appear in your HTML document as codes that begin with an ampersand (&) and end with a semicolon (;). Here are some examples:

| HTML Code | Which Means | Symbol |
|---|---|---|
| &amp; | Ampersand | & |
| &gt; | Greater-Than | > |
| &lt; | Less-Than | < |
| &reg; | Registered Trademark | ® |
| &copy; | Copyright | © |
|   | Non-breaking space | |

# Appendix C

# ESSENTIAL LINKS

As you work on designing and publishing your Web pages, you'll find that the World Wide Web itself can become one of your most valuable resources. You can find Web sites that provide information and advice on everything from the software and utilities you use to create Web pages to the content and style of those pages.

Throughout this book you'll find notes containing the addresses of interesting and helpful Web sites. But be aware, Web sites come and go and change location. For this reason, Sybex and I have set up an area of the Sybex Web site (see the address below) where we can make an up-to-date list of Web resources available. This appendix is intended to be a quick reference for a few of the Web sites you would use most frequently.

## Links to Netscape

Of course, since you're using Netscape Composer, you'll want to stay informed about any developments relating to the Netscape Communicator software suite. You'll find that news, and much more, on Netscape's corporate Web site. The URL is:

```
http://www.netscape.com
```

From the Netscape home page, you can follow links to a rich assortment of information, helpful utilities, and sources of plug-ins. One helpful Web-based utility is the Netscape Web Page Wizard located at:

```
http://home.netscape.com/home/gold4.0_wizard.html
```

The following URL will take you directly to the selection of predesigned pages templates:

```
http://home.netscape.com/home/gold3.0_templates.html
```

## Sybex

Sybex, the publisher of this book, maintains a Web site providing information about the company and the other books it publishes. The following address will take you there:

```
http://www.sybex.com
```

In addition to the other information at the Sybex Web site, there is an area devoted to this book. There you'll find links to many of the Web resources already mentioned in this book and other pertinent information as well.

**NOTE**  When you reach the Home Page at `http://www.sybex.com` just click the picture of books in the upper-left corner. This will take you to the Catalog page. In the search window near the bottom, type this book's ISBN number (2065), and hit return. You will be transported to the book's own page, from which you can access any information associated with the book.

# Search Engines

When you need to find something on the Web but don't know the address of the Web site you're looking for, Web directories and search engines can save the day. They have the ability to index millions of Web sites, so you can enter a search term and get back a list of links to Web sites that match your query. Here's a reference list of the leading search engines:

## AltaVista

```
http://www.altavista.digital.com/
```

## Excite

```
http://www.excite.com
```

## HotBot

```
http://www.hotbot.com
```

## InfoSeek

```
http://www.infoseek.com
```

## Lycos

```
http://www.lycos.com
```

## Magellan

```
http://www.mckinley.com
```

## MetaCrawler

```
http://www.metacrawler.com/
```

## WebCrawler

```
http://www.webcrawler.com
```

## Yahoo!

```
http://www.yahoo.com
```

# Glossary

If you run across a term in this book that you aren't familiar with, look for it here. I've tried to provide simple, succinct definitions in layperson's terms.

**absolute address**   An Internet address that includes the full URL, (host or server name, directory, and file name). An absolute address (such as `http://www.sybex.com/directory/pagename.html`) is the opposite of a relative address (such as `directory/pagename.html`) which includes only the directory and file name of a file on the same server has the Web page in which the address is found.

**active link**   A hyperlink on a Web page that is currently selected—the user has clicked the link and the Web browser is in the process of establishing a connection to the server and displaying the target of the link.

**ActiveX**   A programming technology, developed by Microsoft, where programming commands can be embedded into the HTML source code for a Web page. By using ActiveX, a Web designer can achieve effects ranging from animation to interaction with the viewer to full-fledged applications that would not be possible with normal HTML codes. ActiveX and Java give Web developers similar capabilities although the technologies are quite different.

**adjacent colors**   Colors that appear next to each other on the artist's color wheel (red and yellow, green and cyan, blue and magenta). Using adjacent colors together usually has a harmonious effect.

**AIF**   A common file format for Macintosh audio files. Also the file the extension for those files.

**Alta Vista**   One of the leading search engine/database sites that index Web pages. Web surfers can visit the Alta Vista Web site, type in a keyword, and get a list of links to Web sites related to that keyword. Alta Vista also provides the search technology used by several other Web indexes, such as Yahoo.

**anonymous FTP**  A server that allows users who don't have a user account on that system to download files by entering **anonymous** in place of the user ID and an e-mail address as the password.

**applet**  The nickname given to mini-applications written in Java. Applets are commonly found performing animation and other tasks on Web pages, but might also show up in non-Web related situations as well.

**ASCII**  (pronounced *ask-ee*) Originally, an acronym for the standards organization that established standard computer codes for each character of the alphabet. Now, ASCII has come to mean any text conforming to that standard or, more specifically, a text file containing only ASCII text and no extraneous information such as the binary formatting codes in a proprietary word processing format.

**AVI**  The file name extension for Windows video files.

**background color**  A solid-color background for a Web page, usually referring to a color that is different from the default light gray.

**background image**  An image displayed by the Web browser as the background of a Web page appearing behind the text and other foreground elements. The background image needn't be big enough to fill the entire browser window since the browser will automatically tile (repeat) the image as many times as necessary to fill the available page size.

**backlink**  A hyperlink from another Web site to a page on your Web site—usually as a result of a reciprocity agreement with another Web developer to provide links to each other's sites in an effort to build traffic to both sites.

**bandwidth**  A term for network capacity—the amount of data that move from place to place on the Internet, like the amount of water that can be pushed through a garden hose.

**bps**  Bits Per Second—a measure of network speed and bandwidth.

**browser**  A software program for viewing HTML documents like Web pages. The browser displays text, images, and hyperlinks and all the other elements of a Web page. The browser also handles communications with the server to request and download pages and supplemental files as needed.

**button**  In the context of a Web page, a button is an image with an associated hyperlink. Clicking the image causes the browser to load another Web page and take some other action. Originally, the images used as buttons mimicked the physical buttons commonly used to control appliances. Now, any clickable (hyperlinked) image may be called a button.

**CNET**  Both a syndicated TV show, a Web-based magazine, and an extensive Web site (`www.cnet.com`) covering the Internet, World Wide Web, and related topics. CNET is a great source of news, product reviews, and other interesting information. CNET also sponsors related Web sites that provide easy access to the popular search engines (at `www.search.com`) and shareware (at `www.download.com`).

**cache**  (pronounced cash) A fast local memory store for frequently used files. Navigator and most browsers store recently accessed Web pages and images in a cache on your hard disk.

**CGI**  Common Gateway Interface—a programming standard where programs are run on a server to process input from and output to Web pages.

**code**  As in programming code or source code—the instructions for a computer or computer program.

**color wheel**  An artist's tool for visualizing color relationships. The colors of the spectrum are arranged in a pie chart starting with red and proceeding through yellow, green, cyan, blue, magenta, and back to red.

**complementary colors**  Pairs of colors that are opposite each other on the color wheel. Complementary colors have maximum color contrast and tend to clash when used together.

**compression**  Storing data in a special file format so as to reduce the file size. Compression is important for images, sounds, and other multimedia files in order to minimize the time required to download the files.

**crawler**  A program that automatically goes from Web site to Web site following links and building an index of the pages it encounters. Also called a Web spider or robot.

**domain name**  The network name assigned to a server or a group of servers. Internet domain names are hierarchical starting with the "top level" domains such as .com, .org, .mil, and .edu. These top level domains are subdivided into smaller domains for individual networks, groups, businesses, and so on. For example, whitehouse.gov and sybex.com are both specific domain names.

**e-mail**  Short for electronic mail. E-mail is the common name for the person-to-person computer messages that are the electronic counterpart to letters and memos.

**Excite**  One of the leading search engine/database sites that index Web pages. Web surfers can visit the Excite Web site, type in a keyword, and get a list of links to Web sites related to that keyword.

**FAQ**  Frequently Asked Questions—the term originated on usenet newsgroups where it referred to a resource for new participants that was intended to prevent the regulars from having to repeatedly answer the same commonly asked questions. Now, FAQ may be used to refer to any text file or Web page presenting information in a question and answer format.

**firewall**  Software that serves to limit and control Internet access for users on a network connected to the Internet. The firewall acts as a filter on incoming and outgoing data exchanged with the Internet, protecting the privacy and security of the protected users.

**followed link**  A hyperlink that has been visited recently. Most Web browsers maintain a list of recently visited pages and display links to those pages in a different color from other not yet visited hyperlinks.

**font**  A distinctively shaped set of characters used to display text—in other words, a typeface. Technically, a font is a specific size and style ( normal, bold, or italic) of a particular typeface. However, in common usage, font and typeface are interchangeable.

**form**    A Web page with text boxes, list boxes, and radio buttons to solicit information from the viewer of the Web page. Web forms serve much the same purpose as their paper counterparts.

**FTP**    File Transfer Protocol—as the name implies, is the standard protocol for transferring files from computer to computer across the Internet.

**FTP server**    A server set up to handle requests for file transfers from the inventory on the server to other computers using the FTP protocol.

**GIF**    Graphics Interchange Format—an image file format, developed by CompuServe, that has been widely adopted as a standard for images in Web pages. Also the file name extension for those image files. The GIF format is popular because it compresses the image into a compact file and also because the format supports special effects such as transparent backgrounds and animations.

**home page**    The introductory page of a Web site—the home base that serves as an index or table of contents for the site. The term home page can also refer to the Web page that appears by default when you launch your Web browser. Typically, clicking a button labeled Home in the browser's toolbar will cause the browser to jump back to the default home page.

**Hot Bot**    One of the leading search engine/database sites that index Web pages. Web surfers can visit the Hot Bot Web site, type in a keyword, and get a list of links to Web sites related to that keyword.

**HTML**    HyperText Markup Language—the system of embedding coded instructions called tags in a text document to control the formatting of the text and to create hyperlinks between the text document and other files. The Web browser program interprets the HTML tags and displays the resulting Web page with the proper formatting and hyperlinks. The combination of HTML and browser programs makes the World Wide Web possible. HTML is also the file name extension for Web page source files.

**HTM**    An alternate file name extension for HTML files used on systems (such as DOS and Windows 3.1) that are restricted to three-letter extensions.

**HTTP**   HyperText Transfer Protocol—the standard protocol used to transfer Web pages across the Internet. In addition to transferring the Web page to the viewer, the protocol handles feedback from the viewer as they click hyperlinks. The protocol also appears as part of the full URL for a Web site as in `http://www.sybex.com`.

**HTTP server**   A server, or host computer, set up to handle requests for documents using the HTTP protocol—in other words, a Web server.

**hyperlink**   The fundamental feature of a Web page that allows a Web author to create an association between a text selection or image on a Web page, and another Web page, image, or other Web address. When the user clicks the source of the hyperlink, the Web browser will search out and load the predefined target of the link.

**hypertext**   This is essentially an older term for hyperlink—a holdover from the days when both the source and target of most hyperlinks were text.

**image map**   An image with one or more hyperlinks connected to specific areas, instead of a single hyperlink defined for the entire image. Clicking different portions of an image map will activate different hyperlinks and load different targets of those links.

**InfoSeek**   One of the leading search engine/database sites that index Web pages. Web surfers can visit the InfoSeek Web site, type in a keyword, and get a list of links to Web sites related to that keyword.

**Internet**   The global network of interconnected networks linked together with a common set of communication protocols that allow computers anywhere on the Internet to exchange information with other computers anywhere else on the Net.

**Intranet**   Internal computer networks within a company, institution, or facility that use the same communication protocols and software (such as Web browsers) as the larger Internet.

**ISP**   Internet Service Provider—a business that establishes a permanent, high-capacity connection to the Internet and then sells access to the Internet via its system to others. End users might get Internet access through direct connections between their network and the ISP or, more commonly, via dial-up access via modem. Most ISPs also maintain e-mail and Web servers, and provide Web site hosting (for a fee).

**Java**   A programming technology, developed by Sun Microsystems, that allows a Java program to be embedded into a Web page. By using Java, a Web designer can achieve effects ranging from animation to interaction with the viewer to full-fledged applications that would not be possible with normal HTML codes. Java and ActiveX give Web developers similar capabilities although the technologies are quite different.

**JavaScript**   A simplified subset of Java developed by Netscape for use with its Navigator browser. (Microsoft Internet Explorer now supports a variation of JavaScript called Jscript.)

**JPEG**   (pronounced "jay-peg") JPEG is an acronym for Joint Photographic Experts Group. It's also the name of the second most popular image file format on the Web. The JPEG format provides for varying degrees of image compression with corresponding variations in the quality of the image. The JPEG format works best with photographic images and other images containing lots of colors.

**LAN**   Local Area Network—a network of computers in one physical location.

**link**   Short for hyperlink.

**link color**   Most Web browsers display the text of hyperlinks in a different color from the rest of the text on the page. The link color is the color used to display a link that has not yet been clicked by the viewer.

**Lycos**   One of the leading search engine/database sites that index Web pages. Web surfers can visit the Lycos Web site, type in a keyword, and get a list of links to Web sites related to that keyword.

**Lynx**   A text-only Web browser program that enables users of text-only computer terminals to view at least the text portions of Web pages.

**mailto**   An HTML tag or command that instructs the browser to create and send an e-mail message to the specified address.

**meta tag** Any of several special HTML tags that record information about the Web page (such as the author's name) that is not displayed by the browser.

**MIDI** (pronounced middy) Musical Instrument Device Interface—the standard that defines the interface between electronic musical instruments and the computers that control them. Also the file format for recording the control sequences for MIDI instruments. Playing a MIDI file through a sound synthesizer (such as the one found on a computer sound card) or other instrument reproduces the sounds or music described in the file. MIDI is a very compact and efficient sound file format because its like recording the sheet music for a song instead of recording the sound itself.

**MPEG** (pronounced "em-peg") Motion Picture Experts Group—a compressed file format for audio and video data.

**multimedia** A generic term for sounds, animation, video and other media effects incorporated into Web pages. Basically, anything other than text and static images falls under the umbrella of multimedia.

**navigation** The process of moving around from page to page on a Web site or from site to site.

**Net** A common short form for Internet.

**pixel** A single dot of color on a computer screen or in an image file. When viewed from an appropriate distance, the dots blend together to create the illusion of a whole image.

**PNG** Portable Network Graphics—an image file format similar to GIF and incorporating some interesting new features. This format has been proposed as a replacement for the GIF format but it hasn't caught on yet.

**POP3** Post Office Protocol 3—the protocol used by most email programs to get e-mail from an e-mail server.

**PPP** Point to Point Protocol—a protocol for connecting computers to the Internet over a telephone line and modem instead of a direct network connection.

**protocol**    The rules and procedures established to enable computers to handle a certain type of data communications.

**relative address**    An Internet address which includes only the file name (and, if necessary, the directory) of a file located on the same server as the Web page in which the address is found. This is distinct from an absolute address that includes the full URL, (host or server name, directory, and file name). For example, `directory/pagename.html` is a relative address while `http://www.sybex.com/directory/pagename.html` is an absolute address.

**script**    A set of instructions or programming code that instruct a computer program to perform a series of steps or tasks. A script is similar to a computer program, but it often refers to instructions for a single, relatively simple operation, in contrast to a program that would normally involve more complex operations and be compiled or optimized.

**server**    A host computer that handles requests for access to resources such as Web pages, files for download, or e-mail messages.

**SGML**    Standard Generalized Markup Language—this is a superset of HTML and a precursor to the language we use to create Web pages. SGML was developed as a system for formatting documents for cross-platform desktop publishing.

**SMTP**    Simple Mail Transfer Protocol—one of the standards for sending e-mail messages.

**source**    As in source code—a document containing instructions for a computer program. In the case of Web pages, the source code is the HTML file containing the text and HTML tags that instruct a Web browser how to display the page.

**spam**    Unsolicited e-mail messages—the electronic equivalent of junk mail.

**spider**    A program that automatically goes from Web site to Web site following links and building an index of the pages it encounters. Also called a crawler or robot.

**streaming**    A system for sending large multimedia files across the net to a special player program that can simultaneously download and play the file. The player begins playing the first part of the sound or video clip as soon as it is received without waiting for the entire file to be downloaded. The next portion of the file is being downloaded while the previous portion is being played, and so on. Theoretically, this allows a large file to play smoothly and continuously after only a short delay at the beginning of the download. Unfortunately, the realities of network delays and poor connections conspire to make the playback less than ideal.

**TCP/IP**    Transmission Control Protocol/Internet Protocol—this is the set of communications standards that governs how the bits and bytes of information travel over the Internet.

**text-only**    A computer system that is restricted to displaying only plain ASCII text characters—no images or graphic elements. Some computer terminals connected to mainframe and mini-computers fall into this category. Also a Web page or other document consisting of just text and no images. Text-only pages are useful for viewing on text-only terminals and also for users who have computers capable of displaying graphics but choose to disable the feature because of the time required to download large graphics files over slow Internet connections.

**TIFF**    Tagged Image File Format—this is a popular file format for images, especially those produced by scanners and various graphics and image editing programs. Some Web browsers can display TIFF images, but normally, you'll need to convert TIFF images to the GIF or JPEG format if you want to ensure the widest possible compatibility.

**TXT**    The file name extension for text files containing nothing but plain ASCII text, no formatting codes or other binary information such as images or programming codes.

**typeface**    A distinctively shaped set of text characters—sometimes called a font. Technically, a typeface is the full set of distinctively styled characters and a font is a specific size and style (normal, bold, or italic) of a particular typeface. However, in common usage, font and typeface are interchangeable.

**URL**    Uniform Resource Locator—the Web address of a Web page or other file. A full URL consists of a protocol (`http://`), host name (`www.sybex.com`), directory

(`/directory/`), and file name (`mypage.html`). Often a shortened form of the URL can be used. Specifying just the host name will usually result in the browser using the default protocol to load the default file in the root directory. A relative address consists of just a file name and directory; the rest of the URL is assumed to be the same as the current Web page.

**VRML**    Virtual Reality Modeling Language—a language similar, to HTML in some respects, that allows authors to create three-dimensional worlds that visitors can view much like they view Web pages. Using the appropriate viewing software (often a Web browser with a VRML plug-in) viewers can move through the 3-D world and interact with objects there.

**W3C**    World Wide Web Consortium—an industry association that promotes standards and helps to define the "official" version of HTML and some of the other languages, protocols, and file formats used on the Web.

**WAN**    Wide Area Network—a network, similar to a LAN, but composed of computers that are separated by significant distance.

**WAV**    The file name extension for Windows wave sound files.

**Web**    Short for the World Wide Web. Also used as a more generic term to refer to anything associated with the World Wide Web or using the same HTML and browser technology. For example, in this book, I often use Web as an adjective (as in Web fonts) and as an all inclusive noun to encompass the World Wide Web and the not-so-wide Webs found on intranets.

**Web hosting service**    A company or other entity (usually an ISP) that maintains a Web server with a full-time connection to the Internet and rents space on that server to individuals and companies that want to set up a Web site and don't have (or don't want to maintain) their own Web server.

**Web page**    An individual HTML document formatted to be displayed in a Web browser.

**Web server**    A host computer set up to make Web pages available to users on the Internet or an intranet.

**Web site**    A collection of related and interlinked Web pages—usually, a Web site is composed of pages on the same server, pertaining to the same topic, and posted by the same sponsor (company) or author.

**WebCrawler**    One of the leading search engine/database sites that index Web pages. Web surfers can visit the WebCrawler Web site, type in a keyword, and get a list of links to Web sites related to that keyword.

**World Wide Web**    The phenomenon of graphically-rich hypertext documents being available to users around the world via the Internet. The wide acceptance of the HTML standard and the availability of Web browsers such as Navigator makes the World Wide Web possible. The global reach of the Internet gives the Web its worldwide scope. The essential aspect of hypertext, with its myriad links between documents, gives the World Wide Web its interlocking, spiderweb-like character.

**WYSIWYG**    (pronounced Wizy-wig) What You See Is What You Get—it means that the program's working editing window attempts to display the document you are editing as it will appear as a finished product. In Composer's case, that means that Composer shows you what your Web page will look like, not the HTML source code Composer generates to produce that page.

**Yahoo!**    One of the leading search engine/database sites that index Web pages. Web surfers can visit the Yahoo! Web site, type in a keyword, and get a list of links to Web sites related to that keyword.

# Index

Note to the Reader:   First level entries are in **bold**. Page numbers in **bold** indicate the principal discussion of a topic or the definition of a term. Page numbers in *italic* indicate illustrations.

## G

## Y